FIRST

EXPERT

TEACHER'S RESOURCE BOOK

Drew Hyde, Jan Bell, Roger Gower, Nick Kenny

Pearson Education Limited
Edinburgh Gate
Harlow
Essex CM20 2JE
England
and Associated Companies throughout the world.

www.pearsonelt.com

First published 2014
Sixth impression 2015

ISBN 978-1-4479-7377-5
Set in 10/12pt Text Arial

Printed in Slovakia by Neografia

Acknowledgements
Every effort has been made to trace the copyright holders and we apologise in
advance for any unintentional omissions. We would be pleased to insert the
appropriate acknowledgement in any subsequent edition of this publication.

Contents

Components

First Expert consists of:

- a Coursebook for classroom use with two audio CDs packaged in the back of the book.

- a set of Teacher's Online Resource Material that provides a collection of editable Word tests, based on the course content. These comprise: quick and full entry tests, module tests, progress tests and an end-of-course test.

- Teacher's eText software for Interactive White Board: the Coursebook in interactive format, plus testing materials and reference sections.

- Student's eText software for Interactive White Board: the Coursebook in interactive format.

Six key features

1 *First Expert* is flexible. It is designed in a modular way so that teachers can either follow the order of the material in the book or choose their own route through the course to meet the needs of specific classes. Each page or double-page spread is free-standing and almost always follows the same order in each module, making it easy to access and isolate separate elements of the course and integrate them in different ways.

   So, a teacher might follow a linear route through each module and through the book. Alternatively, you might decide to follow different, tailored routes through each module, for example, starting with Speaking or Listening rather than Reading. And you might choose to do the modules in a different sequence, depending on your students' interests.

2 While each section can be taught independently, there are links between the sections to provide a coherent progression when the more linear route is chosen. For example, the Language development in the 'A' units provides language which will be useful for students in the following Writing section. The Speaking has a topic which relates to the Listening in the same unit. In the 'B' units, the grammar and vocabulary in the Language development sections are practised in the Use of English sections.

3 Most of the Use of English/Language development sections follow a test–teach approach, in which the language is first tested by means of a Use of English task, then focused on in the Language development section, using the examples from the Use of English task to clarify form and meaning.

4 The sub-skills needed for the different parts of Paper 1 Reading and Use of English and Paper 3 Listening (e.g. skimming, scanning, predicting) are presented first in the early units, through tasks which simulate the exam but are graded in terms of their level of difficulty.

5 The Writing and Speaking sections provide practice for each part of Paper 2 Writing and Paper 4 Speaking. However, the focus is more on process than end product. In other words, students are trained to build up good habits, develop the skill of self-monitoring and so become more independent learners.

6 Most sections contain a Help feature, with clues that help students complete the task at hand. These often focus attention on how the task is constructed and thus help students to help themselves in the exam.

Coursebook

The Coursebook consists of 12 modules, each of which is divided into two units (A and B). Each module practises all the papers of the exam and includes grammar and vocabulary consolidation and development.

Each module is designed around a theme and comprises a Lead-in page, with an Overview listing the contents of the module, which facilitates planning. Photos and questions prompt discussion aimed at sparking students' interest in each theme.

Then each of the two units in the module is based on a topic that relates to the overall theme of the module.

Other elements of the Coursebook are:

- Exam overview at the front of the book, presenting an outline of what each paper consists of and the skills which are tested in each section.

- Exam reference section at the end of the book, providing more detailed information about what to expect in each part of each paper, along with a list of recommended strategies for each task type.

- Expert grammar section: grammar reference, giving more detailed information about the main grammar points focused on in each module.

- Expert writing section: writing reference, which provides:

    - a checklist to help students monitor and edit their own writing.

    - a sample question for each type of writing task in the exam, with a model answer, specific guidance and another question for further practice.

    - sections to provide useful support on areas practised in the Writing sections, such as punctuation and spelling.

- Expert speaking section: speaking material, with additional tasks for some modules.

Module and unit structure

Each module contains the sections listed below. For ease of use and flexibility, the sections are nearly always in the same order. The teacher's notes indicate when the photocopiable activities at the back of this Teacher's Resource Book may be used to expand or supplement the lessons.

Overview and Lead-in questions

Use the Overview to introduce the module contents. You could discuss with the class the order in which they would like to cover the module. Use the photos and Lead-in questions to generate interest in the overall theme of the module.

'A' units

➤ Reading

The reading texts have been selected for their interest value, as well as their potential to provide a 'window on the world' and generate discussion. There is a three-stage approach.

Stage 1: The *Before you read* exercise establishes the topic and gives a purpose for reading the text. It also aims to motivate students and generate vocabulary. For example, in Module 4A (*Personal challenges*) students look at the title of the article and the introduction and write three questions they would like to find the answers to in the text.

Stage 2: Students do an activity to encourage reading for gist, followed by an exam-style reading task. They should look at or be referred to the relevant task strategy points before attempting the task for the first time. These can be found next to the corresponding task, within the unit, and at the back of the book in the Exam reference section. As the exam preparation is carefully graded and stepped throughout the course, the strategy boxes within the main units are reduced as the course progresses. Many of the reading tasks are followed by a *Task analysis* exercise, in which students are encouraged to discuss and compare how they performed and which strategies they found useful.

Stage 3: A discussion and/or a vocabulary activity, based on the text. Questions for discussion relate to the students' own lives and encourage them to give their opinions.

➤ Language development 1

This section can be used independently of any exam training. However, it revises and extends general grammar areas which students will need for the exam.

The section contains short grammar summaries and a range of controlled and less controlled practice activities, linked to the topic of the unit. Opportunities are given for personalisation.

There is often a cross-reference to the Expert grammar section, which provides a detailed summary of the language point being practised. Students should be encouraged to use this resource to check their answers.

Further communicative practice of the language area is often provided in the photocopiable activities.

➤ Writing

The Writing sections cover all the types of writing that students may be required to do in the exam. The principle behind the section is to establish 'good practice' through a clear set of procedures consistently applied, which can be used when answering any exam Writing task.

The approach focuses on process more than end product. Each spread is graded and the aim is to give carefully guided preparation so that students build up to complete the main task at the end of the section. In each section, there is considerable language support; in particular, a range of functional exponents is given and linked to the task. At the end of the section there is usually an *Expert language* feature, which practises an important area of language needed for writing.

In the Expert writing section, there is a model answer for each type of writing in the exam, notes for guidance and a second task for further practice if desired.

The procedure in the Writing sections is as follows:

1 lead-in

2 understanding the task

3 planning the task

4 thinking about the language and content

5 writing the answer

6 checking and improving the answer

The *Expert language* feature gives practice in making language vivid. It is linked to but not integrated with this procedure and could be used at any point in the lesson, including the beginning.

'B' units

➤ Speaking

Each section provides relevant vocabulary for the exam-style task students have to do, covers the strategies needed for the task and provides useful functional exponents. In the earlier modules, there are recorded sample answers for students to evaluate from the point of view of appropriate language and effective strategies. Again, there is a three-stage approach.

Stage 1: Vocabulary that students might find useful for the Speaking task is introduced and practised.

Stage 2: Guided preparation for the exam task. In the earlier modules, students listen to the examiner's instructions and an example of a student or students doing the task. They evaluate the performance of the speaker or speakers. Then they listen again to focus on useful language exponents.

Stage 3: Students perform the exam task themselves. A *Task analysis* exercise then encourages them to reflect on how well they performed.

In Module 12 there is a complete Speaking paper (Paper 4).

➤ Listening

This section can be covered before or after the Speaking section, which has a linked topic.

In the earlier modules, the section develops the listening skills needed for the different parts of Paper 3 Listening. The remaining modules provide further exam-style practice tasks.

Stage 1: The *Before you listen* exercise encourages students to think about the topic and introduces or generates vocabulary from the students. For example, in Module 3, students are asked to look at the sentences in the exam task and think about what the man's experience in the Amazon rainforest was like.

Stage 2: Exercises focus on and develop the sub-skills needed for Paper 3 Listening. For example, Module 3 practises listening for specific information, which is an important skill for Paper 3, Part 2, and then introduces the exam task.

Stage 3: There is usually a *Task analysis* exercise that encourages students to reflect on the task they have completed, followed by discussion and/or further vocabulary work based on the topic of the text.

➤ Use of English 1

This section usually focuses on the more 'grammatical' Use of English tasks and so it is usually either Paper 1 Part 2 (open cloze) or Paper 1 Part 4 (key word transformations). Its aim is to develop the exam strategies needed for each task and, in terms of language development, to follow a test–teach procedure, as some of the language tested here is then practised in Language development 2.

The sections which practise Paper 1 Part 2 (open cloze) include texts related to the topic of the unit and have the following structure:

Stage 1: The *Lead-in* exercise aims to build up motivation in relation to the topic of the text and generate some of the vocabulary needed. This is usually done through a short discussion.

Stage 2: Students complete the task. Graded guidance is supplied, e.g. students are usually asked to read the text quickly first for general comprehension. They are further supported by Help notes, which give specific guidance for individual answers. This support is reduced as students work through the modules.

Stage 3: A discussion based on the content of the text and/ or analysis of the language tested in the task.

A similar procedure is followed in the sections which practise Paper 1 Part 4 (key word transformations) but since there is no specific text or topic, more attention is given to the exam strategies needed.

➤ **Language development 2**

This section generally focuses on some of the language tested in Use of English 1.

Stage 1: Analysis of examples of the target language from the preceding Use of English task where appropriate. Students are either guided to the grammar rules or given input on the page.

Stage 2: A range of controlled and less controlled practice activities.

Stage 3: A short personalised task.

There is often a cross-reference to the Expert grammar section, which provides a detailed summary of the language point being practised. Students should be encouraged to use this resource to check their answers.

Further communicative practice of the language area is often provided in the photocopiable activities.

➤ **Use of English 2**

The task in this section focuses on vocabulary and is usually Paper 1 Part 1 (multiple-choice cloze) or Paper 1 Part 3 (word formation). Since vocabulary is also tested in Paper 1 Part 4 (key word transformations), Module 8 has a key word transformations task.

The texts are related to the topic of the unit and the section has a similar structure to Use of English 1 (see above).

➤ **Language development 3**

This section practises and extends the vocabulary tested in Use of English 2. It has a similar structure to Language development 2 (see above).

Teacher's Resource Book

As well as this introduction, this Teacher's Resource Book contains:

Unit-by-unit teacher's notes

Guidance on how to use the Coursebook material, with further suggestions; 'books closed' activities to get things going at the beginning of modules and sections; background information on the texts and exercises; answers to all exercises, with explanations where helpful.

Photocopiable activities

A pre-course exam quiz, to see how much students already know about the *Cambridge English: First* exam; two photocopiable activities to supplement each Coursebook module, providing communicative classroom practice for grammar, vocabulary and skills; full teacher's notes and answer keys for each activity.

Audioscripts (photocopiable)

These are all at the back of the book for ease of reference and photocopying.

Test bank

The Teacher's Online Resource Material contains photocopiable tests to check on students' progress and comprehension of aspects covered in the course materials. The tests reflect the style of the exam and test the appropriate language skills required to pass the exam; their principal purpose is to test the vocabulary, grammar and skills development of the Coursebook and they are therefore not in the exact format of the exam itself.

Entry test

This test is intended for use at the beginning of the course, to give teachers an idea about their students' level of English. There are two versions of this test, both of which cover key areas of grammar and vocabulary. The full one comprises three exercises with a total of 100 items whilst the quick test, which can be used when there are time constraints to testing, consists of the first 50 multiple-choice questions from the full test. The full entry test should take about 40 minutes to administer, whereas the quick test should take 15 minutes. The answer keys to these tests can be found in the same menu as the tests.

Module tests

These would normally be given after a module has been studied. However, in the case where modules are not followed sequentially or where new students join a class, they can also be used to check on prior knowledge. Each module test focuses on grammar and vocabulary from the Coursebook and comprises 25 items. There are 12 module tests, each of which should take 15 minutes to administer. The answer keys can be found in the same menu as the tests.

Progress tests

There is a progress test after every two modules of the Coursebook. These focus on grammar, vocabulary, listening, reading and writing (conventions and functions). These tests are a useful way of revising aspects covered in the preceding two modules: Progress test 1 covers Modules 1–2, Progress test 2 covers Modules 3–4 and so on. Both the reading and listening sections of these tests are based on texts and recordings originating from the Coursebook, although the questions themselves are different. In effect, these tests can help to pinpoint any aspects requiring revision or extended work. Each test should take about 40 minutes to administer. The answer keys and audioscripts can be found in the same menu as the tests.

End-of-course test

This test comprises exercises on grammar, vocabulary, listening, reading and writing, as covered in the Coursebook. Ideally, 40 minutes should be spent administering this test. The answer keys and audio script can be found in the same menu as the tests.

OMR answer sheets (photocopiable)

Replicas of the answer sheets students have to use in the exam for the Reading and Use of English (Paper 1) and Listening (Paper 3) papers are available online with the Teacher's Online Resource Material at www.pearsonelt.com/expert.

CD pack

The CD pack contains all the listening material from the Coursebook. There are two CDs for the Coursebook. The listening tests in the Teacher's Online Resource Material (Test bank) and the listening exercises for the Progress Tests and End-of-course test come from the Coursebook, so you will require the Coursebook audio CD to use these tests. Audioscripts are provided separately for all listening exercises that appear in these tests.

1 Lifestyles

Module 1 includes topics such as family, homes, routines, festivals and celebrations.

Photocopiable activity

The pre-course photocopiable activity on page 87 provides an introduction to the *Cambridge English: First* exam. Students find out how much they know about the exam by completing a quiz about it, referring to the Exam reference section on pages 175–181 of the coursebook where necessary.

After the quiz, it would be useful to show students other features of the book. This could be done as a quick quiz, with questions such as: *Where can you find the Expert grammar section?* (pages 182–197) and *What can you find on pages 198–207?* (the Expert writing section). Use the contents map on pages 2–5 to ask questions such as *What type of writing is practised in Module 6?* (a review).

Lead-in p. 7

Get students to discuss the dictionary entry in pairs or as a class. Then ask them to mark the key points that define *lifestyle* (*way a person or group of people live*, *place they live in*, *things they own*, *job they do*, *activities they enjoy*). Students then discuss the other questions in pairs or small groups before comparing ideas as a whole class.

1A Family life

Reading pp. 8–9

With books closed, get students to tell a partner about their family and childhood. If necessary, provide prompts such as: *Who did you live with? Were you happy? Were you ever bored? Were your parents strict?*

1   Ask students to look at the first strategy box before they do this. Ask them to give reasons and so encourage them to give fuller answers.

2   Use the strategy box to clarify what the term *skimming* means and why it is important. As well as giving a general understanding, skimming helps to establish the type and style of the text, the writer's intention (to inform, amuse, entertain, etc.) and the general organisation and layout of the text. Suggest a suitable time to skim the article (e.g. 2–3 minutes).

1 D	2 A	3 B	4 C

3   Focus students' attention on the highlighted key words in the example and explain that they link back to the highlighted part of section C in the text. Then, before students do the task, use the second strategy box to clarify what scanning is and why it is useful. Point out that in the exam, it is important to use time well and scanning will help students do this.

1 D	2 A	3 B	4 D	5 C	6 D	7 B	8 C	9 A	10 B

4   Discuss the questions with the class.

5   This would be a good point to introduce the concept of phrasal verbs and ways in which students should record them in their vocabulary notebooks. Ask them to find the underlined words in the text and to try to guess what they mean. If they find this difficult, put the following words on the board and ask students to match them with the underlined words in the text: *sent, practise, relax, replaced, communicate, monitor, test.*

You could follow this up with a discussion, using questions such as: *How do you chill out? Where were you packed off to as a child? What interests would you like to keep up if you had time?*

> chill out = relax   try out = test   packed off = sent
> taken over from = replaced   keep in touch = communicate
> keep up = practise   keep an eye on = (here) monitor

6   This question could be discussed in small groups or as a class.

Photocopiable activity

Activity 1A (p. 88) can be used here. It is a board game about students' lifestyles, containing questions typical of those asked in Paper 4 Part 1.

Language development 1 pp. 10–11

1a   First, ask students to describe the picture. What is the relationship between the people and what are they doing? Check/Clarify the difference between *grow* (become physically bigger – used for people, plants, animals, towns, etc.) and *grow up* (develop from a child to an adult – used only for people). Then ask students to match the people in the picture with the sentences.

1 B	2 C	3 A	4 D	5 A	6 E

1b   Check that students are familiar with the basic names of the verb forms before they do this activity. After checking answers with the class, you may want to refer students to the Expert grammar notes on page 182.

a 6	b 4	c 3	d 1	e 2	f 5

1c Students use the information in Exercise 1b to complete the table.

> 1 a changing situation
> 2 His children are growing up fast!
> 3 a temporary situation
> 4 He's staying with the family at the moment.
> 5 an annoying or surprising habit
> 6 She's always making long calls on the phone.
> 7 a regular action
> 8 She usually goes out in the evening.
> 9 a long-term situation
> 10 She lives in a small house with her husband and children.
> 11 characteristic behaviour
> 12 He'll sit and doze in an armchair all evening.

2a Students work individually to complete the conversations. They then compare answers in pairs before class feedback.

> 1 Do you live, are living, are looking for
> 2 do you get on, will tell/tells
> 3 Does anyone annoy, is always taking
> 4 do you go out, go out, am studying, am only going out
> 5 Do you like, is getting

2b Before students practise the questions in pairs, point out how the answers in the coursebook are more than simple responses: the answers are expanded to give further information (e.g. in 2, the answer *My father* is expanded to say why). Encourage students to do the same.

3a Before students do the activity, you may need to clarify the difference between a state and an action. Say: *I live in [Madrid]. It's not an action – I don't actually do anything, I just live.* Then say: *Every day I ride a bike to work. This is a physical action, something that I do.* Check answers with the class.

> 1 S 2 S 3 S 4 A

3b After students have completed the information, give them time to read the Expert grammar notes on page 182.

> A understand, know B have

4 Students can either refer to the Expert grammar notes as they do the exercise or try on their own. During feedback, ask them to justify their answers and say whether each sentence describes a state or an action.

> 1 I **have** two brothers.
> 2 Jan**'s having** a shower – can you call back later?
> 3 I don't understand this word. What **does it mean**?
> 4 Marina**'s thinking** about getting a car. Do you think it's a good idea?
> 5 We **don't own** our house; we rent it.
> 6 The house **looks** old but it's quite modern inside.
> 7 What **are** you **looking** at? Oh! Yes, I can see it now.
> 8 Phil**'s seeing** a client at the moment. He won't be long.

5a First check that students know who Rihanna is. You could ask them to compare answers in pairs before class feedback.

Background

Rihanna is a Barbadian singer and actress. She moved to the USA at 16 and immediately pursued a recording career. Since her debut solo album, *Music of the Sun*, in 2005, she has recorded a number of studio albums and earned numerous awards. She is the highest-selling digital artist in US history. In 2012, she made her big screen debut in *Battleship*.

> habits: used to sell, would help; state: used to live

5b Discuss the questions as a class.

> 1 many times 2 many times 3 used to, would 4 live, would

5c After students have completed the information, refer them to the Expert grammar notes on page 182.

> A used to, would help B used to, used to live C lived, helped

6 Students should be able to justify their choices and say why other answers are or aren't possible.

> 1 forgot 2 used to live, used to have 3 always used to go/would always go, used to have/would have 4 used to be, often used to work/would often work, retired

7a Ask students to write their answers, to give them time to think about the structures. If necessary, give them one or two examples about you.

7b This activity would work well in small groups.

8 After feedback, use the completed sentences as revision: ask students why the various tenses were used in each sentence or ask for alternative endings for each sentence.

> 1 c 2 e 3 f 4 a 5 d 6 b

Writing pp. 12–13

1 Get students started by asking who you might write a formal letter or email to (e.g. a bank), and who you would write an informal letter or email to (e.g. friends or family). Ask if anyone has ever had a pen friend or an e-pal and if so, how long they kept up correspondence.

> **Possible answers:**
> 1 a friend, a family member, an e-pal
> 2 An email to a new friend would usually contain personal information about family, lifestyle, interests, routines, aspirations, etc.

2 Point out that students should establish the style of any writing task by considering who the reader is, and also establish the purpose in order to use suitable language and complete the task.

> mainly b (but also a)

3a Tell students that in the exam, marks are given for task completion, so they should think about what the task requires and what they need to include in their writing. In this case, they will need to cover three main points: information about themselves, information about their family and suggesting a meeting.

3b When students are completing the paragraph plan, remind them that it is only an exam and not a real life situation. Although it is better to write true things about themselves (e.g. they will know more vocabulary about their own real hobbies), it is not necessary. In this case, for example, it is better to invent a hobby rather than say they don't have one. Remind them that the aim is to demonstrate what they can do in English, not to write a true description of themselves.

4a Check that students understand why the sentences are inappropriate (they are too formal) before they attempt the task. Go through the phrases in the table with the class. Remind them that contractions such as *I'm* are acceptable in informal letters/emails.

Suggested answers:

1 It would be great to meet up sometime.
2 I live in a small town in Spain.
3 My sister and I get on well.
4 Next time I write, I'll send a photo of us all.
5 When I was a child, we would always go on holiday by the sea.
6 She looks like me but she can be a bit talkative.
7 So you'd like to get in touch with someone from my country.
8 Do you ever get the chance to visit my country?
9 I'm glad you're interested.
10 Let me tell you about my family.

4b Students complete the task individually and then compare answers in pairs. During feedback, briefly discuss each statement.

1 R	2 W	3 W	4 W	5 R	6 R

4c Students could do this individually or in pairs.

1 any of the phrases in *Responding to a suggestion* or *Talking about the future*
2 It would be great to meet you sometime.
3 We get on (well) ...
4 Do you ever get the chance to ... ?
5 Let me tell you about my family.
6 My name's ...

4d Ask students to read the exam task again before they do this activity.

1 not appropriate; too formal
2 not appropriate; too formal
3 not appropriate; too informal/personal for this email
4 appropriate; using the other person's first name is an acceptable opening for an informal email
5 fairly neutral, therefore appropriate
6 fairly neutral, therefore appropriate
7 not appropriate; students should never begin an email with *Dear friend* (or *Dear pen friend* in a letter)
8 possibly too informal for a first email to someone you don't yet know, therefore not appropriate; could be used in subsequent emails
9 not appropriate; too formal

5 Students can write their email in class or for homework. Before they do, highlight the word limit.

Sample answer:

Hello Simon,

I'm glad you're interested in my country. As your friend said, I'd like us to email each other to help me improve my English.

Let me start by telling you a bit about myself and my family. My name's Ivo and I live in Kutna Hora, which is about 45 minutes from Prague by car. I used to work for a medical company but now I'm learning to be a salesperson. In the future I want a job where I can travel for my work. I've already been to a few places in Europe but I've never been to an English-speaking country.

I live at home with my parents, which is convenient, as I don't have to do much housework and my meals are cooked for me. My younger brother is studying at university. Although he is four years younger than me, we get on quite well. We both enjoy snowboarding and music.

What about you? Have you ever been to the Czech Republic? It would be great if you could come over one day and we could fix up a meeting. Why don't you let me know your plans?

Best wishes,

Ivo

6 Point out to students that there is a more complete list of points to check when editing their work, on page 198 of the Expert writing section.

Expert language: Sentence word order

The aim of this exercise is to revise basic English sentence structure and word order, in particular with adverbs of frequency and other adverbials. It can be done at any time during the writing lesson or at the end of it, or at another appropriate moment during Module 1.

1 I don't always speak English very well.
2 My mother and father always eat fish on Fridays./On Fridays, my mother and father always eat fish.
3 My sister's having a great time in Paris right now./Right now, my sister's having a great time in Paris.
4 Her friends usually gave her a lot of help./Usually, her friends gave her a lot of help.
5 My grandmother would always listen to music in bed.
6 Everyone enjoyed themselves very much at the party./Everyone at the party enjoyed themselves very much.
7 I'll send you an email on Tuesday next week.
8 Please write back as soon as you can./Write back as soon as you can, please.

1B Customs and traditions

As a lead-in, with books closed, ask students what kinds of festivals or events they celebrate in their country. Give birthdays and national holidays as examples of a range of possible festivals. Ask students to discuss what makes festivals special (e.g. traditional clothes, food, processions).

Speaking pp. 14–15

1 Ask students to spend a moment describing the photos after they have matched them with the special occasions.

> **A** 2   **B** 3   **C** I   **D** 3

2a Use the exercise to introduce students to the concept of collocation, the way that certain words are commonly used together, and the importance of recording and learning vocabulary by collocations. For example, it will be easier to remember the difference between *blow up* and *blow out* if they learn them as *blow up a balloon* and *blow out candles*.

2b Students match the photos with the collocations and briefly discuss the questions.

> be awarded a certificate (A)   blow out the candles (C)   blow up balloons (C)   cut the cake (B, C, D)   exchange presents/photos/rings (B, D)   make a speech/a toast (B, D)   propose a toast (B, D)   rent a marquee (B, D)   send out invitations (B, C, D)   take photos (A, B, C, D)   unwrap presents (B, C, D)   walk down the aisle (B, D)

3a Draw students' attention to the definitions and point out that in the speaking exam, such paraphrasing can be used when students are explaining something and have forgotten an important word (e.g. *I can't remember the name but it's the place where people ...*).

3b Again, use the opportunity to discuss ways of recording the pronunciation of new vocabulary, including sounds and stress, and the importance of doing so.

> **1** registry office   **2** bridesmaid   **3** best man   **4** witnesses
> **5** reception   **6** honeymoon   **7** anniversary

4 This exercise focuses on words that are often confused. You could ask students to compare answers in pairs before checking with the class.

> **1** get   **2** got   **3** hold   **4** guests   **5** up

> **a** registry office   **b** bridesmaids   **c** reception   **d** honeymoon
> **e** send out

5 Students could discuss the questions in small groups or as a class. The discussion can be used to introduce other family celebrations (e.g. engagement, new baby, house warming, retirement). Clarify any new vocabulary and in particular, get students to think about word building (e.g. *to get engaged, to be engaged, engagement*).

6a Point out the strategy box. Remind students that in Paper 4 Part 2, they will be asked to speak for about a minute and compare two photos but they should not describe them in detail. Give students time to make notes under the headings.

6b Play the recording. During feedback, ask students what words/phrases in the recording helped them get to the answers.

> **1** A and C
> **2** The graduation ceremony is an opportunity to share in the girl's success. The birthday party is an opportunity for friends to get together.

6c Give students enough time to read the expressions before they listen for them. You could model them for the students, either before or after listening, so that they can recognise the stress patterns.

> Both of ... are ...   They both seem to be ...   In this one ... and this one ...   The main difference between ... and ... is ...   This one is ... whereas ... is ...   Although ... , I think ...   On the other hand, ... is probably ...

6d Divide students into pairs. Before they do the speaking task, refer them to the strategy box again and get them to think about how long they will speak on each section (similarities, differences and importance). As they speak, encourage their partners to listen attentively but not to interrupt. They could also time the speaker and give feedback on his/her fluency.

7 This could be done in pairs, small groups or as a whole class, and could produce some interesting stories. If any students seem to have little to say, you could prompt them to talk about any planned future celebrations that are not shown in the photos.

Listening p. 16

1 Ask students to look at the photos and say where they think they might have been taken. Point out the first strategy box before they discuss the questions.

2 Before students listen, point out the second strategy box and discuss briefly with the class. Then play the recording for students to match the speakers with the reasons. During feedback, ask students if they remember any words/expressions from the recording that led them to their answers.

> **1** c   **2** b   **3** a

3 Before students listen again, ask them to read the last strategy box and remind them that they are listening for specific information (similar to scanning when reading), not specific words or phrases. Give them time to mark the key words in each statement before listening.

> **1** C   **2** E   **3** A

4 At this stage of the course, it is probably useful to give students time to prepare what they are going to say and to look up key vocabulary if necessary. However, remind them that this is a speaking activity and check that they are just making notes rather than writing out sentences in full. The discussion itself would work best in small groups.

Language development 2 p. 17

1a–b The language in Exercise 1 should largely be revision for students at this level but it is important to check that they have a good grasp of these basics. Ask students to look at the photo and ask if anyone knows anything about Burns Night. Get them to correct the mistakes in the sentences in pairs or at least discuss their answers in pairs before checking in Expert grammar. During feedback, discuss and clarify any points students are not sure about.

Background

Burns Night, celebrated on 25 January in Scotland and by Scottish people all over the world, celebrates the life and works of Robert Burns (1759–1796), Scotland's favourite poet and songwriter. It includes speeches, reciting some of his work and, of course, eating haggis.

1 Burns Night celebrates the birth of the poet Robert Burns. It is one of most **the** important nights in Scotland.
2 For many Scots, Burns supper is the **best** event of the year.
3 Usually, **the later** it gets, **the noisier** it gets.
4 The speech before the toast was **the funniest** I have heard.
5 The music was **louder than** last year.
6 The celebration was **the liveliest** one I've ever been to.
7 Outside, it was just as chilly **as** last year.
8 Next year, I'll leave **earlier**. I couldn't get hold of a taxi.

1c Students may need access to dictionaries for this exercise. If so, encourage them to work out the correct form of the words before they look up the meanings. Again, get them to compare answers in pairs before checking with the class.

1 more enthusiastically 2 most popular 3 more widely
4 better known 5 bigger 6 wider 7 as enthusiastic
8 liveliest 9 most sensational 10 more commercialised

2 Give students plenty of time to study the grammar box before attempting the exercise. Point out that to do well in the exam, it is not enough just to use basic comparative and superlative structures – they should be able to demonstrate use of these modifiers when using adjectives and adverbs.

1 by far the largest 2 much more crowded 3 quite as long as
4 a lot more colourful 5 far spicier 6 easily the mildest
7 just about the worst

3a Remind students to use modifiers in their sentences.
3b This could be done in pairs or small groups, with brief class feedback.

Use of English 1 p. 18

1a–b As this is the first time students encounter key word transformations, and they are an area of the exam that students often find problematic, it is important to go through the examples carefully with the class. Explain or elicit that the two sentences in each pair express the same idea in different ways, and take time to work through the strategy box before students answer the questions and then do the key word transformations.

1a a B **b** A **1b 1** not (nearly) as old as **2** apart from

2a Before students do the task, ask questions to check their understanding of the rubric, e.g. *Can you change the word given?* (no) *Can you use six words?* (no) *Five words?* (yes). Point out the Help notes for questions 1 and 2. You could ask students to compare answers in pairs before checking with the class.

1 aren't as widely read 2 a much better swimmer than
3 (much) less popular than
Help:
1 passive 2 adjective

2b Students do the second part of the task, this time without Help notes. Again, you could ask them to compare answers in pairs before checking with the class.

4 is more difficult to study 5 always borrowing my things without
6 (only) a little more slowly

3 Students could discuss the questions in pairs or small groups before class feedback. You could then discuss strategies for further practice in areas they found difficult, such as using the notes in Expert grammar, referring to grammar practice materials, the school study centre, etc.

1 a 5; **b** 1, 2, 3, 4, 6 **2** Students' own answers

Use of English 2 p. 19

1 Check that students understand *hospitality* (friendly behaviour towards visitors) before they discuss the question.

2a With all text-based exercises, students should understand the gist before attempting to complete the task. Give them a minute to first skim the text and then scan it to find the answers to the three questions.

1 They gave them food and water.
2 an object in the house the guest has admired
3 They might be too embarrassed to refuse food when it is offered.

2b Take time to work through the strategy box before students complete the exercise. Remind them to use the Help notes where they have difficulty.

1 C **2** B **3** D **4** C **5** A **6** B **7** D **8** B
Help:
1 world 2 survived 3 want 4 turn

3a This task analysis discussion could be done in pairs, small groups or as a whole class. See if students managed to guess any of the gapped words before looking at the options. Point out that the areas listed in question 2 (words with similar meanings, phrasal verbs and collocations) are frequently tested in Paper 1 Part 1.

1 Students' own answers **2 a** 2; **b** 5, 8; **c** 1, 6, 7

3b Remind students that they will need to learn a lot of vocabulary during the course and discuss with them ways to organise and use a vocabulary notebook to help them.

Language development 3 p. 20

This section is designed to familiarise students with the concept of collocation. They will need encouragement throughout the course to notice collocations as they occur and to record them in their vocabulary notebook.

I When students have found the collocations in the text on page 19, it might be useful to elicit the opposites for some of them (e.g. *heavy meal – light meal*), to further demonstrate how collocation works.

> ancient world, passing travellers, old customs, traditional Japanese household, special cloth, foreign guest

2 Students may be unfamiliar with this type of diagram, which is sometimes known as a spidergram. If so, spend a little time explaining how they can be a useful memory aid, as they help learners with strong visual memories and may help to categorise vocabulary in a similar way to the brain.

> apple(s), milk, look, grapes

3a Students could do this activity in pairs or compare answers in pairs before class feedback. Note that although some other adjective + noun collocations might be possible here (e.g. *strong clothes*, *wide heels*), they are not common and therefore cannot really be regarded as 'strong' collocations.

> strong: argument, feelings, influence, possibility
> plain: English, clothes
> wide: choice, gap, grin, variety
> high: heels, number, speed

3b Students complete the sentences with collocations from Exercise 3a. Point out that more than one answer is possible in one of the items, and get them to compare answers in pairs before you check as a class.

> **I** strong feelings   **2** plain English   **3** wide grin   **4** high speed
> **5** wide choice/wide variety   **6** strong influence   **7** High heels
> **8** strong possibility

Photocopiable activity

Activity 1B (p. 89) can be used here. It practises adjective + noun collocations, including some of the collocations covered in Exercise 3 above.

4 This might be a good point in the course to show students how phrasal verbs are listed in dictionaries. (e.g. *pick sth/ sb* (*up* in the in *Longman Exams Dictionary*, where the symbol (is used to mean that the object can come before or after the participle, i.e. that the verb is separable, compared with *pick on sb/sth*, which is inseparable). Check that students understand the different meanings of *pick up* in the two sentences.

> obvious: 1; idiomatic: 2

5a Point out to students that it is a good idea to learn the phrasal verbs with the nouns they collocate with, e.g. *turn the heat up*, *keep costs down*.

> **I** up   **2** down   **3** down   **4** up   **5** down   **6** up

5b After checking answers with the class, you could ask students to work in pairs and write alternative endings for the sentence beginnings 1–8.

> **I** d   **2** f   **3** e   **4** g   **5** c   **6** h   **7** b   **8** a

5c Get students to compare answers in pairs before you check with the class.

> **I** h   **2** e   **3** f   **4** g   **5** b   **6** d   **7** c   **8** a

6 Ask students to record the phrasal verbs in their vocabulary notebooks. It would be useful to revise some of these verbs in a future lesson. One good way of doing so is to play *Noughts and crosses*. Divide the class into teams. The object of the game is for one team to complete a row of three squares (vertical, horizontal or diagonal) in a grid with their symbol, either 'noughts' (0) or crosses (x). Draw a square on the board and divide it into nine smaller squares by drawing two horizontal lines and two vertical lines inside it. Write one phrasal verb into each square. Teams take it in turns to choose a verb and put it into a sentence. If it is correct, they can put their symbol in the square. The first team with three squares in a row wins.

7 This activity would work well in pairs or small groups.

2 | Earning a living

Module 2 includes topics such as growing up, schools/education and work.

Lead-in p. 21

Elicit the difference between the words *job* and *work* (*job* (countable): the specific thing that you do for a living; *work* (uncountable): the general concept) and between *job* and *career* (*career*: a job or profession that you plan to do for several years). Then elicit the names of the jobs shown in the photos (barrister, artist, clothes designer, stockbroker). Ask students if they would like to do any of the jobs shown and to give reasons for their answers. Finally, get them to discuss the lead-in questions.

Background

In the UK *lawyers* are divided into *solicitors*, who give legal advice and prepare documents, and *barristers* (shown in the photo), who represent people in court.

2A Work

Reading pp. 22–23

1 Ask students if they know of anyone that has quit a job to start their own business and why they did so. Then ask them to look at the photo and title of the article and discuss the questions. You could add a third question: *Why do you think the company is called Innocent?*

2 Refer students back to the first strategy box on page 8, then ask them to read the article and check their answers to the questions in Exercise 1. You could get them to discuss/compare answers in pairs before you check as a class.

3 Start by looking at the strategy boxes, then get students to mark the key words in the questions before they do the task. You could also suggest a different technique for answering multiple-choice questions here: students look at the question first and then try to find the answer in the text without looking at the options. Remind students that for each question, they should mark the parts of the text that contain the information they need. Do not confirm answers yet.

1 B   **2** C   **3** A   **4** D   **5** C   **6** B

4 Ask students to discuss their answers to Exercise 3, explaining why they chose each option. They could do this in pairs or small groups. Then check answers as a class.

5 Students are likely to encounter words with which they are unfamiliar. If the words are in an important part of the text, students should use the strategy highlighted here to deduce the meanings. Ask students to look at the underlined words in the text and try to work out the meanings from the context. If they find this difficult, put the following definitions on the board and ask students to match them with the underlined words.

1 encouragement to work harder

2 very little

3 keep something in order to sell it

4 tell your employer officially that you are leaving your job

5 unusual behaviour or appearance

6 something put in food, usually to make it taste better or to preserve it

Get students to find other new words in the text and use the strategy to guess the meanings. Use the opportunity to advise students on how to organise their vocabulary notebooks – they often need a lot of encouragement initially.

You could finish off with a brief class discussion, using the following questions:

1 Would you prefer to have your own business or work for someone else?

2 What are the benefits and drawbacks of setting up your own business?

3 What type of business would you like to have?

resigned = tell your employer officially that you are leaving your job
additives = something put in food, usually to make it taste better or to preserve it
stock = keep something in order to sell it
quirkiness = unusual behaviour or appearance
minimal = very little
incentives = something that encourages you to work harder

Photocopiable activity

Activity 2A (p. 91) can be used here. It is a group discussion on various aspects of a variety of jobs.

Language development 1 pp. 24–25

With books closed, ask students for ways of finding jobs (e.g. asking around, job centres, advertisements, relatives) and the process of getting them (e.g. see an advertisement, write a letter of application, attend an interview). Discuss students' experiences of applying for jobs and/or attending interviews.

1a Get students to read the advert and letter and discuss the question in pairs. Note the spelling variation: *program* (AmE), *programme* (BrE). Point out that either is acceptable in the exam as long as there is consistency.

Yes, she is. Her first language is Spanish, her English is good and she has some experience of working with children.

1b If students are not familiar with the names of the tenses, give them some examples before they do the exercise.

past simple: spent, helped
present perfect simple: have (often) been, have learned, haven't worked

1c This is to draw students' attention to the different uses of the tenses and is also preparation for completing the grammar box in the next exercise. You may want to let students discuss the questions in pairs before class feedback.

1 no **2** no **3** yes (last year) **4** yes (two years ago)

1d Give students enough time to complete the grammar box, then check answers with the class.

A
1 I have often been to California ...
2 I have learned a lot of English over the years.
3 I haven't worked at a summer camp before.
B
1 Last year I spent two months on an internship program in San Francisco.
2 Two years ago I helped at a children's charity here in Peru for a month.

2a Ask students to complete the extracts individually and then compare answers in pairs. It would be helpful to compare/contrast the two perfect forms of *go* at this stage (e.g. *He has gone to the USA./He has been to the USA.*) with suitable concept questions (e.g. *Where is he now? Has he returned?*).

1
A: Have you ever lived abroad?
B: Yes, I have.
A: Where did you live?
A: When did you go there?
2
A: Have you ever worked in an office?
B: No, I haven't.
3
A: Have you ever been to the USA?
B: Yes, I have.
A: When did you go there?
A: Why did you go there?

4
A: Have you used English in your work before?
B: No, I haven't.

2b This activity would work well in pairs.

3a Students complete the exercise individually, then check answers as a class.

present perfect simple: have lived, have (just) taken, haven't had
present perfect continuous: have been studying, have been taking

3b Like Exercise 1c, this is to draw students' attention to the different uses of the tenses and also to prepare them for the next exercise, where they complete the grammar box.

1 yes **2** yes **3** I **4** yes **5** maybe – we don't know

3c Give students enough time to complete the grammar box, then check answers with the class.

A I have lived in Lima since 2011.
B I have been studying for a degree in education for two years.
C I have just taken my second-year exams.
D I have been taking part in a series of workshops on children's games.

4 *For* and *since* are frequently tested in the exam and also often confused by students. Ask students to read the information and complete the phrases, then check answers with the class. One way to give further practice is to give each student two pieces of paper, one with the word *for* and the other with the word *since*. Then call out a list of time expressions (e.g. *six months*, *last year*, *October*, *Friday*, *five days*, *five o'clock*, *Christmas*), and as you say each one, students hold up the correct piece of paper. To make it a game, you could award points for correct answers.

1 for **2** since **3** for **4** since **5** for **6** since

5 Remind students that this type of checking and correcting is important with their own written work. Get them to justify their answers.

1 ✓
2 I**'ve had** some good news. I've got the job!
3 ✓
4 ✓
5 Emma**'s fallen over** and hurt her knee.
6 The lift isn't working, so we**'ve been using** the stairs all day.

6 Students complete the extract with the correct verb forms. Point out that more than one answer may be possible in some items. You could get students to compare answers in pairs before checking with the class.

1 have been **2** haven't written **3** haven't been waiting **4** have been working **5** haven't had **6** felt **7** have made/have been making **8** have been trying **9** have found **10** have been staying

7 This is an opportunity for less controlled personalised practice of the structures. Encourage students to try and write interesting true sentences but to use their imagination if they can't think of anything true to write.

8 This could be done with a competitive element: you could ask students to work in pairs and see which pair is the quickest to find and correct the eight mistakes.

I **was** born in Peru 26 years ago and I've lived here all my life. I **have been** married for two years but we don't have any children yet. I've been working in a bank **for** four years and I enjoy it a lot. In my spare time I'm trying to improve my English – I**'ve been having** private lessons for six months now. I also love reading. Last year I **tried** to read a novel in English. I **have been going** to the mountains for my holidays **for** six years because I love walking. I **also went** to Brazil two years ago to stay with some friends.

Writing pp. 26–27

1 Point out to students that in Paper 2 Part 2, they may be asked to write a formal letter or email. Go through the list of different types of email/letter and discuss the questions with the class.

very formal: d, e; semi-formal: c and possibly a and b, depending on the relationship; informal: f;
It depends on the relationship, e.g. how friendly you are with your neighbour.

2 In the exam, as with all writing, the writer needs a clear focus on the reason for writing. Students should consider these four questions for every piece of writing they do now.

1 the Lifeguard Manager **2** to apply for a job **3** personal information, experience, qualifications, suitability (and possibly availability) **4** positive, enthusiastic

3a Again, emphasise that the planning stage is vital if students are to include all the important information within the word count and use a range of structures/vocabulary. You could ask students to discuss their answers in pairs before class feedback.

1 b (The name comes at the end.)
2 a, c, e, f, g, j
3 c
4 a (Referees would normally be given in the accompanying CV.)

3b Encourage students just to make notes at this stage, not to start writing the actual paragraphs.

4a Point out that the only problem here is the level of formality. All the sentences contain good English and interesting phrases.

appropriately formal: 2, 6, 10
too informal: 1, 3, 4, 5, 7, 8, 9

4b Give students enough time to study the phrases in the table before they rewrite the sentences. Point out that more than one answer may be possible.

Suggested answers:
1 I would like to apply for the position of lifeguard assistant, which I saw advertised in a student newspaper.
3 At present I am studying at university and I am a good swimmer.
4 I regret I have had no experience of this kind of work but I am a good swimmer.
5 I very much enjoy working with people.
7 I think I would be a suitable candidate for this job because …
8 I would be happy to attend an interview.
9 I hope you will consider my application.

4c Point out to students that it is important that their letter/email has a suitable opening and closing. Check answers with the class.

opening: 2 (As the name of the manager is unknown, this is the only suitable opening.)
closing: 7 (This is the best ending when no name has been used at the beginning. In British English, if there is a name at the beginning (e.g. *Dear Mr Smith*), *Yours sincerely* is usually used at the end.)

5 Now that students have done detailed work on the planning of their email, the writing should not take more than 20 minutes.

Sample answer:
Dear Sir or Madam,
I am looking for outdoor work during the summer holidays and I would like to apply for the position of lifeguard assistant, which I saw advertised in my university's student newspaper.
I am 20 years old and at present I am studying Physical Education. I am a strong swimmer and have recently had first aid training.
I very much enjoy working with people and for the last two summers I have been working as an assistant ranger in a National Park, where I had to provide information to the public about using the park and provide emergency assistance to park users. Now I am looking for something different.
I think I would be a suitable candidate for the position because I have been described as calm in a crisis and someone who works well with others.
I am available for the whole of August and would be happy to attend an interview at any time. I look forward to hearing from you at any time in the near future.
Yours faithfully,

6 Checking and editing should take another ten minutes. Remind students that contractions and direct questions are not used in formal letters/emails. When they check the number of words, teach them at this stage to calculate the average number of words per line and then just count the lines. By the time of the exam, they should have a good feel for the right number of words in their handwriting and therefore won't need to waste time counting every word.

2B A learning experience

As a lead-in, with books closed, put students in pairs or groups to talk briefly about the school(s) they go/went to. Give suitable prompts if necessary (e.g. *State or private? Single-sex or mixed? Strict or relaxed?*).

Speaking pp. 28–29

I Ask students to look at the photos and match them with the stages of education. Check answers, then discuss the question about schools/colleges in the students' country/countries.

> I C   2 B   3 D   4 A

2a You could ask students to work in pairs to match the words with the different stages of education, then discuss as a class. Point out that some of the words might go with more than one photo.

Background

Continuous assessment is a way of judging a student's work by looking at what they have achieved during the year in tests, essays and projects rather than by testing them in a final year exam. It is said to give a more complete picture of a student's ability and understanding as they are free from time pressures. However, with students increasingly using the internet to research assignments, many institutions are considering returning to the use of exams.

2b This exercise gives students practice in identifying syllable stress. Encourage students to compare answers in pairs after completing it and play the recording for them to check their answers. You could then play it a second time, pausing after each word for students to repeat it, checking that their pronunciation is correct as required.

> continuous assessment   curriculum   degree   exams
> head teacher   higher education   homework   lecturer
> playground   playgroup   strict discipline   tutorial
> undergraduate   uniform

3 Check that students know the meaning and pronunciation of the items. A list of school subjects is a useful lexical set under the topic of education. A spidergram in a vocabulary notebook would be a good way to record them. When checking answers to question 2, ensure students are pronouncing the words correctly.

> **2** dramatist   economist   engineer   historian   linguist
> mathematician   philosopher   scientist   sociologist

Background

Many school subjects are abbreviated: *PE* = physical education, *ICT* = Information and Communications Technology, *DT* = Design and Technology, *RP* = Religion and Philosophy, *PSHE* = Personal, Social and Health Education.

4 Point out that students should notice the collocations as they do the exercise (e.g. *sit/pass/fail exams*, *attend lectures*).

> **I** paid   **2** skipped   **3** failed   **4** resit   **5** passed   **6** apply
> **7** doing   **8** get   **9** study   **10** attends   **11** revises

5 Students can discuss the questions in pairs, small groups or as a whole class.

6a Draw students' attention to the spidergram, then play the recording for them to answer the question. They should not discuss the question in the spidergram at this stage – they will do this later.

> They have to discuss the question between them for about two minutes. In this task, they are asked to talk about how the changes would benefit the students.

6b Ask students to read the strategy first, then explain that they are going to hear two candidates doing the first part of a collaborative task. Play the recording, then ask students which points of view they agree/disagree with, and why.

6c Give students time to study the table, then play the recording again for them to complete the phrases.

> **I** personally, I think   **2** me   **3** least important   **4** agree more
> **5** true   **6** suppose   **7** up to a point   **8** think   **9** not so sure
> **10** what you mean but   **11** don't think that matters

7 Divide students in pairs and give them time to look at the spidergram again and to prepare before the discussion. Monitor and check that they are using the language for giving opinions, agreeing and disagreeing, and give feedback on this afterwards.

8 Refer students back to the strategy box and get them to briefly discuss the question. They could do this in pairs, small groups or as a whole class.

9a–b Give students time to look at the statements and think about them first. Remind them to use the functional language as they discuss the points, and again give feedback on this afterwards.

Listening p. 30

Ia Start by getting students to briefly describe the photo and then ask them to discuss the questions in pairs, small groups or as a whole class.

Ib Ask students to look at questions I and 2 first, and the highlighted key words. Ask them what they think the answers might be. They should then mark the key words in the rest of the questions and try to predict what they might hear. Point out that they should *not* read the options yet.

2 Go through the strategy box before students do the task. Before they listen, remind them that opinions might be expressed in different words from those written in the options. Do not confirm answers yet.

> **I** B   **2** A   **3** C   **4** C   **5** B   **6** A   **7** C

3 Ask students to compare and discuss their answers in pairs, then play the recording for them to check. Finally, check answers with the class.

4 Students could also discuss their opinions on whether it is good to work while studying.

5 After checking answers, you could ask students to make sentences of their own using the collocations. Encourage them to record the collocations in their vocabulary notebooks.

1 g **2** h **3** f **4** b **5** a **6** e **7** c **8** d

Use of English 1 p. 31

1 This exercise is a quick introduction to the topic of the text. Don't spend long on it and don't expect students to come up with too much detail!

Background

Albert Einstein (1879–1955) was born German but became a Swiss citizen in 1901. He emigrated to the USA in 1933. His theory of relativity was just one of many great theories. When the first atom bomb was used, he said that if he had known what his discoveries would be used for, he would have been a watchmaker. After the Second World War, he campaigned against nuclear weapons.

2a Explain to students that the purpose of the two questions is to get a general understanding of the text and that they should only spend a minute or so looking at the text to find the answers.

1 science
2 He didn't like exams or going to classes.

2b First go through the strategy box with the class. Elicit ways of identifying whether the missing word is a noun, article, verb, pronoun, etc. (e.g. *What word follows the gap? What type of words are followed by -ing forms?*). When students first work through the text, point out that they don't have to fill in the gaps in order; harder ones can be left until others have been filled in, by which time they might seem easier. Remind students that they can use the Help notes for support with certain items.

1 a **2** all **3** what/as **4** neither/nor **5** Despite/After
6 the **7** where **8** was

2c It might be useful for students to discuss these questions in pairs before giving them the answers and explanations.

1 0, 1, 2, 3, 6 **2** b

3 Another question to discuss could be: *Do you think that, generally speaking, school/university exams are a good indication of how successful someone will be?*

Language development 2 p. 32

1a It might be useful to elicit some uses of articles with books closed before students read the grammar box and look for examples in the text.

A
before singular, countable nouns: he was unable to get a job in a university, he worked in a secondary school, Einstein got a job with jobs: he was not a particularly good student
B
in certain expressions: one of the best, one of the greatest when there is only one of something: the entrance exam, the Swiss Federal Institute of Technology
C
when talking about something in general: At school, he didn't like exams
before subjects of study: outstanding in mathematics and physics
before most countries, continents, towns and streets: in Munich, in Zurich, in Bern
in certain expressions: in the history of

1b Do the first question as an example with the class, asking suitable concept questions for each part, e.g.: *How many best courses can you have?* (only one) '*... the one I did*': do *we know which one?* (yes) '*the economics*': what type of word is '*economics*'? (a subject of study) '*The teacher*': do *we know which teacher?* (yes) '*a good progress*': is progress countable or uncountable? (uncountable)

Encourage students to work through the other sentences in the same way.

1 The best course was the one I did on the~~the~~ economics.
The teacher was very good and I made a~~a~~ good progress.
2 Nina's studying the~~the~~ German at evening classes in the~~the~~ London.
3 My brother is 19. He's at the~~the~~ university in the~~the~~ Africa and wants to become **an** English teacher because it would give him **a** good opportunity to travel.
4 When we were in Japan, we noticed that most Japanese students work harder than the American students I met in **the** USA.
5 I go to college by the~~the~~ train. Unfortunately, the train is often late.

1c Students should work through the gapped text with the same systematic approach. Note how *college* is used in different ways in the text, illustrating different uses of articles; *students wanted a college* (indefinite), *the location of the college* (definite), *go to college* (fixed phrase).

1 – **2** a **3** – **4** the **5** the **6** the **7** the **8** the **9** the
10 The **11** a **12** – **13** a **14** a **15** – **16** – **17** –

2 Give students time to read through the grammar box before doing the exercise. You could then get them to compare answers in pairs before checking with the class.

> **1** some **2** any **3** anything **4** some **5** anything **6** some
> **7** hardly any **8** some **9** some **10** anything

Photocopiable activity

Activity 2B (p. 92) can be used here. Students complete the missing articles in a story and retell it to a partner.

Use of English 2 p. 33

1 Start by asking students to briefly describe the photo. They then discuss the questions in pairs, small groups or as a whole class.

2a As with other Use of English tasks, it is important for students to have a general understanding of the text before attempting the task. Ask them to read the text quickly, ignoring the gaps at this stage, and answer the two questions.

> **1** trying to remember things **2** Use all senses, so listen to as well as read the information. Study at the right time (before bed) and in the right atmosphere (peaceful).

2b Go through the strategy box before students do the task. Look at the example and do question 1 together, to help students with the strategy. You could get students to compare answers in pairs before checking with the class.

> **1** countless **2** valuable **3** silently **4** combination **5** written
> **6** unlikely **7** possibility **8** peaceful
> **Help:**
> **3** an adverb

3 These questions focus students on the strategy and introduce words such as *suffix* and *prefix*, which students may not be familiar with.

> **1** Students' own answers
> **2 a** 0, 4, 7; **b** 1, 2, 5, 6, 8; **c** 3
> **3 a** 1, 2, 3, 4, 7, 8; **b** 6
> **4** Students' own answers

4 You could also ask students whether they think listening to music helps people study or when the best time to revise something is.

Language development 3 p. 34

1a This is the first time suffixes are dealt with in the book. Emphasise that many types of words are formed by adding suffixes and that this section only looks at adjectives. Give students advice on recording suffixes in their vocabulary notebooks. Suggest that each time they learn a new word they also record the related words formed with suffixes (e.g. *suit*, *suitable*, *unsuitable*, *suitability*, *suitably*). As you check answers, point out changes in stress as the nouns change to adjectives (*courage* – *cour*a*geous*; *drama* – *dra*ma*tic*).

> **1** harmless **2** natural **3** courageous **4** childish **5** helpful
> **6** passionate **7** dirty **8** horrible **9** dramatic **10** lively

1b Students can discuss the questions in pairs, small groups or as a whole class.

2a Students could either do this in pairs or individually, using dictionaries. If they use dictionaries, explain how phrasal verbs are listed in the dictionary. This is another useful lexical set under the topic of education, so a spidergram in students' vocabulary notebooks would be a good way to record these phrasal verbs.

> **1** g **2** a **3** h **4** c **5** j **6** i **7** b **8** d **9** e **10** f

2b Do the first question as an example with the class, to ensure they are thinking about both the correct verb and the correct tense.

> **1** turned up **2** staying on **3** carry out **4** work out
> **5** Go over **6** handed in **7** keep up with **8** pick up
> **9** get, across **10** got down to

3 The world around us

Module 3 includes topics such as cultural heritage, the environment, weather and animals.

Lead-in p. 35

With books closed, get students to think of three man-made and three natural things which they see around them on a normal day. Compare ideas as a class. Then ask them to look at the photos and say which place they would prefer to visit and why. Explain *World Heritage Sites* briefly (see Background below). Then get students to discuss the questions in pairs or small groups, followed by class feedback.

Background

A World Heritage Site is a place listed by the UNESCO (United Nations Educational, Scientific and Cultural Organization) as one of special cultural or natural significance. The World Heritage List includes over 980 properties which the World Heritage Committee considers as having outstanding universal value.

The Historic Centre of Kraków, the former capital of Poland, is situated at the foot of the Royal Wawel Castle. The town has Europe's largest market square and numerous historical houses, palaces, churches and monasteries, with magnificent interiors. The entire medieval old town is among the first sites chosen for UNESCO's World Heritage List.

The Los Glaciares National Park in Santa Cruz, Argentina was chosen as a World Heritage Site as an area of exceptional natural beauty. The park has two distinct regions: forests and grassy plains in the east, and needle-like peaks, lakes, large glaciers and snowfields in the west. Wildlife includes chinchillas, pudu and guemal (two species of deer), condors and rheas.

3A Our cultural heritage

Reading pp. 36–37

1   With books closed, ask students what they know about London and its history.

2   Refer students back to the strategy boxes on page 8 and remind them of the difference between skimming and scanning. Ask them first to skim to get a general idea of its content. If necessary, set a time limit of about 2–3 minutes. They then scan the text to find information about the items listed.

the Romans: developed the area around the River Thames into a trading centre, in the hope of establishing the city as the future capital of England
the Vikings: burnt the city to the ground in the ninth century
the Normans: the city continued to grow, although overcrowding resulted in fires and illness
Henry VIII: gave away much of the land previously owned by the church for private development, the first theatres were built
the Plague: caused panic and wiped out much of the population.
the Great Fire: ended the Plague, but burnt down four-fifths of the city
the Industrial Revolution: arrival of the railways, London became the centre of trade, population increased to six million
World War II: bombs ruined much of the city

3   As this is the first time students have encountered a gapped text, spend some time going through the rubric and strategy box with them. Point out that the sentences must fit logically with both the preceding and following sentences, and also grammatically. The example demonstrates this. Do not confirm answers at this stage, as students are asked to compare and discuss their answers in the next exercise.

2 F   **3** C   **4** E   **5** B   **6** A

4   Allow enough time for students to compare and discuss their answers in pairs or small groups, then check answers with the class.

5   Give students time to think about the questions before they discuss them in pairs or small groups, then as a whole class.

6   Students could do this exercise in pairs or individually. Encourage them to record near synonyms in their vocabulary notebooks.

1 put off   **2** hygiene   **3** wipe out   **4** fatal   **5** calamity
6 sprang up

Language development 1 pp. 38–39

1a Ask students to look at the photos. Do they know what the three sites are and where they are?

The sites in the photos are (top to bottom): the Taj Mahal (India), the Statue of Liberty (New York, USA) and the Islamic centre of Marrakesh (Morocco).

21

Background

The Taj Mahal, near Agra in India, was built by the Mughal emperor Shah Jahan in memory of his wife, Mumtaz Mahal ('Chosen One of the Palace'), of which the name Taj Mahal is a corruption. She died in 1631 and the building was commenced around 1632. It took 16 years to complete and is estimated to have cost 32 million rupees (530,000 US dollars).

The Statue of Liberty stands in New York Harbor. It is 92 metres high and made of copper sheets over a steel frame. Begun by the French sculptor Frédéric-Auguste Bartholdi in 1875, it was dismantled in 1885, shipped to New York and reassembled.

Marrakesh, a major city in central Morocco, was founded in 1070–1072. The lively medina contains an impressive number of architectural masterpieces, including the walls and the monumental gates, the Kutubiya Mosque with its 77-metre-high minaret, the Saadian tombs and characteristic old houses.

1b After they have read the text, ask students if they know any other World Heritage Sites, perhaps in their own country.

They are all World Heritage Sites.

2a Students write the words in italics from the text in the correct column. You could ask them to compare answers in pairs before checking with the class.

Adjectives: cultural, best-known, lively, impressive, fascinating, bleak, worrying, political, full
Adverbs: fast, hard, actively, extremely, hardly, well

2b/c Before feedback, refer students to the Expert grammar section (page 186) and ask them to check their answers. During feedback, go through the questions one by one with the class. If necessary, use further examples to highlight the difference between the adverbs *hard* and *hardly* (e.g. *He works hard. = He works a lot. He hardly works. = He doesn't work very much at all – he does almost no work.*).

1 fast, hard, well   2 lively   3 hard – hardly

3a You could ask students to compare answers in pairs before checking with the class.

1 easy   2 incredibly   3 fast   4 classic   5 late, hard
6 surprising, imaginatively

3b Remind students that World Heritage Sites can be cultural and/or natural and should be of 'outstanding universal value'. It would be interesting for students to check whether their chosen place is already a World Heritage Site – they may not even know that it is!

4 Tell students that this language is frequently tested in Paper 1 and that it can make their writing and speaking more interesting in Papers 2 and 4. Get them to compare answers in pairs before checking with the class.

1 D   2 C   3 A   4 C   5 B   6 D   7 B

5 This is an opportunity for less controlled, personalised practice of the language, probably best in small groups followed by class discussion.

6 Correcting is a vital element of writing and students should be encouraged to check their own writing, looking for typical mistakes such as these. Get students to compare answers in pairs before checking with the class.

1 It's easy to find my house. There's **a huge/an absolutely huge** statue on the other side of the road.
2 The park is really lovely and the new theatre is **fantastic/absolutely fantastic**.
3 You don't need to be **smartly** dressed. People dress casually here in summer.
4 They are working very **hard** to restore the Town Hall before the president's visit next month.
5 It's a fairly lively town, which I like, but the streets are sometimes **a** bit noisy at night.

Photocopiable activity

Activity 3A (p. 94) can be used here. It gives further practice of adjectives and adverbs.

Writing pp. 40–41

1 This exercise introduces the topic of the essay. Students could discuss the questions in pairs or small groups, making notes which they will later use to plan their essay.

2 Remind students that in the exam, they will be required to write an essay for Part 1 and that they should aim to write 140–190 words. Ask them to read the task carefully and discuss the questions in pairs. Then go through the answers with the whole class. Emphasise that it is very important for students to think about these questions in all their essay writing. It would be useful to encourage students to get into the habit of underlining the key words in all tasks.

1 a teacher; to summarise a discussion and give an opinion
2 most likely: for and against
3 the past, the future and your own idea
4 fairly formal
5 a balanced discussion, good organisation, inclusion of all the ideas and supporting information, clear linking of ideas and a range of structure and vocabulary, a mix of simple and complex sentences, register consistently appropriate, ideas effectively communicated

3a Ask students to look at their notes from Exercise 1 and see if any of their points can be used in the essay. If not, ask them to think about things to include for points 1 and 2 and make notes.

3b Students think about the third point in the essay and make notes. They could do this on their own or in pairs.

3c Remind students that their writing needs to be well organised. A good plan should include key points to include in each paragraph, as well as supporting points for each general/introductory statement. Go through the rubric, strategy box and paragraph plan with the class and then ask students to make notes for each paragraph in their essay.

4a Point out to students that normally, an essay would be semi-formal/neutral. Ask them to choose the best option in each pair, then discuss the answers with the class.

4b Students match the sentences from the previous exercise with the paragraphs in Exercise 3. They could do this individually or in pairs.

4c Again, students could do this exercise on their own or in pairs before class feedback.

> **4a–c**
>
> **A** 1; last paragraph, first sentence
> **B** 2; para 1, first sentence
> **C** 2; para 3/4, second sentence or second part of first sentence
> **D** 1; para 2, first sentence

4d Students think of supporting points for each of the main/introductory sentences in Exercise 4a.

> **Example answers:**
> **A** 1 However, it's not realistic to try and save everything.
> **B** 2 Nevertheless, there is a strong argument we should look forwards, not backwards
> **D** 1 Once it is lost, it is lost for ever.

4e Check answers to the matching task before students write complete sentences for their own essay. When they have written their sentences, you could ask them to swap with a partner and check each other's work.

> **Suggested answers:**
> **1** arguments against (paras 3/4)
> **2** arguments for (paras 2/3)
> **3** arguments against (paras 3/4)
> **4** conclusion (para 4 or 5)
> **5** introduction (para 1)
> **6** arguments for (paras 2/3)
> **7** introduction (para 1)
> **8** conclusion (para 4 or 5)
> **9** arguments against (paras 3/4)

5 As students now have a detailed paragraph plan, the writing should take only about 20 minutes. In the exam, if students aim to spend 15 minutes planning and 20 minutes writing, they will have ten minutes to check their work.

> **Sample answer:**
> Most countries spend large sums of money protecting their national heritage. However, there is strong argument that we should look forwards not backwards, spending less money on preserving the past and more on securing our future.
> On the one hand, it is important that we remember our heritage. Once it is lost, it is lost forever. Caring for important monuments helps with this. It also attracts tourists, which has an economic benefit for everyone.
> On the other hand, governments spend a lot of money on museums and keeping historic sites in good condition when poor people need houses to live in and businesses need better roads for transporting their goods.

Another argument is that by making heritage sites attractive for tourists – for example, by putting on entertainment – we give a very untrue picture of the past and sometimes damage the local environment.

To conclude, while there are strong arguments for not spending too much on preserving the past, I believe it is important to protect the most famous sites for future generations but it is not realistic to try and save everything. We need to invest in the future too.

6 After students have checked their own essay using the checklist here, you could ask them to work in pairs, swap essays and evaluate each other's work using the same checklist.

Expert language: Punctuation

Although poor punctuation is not specifically penalised in the exam, the overall impression mark may be adjusted if communication is impeded. Students could use the Punctuation section in Expert writing (page 206) to help them with any they are not sure about, and/or to help check when they have finished.

> When you're in England you must visit Chester. It dates back to Roman times, so there are lots of fascinating ruins, which I'm sure will interest you and which English Heritage, a branch of the British Government, wants to preserve. The Roman amphitheatre is well worth a visit, with its guides dressed up as Roman soldiers. There is also a cathedral and a church and there are red sandstone walls all around the town. It takes about an hour and a half to walk round them but it's a lovely walk. Henry James, the American writer, wrote about how much he loved these walls. Unfortunately, many of Chester's heritage sites were destroyed in the 20th century to make way for a ring road and more are under threat in this century.

3B Our natural heritage

As a lead-in, with books closed, play a quick game to introduce the topic of animals: go round the class asking different students to name an animal beginning with a different letter of the alphabet (*ant, bee, crocodile, dog, elephant, frog, goat, hamster*, etc.), with those who can't think of one quickly dropping out until one winner remains.

Speaking pp. 42–43

1a Get students to identify the animals in the photos. Many students are confused by the difference between mice and rats (mentioned in the text on London on page 37). Ask students to think of other words ending in *-f* or *-fe* that change to *-ves* in the plural (e.g. *shelf, knife*).

> **A** butterfly – butterflies   **B** goat – goats
> **C** lizard – lizards   **D** goldfish – goldfish   **E** wolf – wolves
> **F** sea lion – sea lions   **G** mouse – mice   **H** parrot – parrots

1b–e Use the photos to get examples of the words listed and then elicit other suggestions from students.

1b
Suggested answers: farm: goat (mouse); jungle: parrot (butterfly, lizard); forest: wolf (butterfly); house: goldfish, mouse (parrot)
Others: butterfly: garden, countryside; lizard: desert, forest, house; sea lion: sea/beach; mouse: field, house
1c
Suggested answers: insect: butterfly, rodent: mouse, reptile: lizard, sea animal: sea lion, domestic pet: parrot, goldfish, mouse
1d
1 mouse, wolf, goat   2 butterfly, parrot   3 lizard, wolf, sea lion, mouse, parrot   4 wolf, sea lion, mouse   5 parrot   6 goat
7 goat, wolf, mouse   8 goldfish, sea lion
1e
1 mouse   2 wolf   3 parrot

2 Students can work individually or in pairs for this exercise. Point out that sorting new vocabulary into lists is a good way to process the language and helps to remember it.

1 guinea pig, hamster, pigeon, rabbit, tortoise   2 bee, bull, calf, sheep   3 ant, bear, beaver, bee, beetle, dolphin, giraffe, leopard, moose, mosquito, penguin, shark, rabbit, squirrel, vulture, whale
4 penguin, pigeon, vulture   5 ant, bee, beetle, mosquito

3 After checking answers with the class, elicit or teach the parts of the animal used for the verbs in 1–4 (*bite*: teeth, *peck*: beak, *sting*: sting, *scratch*: claw).

Example answers:
1 dog, mosquito   2 bird   3 bee, wasp, scorpion   4 cat   5 bear
6 most birds   7 Siberian tiger, sea turtle, mountain gorilla, African black rhino, giant panda

4a–b Allow a certain amount of individual interpretation here.

Example answers:
1 crocodile   2 snake   3 lion   4 tiger   5 fox   6 jaguar
7 cat   8 donkey   9 dog

5 You could add: *What animal would you most like to be and why?*

6 There may be some discussion about exactly what each person's job is, which gives you the opportunity to teach some useful vocabulary. The man in the photo on the left could be a farmer or a shepherd. The woman in the photo on the right could be a vet, a veterinary nurse or a veterinary assistant. In British English, *vet* is the most common word; *veterinary surgeon* is more formal. In American English, *veterinarian* is more common.

7 This activity aims to train students to compare the pictures rather than simply describe each one separately, a common mistake in Paper 4 Part 2.

1 They both showing someone looking after animals.   2 In the one on the left a man (a shepherd or farmer) is looking after sheep outdoors, whereas in the other one a woman vet is helping to make a sick dog better.

8a Point out that the instructions for this part usually have two parts: first *compare* … and then *say* … (i.e. give a personal reaction of some kind).

you think the jobs might be difficult

8b Point out to students that as they listen, they need to think about what the candidate says compared with what they said in Exercise 7.

8c Play the recording again, for students to tick the expressions the candidate uses to express personal opinion.

I

8d Play the recording again and ask students to discuss their answers in pairs. Point out that in Paper 4, if students don't know a word, they should explain it in another way, just as the candidate does on the recording. They will be given credit for this by the examiner. If they make no attempt to explain a word they don't know, they could lose marks.

vet: a kind of doctor who looks after animals, a doctor for animals
pets: small animals who live in the home
upsetting: it must upset her

8e Students could discuss the questions in pairs, small groups or as a whole class.

9 Divide students in pairs and go through the strategy box before they complete the task.

10 Encourage students to discuss their own and each other's performance in the task.

11 Get students to discuss the questions in pairs or small groups, followed by a brief class discussion.

Listening p. 44

1 First ask students to look at and briefly describe the photo. Elicit or teach *jaguar* and *rainforest*. Let students discuss the question in pairs, then explain that they will hear the answer on the recording.

2a Get students to do this in pairs. It is important that students think about what kind of word could go in each gap. Look at the example with them and perhaps do question 2 together, to make sure they know what to do.

1 a plural noun   2 a noun   3 a noun   4 an adjective
5 a measurement   6 a noun   7 a noun   8 a plural noun
9 a noun   10 a noun/noun phrase

2b Go through the strategy box with the students, then play the recording for them to complete the exam task. During feedback, point out that an abbreviation such as *km* in question 5 would be acceptable. The most important thing is to show the examiner that they have understood the material on the recording.

1 tropical birds   2 (day)light   3 motorbikes   4 emotional
5 170 km   6 spider   7 respect   8 landowners   9 dogs
10 lecture tours

3 Let students compare and discuss their answers in pairs. You could finish off by asking students if they would like to do the job that Jay Carter does, and why.

Use of English 1 p. 45

1   This is to generate interest in the topic of animals' unusual abilities – you might want to reassure students that they don't need to know facts like these for the exam! Let students discuss the questions in pairs before you confirm the answers.

All the statements are true.
1 Although cats distinguish some colours better than others, they don't generally distinguish colours very well.
2 It is estimated to be anywhere between 100 and a million times better.
3 They have a very large brain and live for a very long time. They particularly remember extremes of kindness and cruelty on the part of humans.
4 The snowy tree cricket (*Oecanthus fultoni*) is popularly known as 'the thermometer cricket' because the approximate temperature (Fahrenheit) can be estimated by counting the number of chirps in 15 seconds and adding 40.
5 It is believed that they sense changes of air pressure in their digestive system.

2a   Discuss the question with the class and point out that students should always look at the title of a text, as it will give them a clear indication of the content.

Possible answer:
Animals help us to predict when an earthquake is coming.

2b   Again, point out that students should always read any text for a general understanding before they start the exam task.

1 Fish jump onto land. Mice seem dazed.
2 They evacuated a city and saved many lives after the strange behaviour of some animals alerted the authorities to a major earthquake.
3 Some animals' senses are very sensitive, so perhaps they can detect seismic activity before an earthquake.

2c   Ask students to read the strategy on page 31 before they do the task. If you think it necessary, do the first one or two items with the whole class so that they can see the process of deciding what the missing words are.

1 have   **2** to   **3** had   **4** too   **5** the   **6** Since   **7** for   **8** It
Help:
1 present perfect simple   **3** past perfect simple   **5** the

3   This focuses students on choices they made and highlights typical areas tested in this part of the exam.

1 5   **2** 1, 3   **3** 2

Language development 2 p. 46

1a   Students could do this exercise on their own or in pairs.

main verb + *to*-infinitive: scientists began to receive reports
main verb + infinitive without *to*: people have seen fish jump
adjective + infinitive: too frightened to enter buildings

1b   This is a brief lead-in to the grammar exercise that follows. Check that students know the meaning of *solar eclipse*, then discuss the questions.

1 The moon passes exactly in front of the sun and blocks out its light.
2 Students' own answers

1c   Get students to compare answers in pairs before checking answers with the class.

1 to settle down   **2** sleeping   **3** fly   **4** noticing   **5** solving
6 going/go   **7** not recording   **8** feel   **9** to talk   **10** not to drive

2a   After checking answers, you could point out to students that these three verbs are commonly tested in the exam.

1a He remembered that he needed to wear them and then put them on.
b He remembered that he had worn them at some point before then.
2a She experimented with using one to see if it would work or was a good idea.
b She physically attempted to do it. Maybe she didn't succeed.
3a He stopped doing something (e.g. driving) in order to look at the lights.
b He was looking at the lights and then he didn't look at them.

2b   Get students to compare answers in pairs before checking with the class.

1 to buy   **2** to get   **3** drinking   **4** to post   **5** calling   **6** adding

3a   Ask students to look at the photo and tell you what, if anything, they know about this natural phenomenon (see Background below).

Background

The Northern Lights is the popular name for the *aurora borealis*, which occurs when solar particles enter the earth's atmosphere over the North Pole and react with gases, causing them to emit light. In the southern hemisphere, the corresponding phenomenon is known as the Southern Lights or *aurora australis*.

3b   Get students to compare answers in pairs before checking with the class. Encourage them to record the collocations in their vocabulary notebooks.

1 of seeing   **2** to going   **3** in getting   **4** on putting up   **5** for not helping   **6** to go   **7** to her going   **8** on walking   **9** her (from) doing   **10** of getting

4a–b   Encourage students to write true sentences. Get them to compare and discuss their answers in pairs or small groups, then ask a few students to share their sentences with the class.

Photocopiable activity

Activity 3B (p. 96) can be used here. It provides further practice in *-ing* forms and infinitives.

Use of English 2 p. 47

1 Discuss the question with the class. Any students who have seen the film will be familiar with Groundhog Day. Get them to explain it briefly to the others.

Background

In the fantasy comedy film *Groundhog Day* (1993) a weatherman, fed up with reporting on the Punxsutawney story every year, suddenly wakes up and finds himself in a world where every day is 2 February and all the events of that day are repeated daily.

2a Give students one or two minutes to read the text, ignoring the gaps. They could discuss the questions in pairs, small groups or as a whole class.

1 The groundhog 'Punxsutawney Phil' comes out of his hole and people make weather predictions based on his behaviour.
2 The 1993 film *Groundhog Day* has made the event better known in recent years.

2b Remind students to use the strategy on page 19 and the Help notes if they need to.

1 B **2** C **3** A **4** B **5** D **6** A **7** B **8** C

3a Ask students to work on this individually first, then compare answers in pairs.

phrasal verbs: 5, 6
linking words: 7

3b Weather collocations are practised further in Exercise 3a on page 48. Remind students that knowledge of collocation is tested in various parts of the exam. Encourage them to record collocations in their vocabulary notebooks.

clear sky, severe weather, cloudy day, early spring, good weather

Language development 3 p. 48

1 This could be done in pairs or small groups, followed by class discussion. Get students to expand their answers and to support them with reasons.

2a Point out to students that some words may go into more than one category (e.g. *hurricane* could go with both *Wind* and *Storm*; *snow* and *hail* could go with both *Rain* and *Storm*). Encourage students to discuss their answers in pairs or small groups. If they give reasons for their answers, it will help them to understand the meanings of the words. If necessary, use the short definitions in the answer key to help clarify meaning.

Rain: downpour (a lot of rain in a short time), drizzle (light rain), hail (frozen rain), shower (a short period of rain)
Wind: breeze (a light wind), gale (a very strong wind), gust (a sudden, short, strong wind), hurricane (a violent storm, especially in the Western Atlantic; we often associate hurricanes with strong wind)
Storm: lightning (light in the sky caused by electricity), thunder (a loud noise in the sky)

2b If there is time, after feedback you could ask students to write sentences using the incorrect options in italics.

1 lightning **2** gusts **3** hail **4** Hurricanes **5** snow

3a Remind students of the weather collocations they saw in Exercise 3b on page 47. Get them to compare answers in pairs before checking with the class.

1 c, e **2** a, b, c, e, g **3** a, f **4** b, c, e **5** f **6** a, b, e, f **7** d
8 f **9** e **10** e **11** a, f

3b Get students to think of the context of each sentence before completing it. Point out that more than one answer may be possible.

1 high/strong **2** heavy **3** gentle/light **4** loud **5** heavy.
6 chilly **7** torrential/tropical/heavy

4a There may be more than one possibility here, but students should look for the strongest collocations. Get students to compare answers in pairs before checking with the class.

1 d **2** c **3** e **4** a **5** b

4b After feedback, encourage students to record these collocations in their vocabulary notebooks, along with their meaning and possibly an example sentence.

1 a relationship that is full of strong and often angry feelings
2 a discussion that is full of angry and excited feelings
3 a look that shows you feel annoyed with or unfriendly towards someone
4 a friendly smile
5 happy, confident and relaxed manner

5 Check that students understand all the vocabulary in the questions. There are no 'right' answers here but encourage students to give reasons for their choices.

4 Challenges

Module 4 includes topics such as fundraising/charity events, adventurous people and various aspects of sport.

Lead-in p. 49

Check that students know the meaning of *challenge* (something that tests skill, ability or strength). Get students to look at the photos and talk about what challenge the people in each photo are facing. They should then discuss the lead-in questions. For question 2, you may want to start students off by giving one or two examples of your own.

4A Personal challenges

Reading pp. 50–51

1 Students could write the questions individually or in pairs.

Background

Lewis Pugh started his love of the ocean after moving to South Africa as a boy. As well as the swims described in the text, he pioneered more swims around famous landmarks than any other swimmer and can lay claim to having been the greatest cold water swimmer in history. When not swimming, he works as a maritime lawyer in London and does motivational speaking. He says his swims are about competing against himself and his own limits, and campaigning against climate change.

2 Before students skim the article, they could refer back to the strategies on page 8. They should first skim for general understanding (1–2 minutes), then scan to see if they can find answers to their questions. Explain that they may not find all the answers. Check which questions remain unanswered and help students find those answers which you know to be in the text.

3 Refer students to the strategy on page 176 of the Exam reference section. Elicit the best strategy for dealing with multiple-choice questions, then use the technique to do question 1 together. Do not confirm answers yet.

1 D 2 B 3 C 4 A 5 A 6 D

Help:
1 Pugh's childhood dreams were filled with his heroes' ground-breaking expeditions to the Poles, Australia and Mount Everest.
2 do things that have never been done before
3 He 'broke the world record for the most northern swim' and four months later 'he went on to do the same for the most southern part of the Antarctic'.

4 Let students compare, discuss and give reasons for their answers in pairs before you check with the class.

5 The article uses a number of phrasal verbs that students need to identify. Get students to compare answers in pairs before you check with the class. Point out that phrasal verbs are not only used in informal writing.

bring (sb) up = raise
take to = start to like something or someone
speed up = become faster
put on (weight) = gain; become fatter and heavier
put (sb) through (sth) = make somebody do something difficult or unpleasant

6 Get students to discuss the questions in small groups.

Language development 1 pp. 52–53

1a With books closed, write *unlock*, *door* and *noise* on the board and ask students to try and combine them in a sentence. Then ask them to read the sentence in their books and compare it with their own. Finally, ask them how they think the story continues.

1b Students read the next part of the story to check their predictions.

1c Establish that the story takes place in the past. It is not important if students don't know the names of the past verb forms at this stage. Ask students to underline the past verb forms in the story and check answers with the class.

was unlocking, heard, closed, ran, tried, wasn't working, 'd been talking, had run down

1d Students could do this individually or in pairs. Check answers with the class.

Past simple: an action or event at a particular point in the past; ... I heard a noise inside the house ... ; I closed the door ... and ran out into the street; Then I tried to call the police ...
Past continuous: an action in progress at a point in the past; I was unlocking my front door ... ; ... my mobile phone wasn't working ...
Past perfect simple: a single action which happened before a point in the past; ... the battery had run down
Past perfect continuous: an action which continued up to a particular point in the past; I'd been talking to people all day ...

1e Get students to skim the text first and find out what the noise was. They then do the exercise individually and then compare and discuss answers in pairs before class feedback.

> 1 ran 2 was talking 3 was arguing 4 had waited/had been waiting 5 came 6 had been crying 7 arrived 8 told 9 had happened 10 was talking 11 came 12 was carrying 13 was going on 14 was 15 were waiting/had been waiting 16 went 17 laughed/was laughing 18 started 19 felt 20 had reacted

2 As students study the grammar box, check understanding of any words in the examples they may not be familiar with, such as *cross the finish line* and *fill up*. It would also be useful to compare and contrast some of the time conjunctions: rephrase some of the example sentences using different time conjunctions and ask students if there is any change in meaning, e.g. *By the time the police arrived, the robbers had run away. When the police arrived, the robbers had run away. When the police arrived, the robbers ran away. The police arrived after the robbers had run away.*

Get students to compare answers in pairs. As you go through the answers with them, ask concept questions to check understanding, e.g.

1   *How late was he?* (very!)
2   *Did they catch the plane?* (no)
3   *Did she say it during the call or before?* (during)
4   *Did she finish the book?* (no)
5   *Did he see the end of the programme?* (yes)
6   *Did they check during the race?* (no, before)
7   *Was the search before or after we arrived?* (just after)
8   *Why was I relieved?* (I found the purse.)

> 1 C 2 B 3 C 4 D 5 C 6 A 7 A 8 D

3a Students should try to make true statements about themselves, as they are more likely to be remembered. But they could make up sentences if they can't think of any true ones.

3b Get students to compare their sentences in pairs or small groups. Then ask different students to share some of their sentences with the rest of the class.

4 Point out that there may be more than one answer and try to elicit all possible answers when checking with the class.

> **2** After I'd been to see a friend, I went home./I went home after I'd been to see a friend.
> **3** By the time he arrived, I'd been waiting for around an hour./ I'd been waiting for around an hour by the time he arrived.
> **4** When the boss resigned, the business collapsed./The business collapsed when the boss resigned.
> **5** I had been gardening for hours when she phoned me./When she phoned me, I had been gardening for hours.
> **6** While his owner was talking, the dog ran into the road./The dog ran into the road while his owner was talking.
> **7** By the time we got to the airport, the plane had left./The plane had left by the time we got to the airport.
> **8** Before I went to Russia I had never eaten caviar./I had never eaten caviar before I went to Russia.

5 This could be set as a writing task for homework. Encourage students to use a range of tenses.

Writing pp. 54–55

1a This activity aims to introduce the topic of fundraising/charity events. Ask students to look at and briefly describe the photos. They then work in pairs or small groups to discuss the questions. Finally, ask individual students to share their ideas with the class.

1b Remind students that in Paper 2 Part 2, they may be asked to write an article. Here, they are going to write an article about the personal challenge they chose in Exercise 1a. Go through the rubric with them and give them some time to make notes for their article. Make sure students only write notes at this stage and do not start writing the actual article yet.

2 Before students read the task, ask them to read the strategies on page 177–178 of the Exam reference section. Now refer students to the task and ask them to read it, underlining key words. They then discuss the questions in pairs or small groups, followed by class feedback.

> 1 to inform and entertain the reader
> 2 all the questions in the task
> 3 informal and conversational
> 4 by addressing the reader directly and engaging them
> 5 Is the article persuasive, lively, interesting and well organised? Have you given your opinion? Have you used a range of language?

3a–c Students complete the paragraph plan with the questions in the task and in Exercise 3b. They then use their notes from Exercise 1b to answer the questions in their plan. You could ask them to compare and discuss their answers in pairs before class feedback.

> **3a–b**
> Paragraph 1: What did you do? How did you do it? Why did you decide to do it?
> Paragraph 2: What did you have to do? What was the experience like?
> Paragraph 3: Was the event a success? How much did you raise?
> Paragraph 4: Would you do it again? How would it be different?

4a–b Give students time to discuss their ideas in pairs or small groups before you check answers with the class. During feedback, ask students to give reasons for their answers.

> **4a**
> A sounds flat and the short sentences are not engaging. B is more engaging and adds colour because it asks a question to the reader directly, which the article will answer.
> **4b**
> A sounds more enthusiastic. B sounds flat and uninterested. In this context, the short sentences sound as if the writer is not making an effort.

4c Go through the sentences in the box with the students. Ask them why it wouldn't be a good idea to use sentences like these in their article. (They sound flat and uninterested; they do not add 'colour' to the article.) Then give students time to go through the phrases in the table and rewrite the sentences to make them more appropriate for an article. You could ask them to do this in pairs or let them work individually and then compare answers with a partner.

Example answers:

Have you ever wondered what it would be like to walk along the Great Wall of China?

If the answer is yes, you should try doing 90 km in six days.

How would you feel if you had to cycle 400 km across Cuba?

Before I went, I thought it was a flat country but I soon realised that it's quite hilly in places.

When I saw how high the steps were my heart sank.

After a while I started to enjoy the open countryside.

It was the most amazing experience I have ever had.

4d Give students time to write sentences they can use in their own articles, using the phrases in the table. Go round monitoring and helping students as needed.

5 Now that students have done detailed work on the planning of their article, the writing should not take more than 20 minutes. Point out that they should add a title to catch the reader's attention – they can use the one in the question or invent their own. If they use their own title, they need to make sure that it is short and relevant. Finally, remind students that they must not exceed the word limit of 140–190 words.

Sample answer:

A charity event to remember

So why did I decide to do a 90-km walk in six days along the Great Wall of China? Well, the reason was that our local children's hospital needed to raise money or it would close. However, I didn't realise how big a challenge it would be.

Before I went, I thought that I would be walking along a flat surface but when I saw the Great Wall, my heart sank. Part of the time we would be trekking up hundreds of high steps and, worryingly, some of the paths had steep falls on either side and there was nowhere to go because we were surrounded by mountains and forests. However, after a while, I started to love the experience. I was in one of the most amazing places on earth and the views were incredible.

In the end, the adventure was a great success. The hospital was delighted because a group of us managed to raise several thousand pounds.

Would I be keen to help the hospital again next year? Yes, but I think I'll try and find an easier challenge next time!

6 Allow ten minutes for this stage. Go through the checklist here with the students and also refer them to the full checklist on page 198. If time allows, ask students to work in pairs and check each other's work first.

Photocopiable activity

Activity 4A (p. 98) can be used here. It is a discussion similar in format to Paper 4 Part 3, with students deciding on the best way to raise money for their club/society.

Expert language: Attitude adverbs

This exercise practises a number of adverbs that can be used in this type of writing. As you check answers, make sure students know the meaning of the alternatives.

1 absolutely   2 importantly   3 surprisingly   4 Personally
5 exactly   6 Naturally   7 Luckily   8 worryingly

4B Sport

As a lead-in, with books closed, ask students in pairs to write a definition of *sport*. Compare definitions, then give students a dictionary definition of the word. The *Longman Exams Dictionary* defines *sport* as 'a physical activity in which people compete against each other'.

Speaking pp. 56–57

1 Before students discuss the questions, ask them to name the sports in the photos (cycling, tennis, baseball) and check that they know the sports in the spidergram.

2a–b Before students give examples of sports for each item, check that they know the meaning of the target vocabulary. You could ask them to work in pairs for both exercises, then share ideas with the class.

2a

Suggested answers:

1 tennis, basketball, squash   2 running, cycling   3 horse-riding, boxing   4 swimming   5 baseball, football, cricket

2b

Suggested answers:

1 tennis, squash   2 baseball, cricket   3 swimming   4 swimming, cycling, motor racing, skiing   5 horse-riding, cycling, baseball, motor racing   6 running

3a Give students time to do the matching task, then check answers with the class. See if students can name more sports for each verb (see answer key below for examples), and encourage them to record the collocations in their vocabulary notebooks.

1 judo   2 tennis, baseball, basketball   3 cycling, swimming, horse-riding, running

More examples:

do: aerobics, gymnastics, taekwondo, karate, kung-fu, ballet, yoga, athletics, archery, tai chi

play: football, chess, cricket, hockey, rugby, volleyball, squash

go: riding, jogging, fishing, sailing, windsurfing, skiing, snowboarding, skating

3b Give students time to do the exercise, individually or in pairs, then check answers with the class.

3c This exercise highlights words that are often confused, so time should be spent examining the differences of use in each pair, with students making up sentences for the alternative word (e.g. *win* is intransitive: *Brazil won*, whereas *beat* is transitive and requires an object: *Brazil beat France*).

4a After checking answers, point out that it is not important to come to an agreement – it is the interactive communication that matters.

4b After listening, students could discuss the questions in pairs, small groups or as a whole class, giving reasons for their answers.

4c Give students some time to study the phrases in the table, then play the recording again for them to tick the ones the candidates use.

4d Before students answer the question here, ask them what the interlocutor's instructions were and what the candidates had to do (in about a minute, decide which sport would be best to encourage).

5 Refer students to the strategy box and remind them of the importance of turn-taking. If your class is not divisible by three, it would be better to have extra examiner/interlocutor with some pairs than a pair without an examiner, so everyone can have some feedback. Remind the interlocutors that as well as giving the instructions and keeping time, they will need to be noting the two candidates' performances.

6 Try to encourage students to be constructive rather than just polite.

Listening p. 58

I Discuss question I with the class. Then, for question 2, establish a definition for *extreme sport* (a sport that is done in a way that has much more risk and so is more dangerous than 'normal' sports) before eliciting examples.

2
Examples:

2a As this is the first time students encounter a Paper 3 multiple matching task, give them plenty of time to read the rubric and answer the questions.

2b Give students time to read through the statements and check that they understand *persuaded* and *join in*. They could discuss the questions in pairs or as a whole class.

2c Go through the strategy box before students do the task. Before they listen, remind them that opinions might be expressed in different words from those in the statements. Check answers with the class.

3 Discuss the questions with the class. Play the recording again if necessary.

4 If students find any of the words in italics difficult (e.g. *keen on*, *enrol*), remind them of strategies for guessing unknown words. Give them time to complete the exercise, then check answers with the class.

5 Students could discuss the questions in small groups or as a whole class. Encourage them to use some of the vocabulary in Exercise 4 in the discussion.

Language development 2 p. 59

1 The concept of countable and uncountable nouns is not usually a problem for students at this level but it can be difficult for them to know which nouns are which. It might be useful to show students how countable and uncountable nouns are marked in a dictionary ([C] and [U]) before they do this exercise, so they can check any that they are unsure of.

1 spectator: C, fan: C, excitement: U
2 advice: U, fact: C, information: U
3 skiing: U, athletics: U, football (both)
4 money: U, salary: C, coin: C
5 racket: C, equipment: U, glove: C
6 temperature: C, weather: U, sunshine: U
7 exercise: both, tracksuit: C, trainer: C

2 These are typical B2 level mistakes; remind students to check their own work for similar mistakes.

1 Our trainer gives us good **advice**.
2 I've heard the results. The news **is** very bad.
3 People **like** Lionel Messi.
4 Some footballers have long **hair**.
5 It was **terrible weather**, so the match was cancelled.
6 Ronaldo has very expensive **furniture** in his house.
7 My shorts **were** very dirty after the match.
8 I had to do some hard **work** to beat the champion.
9 The national team stayed in **luxury accommodation**.
10 I need **information** about tickets.

3 Get students to skim the text first and answer the following question: *Who was most seriously injured?* (Camille Jenatzy). Give them time to read the grammar box and complete the task, then check answers with the class. As a follow-up, you could put students in groups to discuss which sports are popular in their country, which are more popular with men and with women, and whether any dangerous sports are popular. Give an example first, such as: *In the UK a lot of people play football, but not so many play basketball and very few play baseball.*

1 Many 2 a number of 3 much 4 several 5 any 6 lots
7 much 8 a lot of 9 few 10 a few 11 a few

Use of English 1 p. 60

1 Remind students that this exam task tests their knowledge of grammar and vocabulary by getting them to express the same idea in two different ways. Check answers with the class.

1 b 2 a 3 c

2 Let students read the rubric and remind them of the strategy for approaching Key word transformations tasks. Point out the Help notes that they can use if necessary. You could ask students to compare answers in pairs before checking with the class.

1 wasn't much interest 2 quite a nice 3 great deal of work
4 people like 5 doesn't belong to me 6 to be fewer
Help:
1 a noun 4 plural

3 You could ask students to discuss the questions in pairs before checking answers with the class.

1 a 3, 6; b 1, 2; c 4
2 Students' own answers

Use of English 2 p. 61

1 Some of the more dangerous popular sports include rugby and horse-riding. Many extreme sports can be considered as new. (For examples of extreme sports see the answer key to Exercise 2 in Listening on page 30.)

2a Remind students that it is good to get into the habit of using the title and a skim-read to get a general idea of the text.

Background

The most famous 'traceurs' are the founder David Belle and Sebastien Foucan (who appeared in the opening scenes of the James Bond film *Casino Royale*). To many people, *Parkour* and the English term *Freerunning* are the same things. However, purists insist that whereas Parkour focuses on the most efficient uninterrupted forward motion over and around objects, Freerunning has more emphasis on aesthetics, fun and creativity, using more flips and somersaults. There are now groups all over the world and Parkour games have been created for games consoles.

2b You could refer students to the strategy in the Exam reference section before they do the task. Point out the Help notes that they can use for support with certain items. If time allows, ask students to compare and discuss answers in pairs before you check with the class.

1 B 2 C 3 D 4 B 5 A 6 C 7 B 8 D

3 Give students examples of verbs, phrasal verbs and collocations that they should record (e.g. *demand, improvise, rehearse, go off, get up, come about, good technique*).

Language development 3 p. 62

To introduce the language point, ask students to close their books and write the following pairs of words on the board: *actual/current, old/ancient, great/big*. Ask students if the words in each pair are the same or different and if they are different, what that difference is. They then look at the examples and explanations in the grammar summary.

1   Check students understand that the words and definitions are in pairs. They may need to use a dictionary to check some of the words. Check answers with the class.

> 1 pleasant: b, sympathetic: a   2 sensitive: a, sensible: b
> 3 nervous: b, excited: a   4 usual: b, typical: a

2   Get students to discuss the questions in pairs or small groups. Then ask individual students to share their answers with the class.

Photocopiable activity

Activity 4B (p. 99) can be used here. It is a board game in which students answer questions using adjectives that are often confused.

3a Adjectives ending in -ed and -ing are often confused. Further help could be given with a drawing on the board of a person reading. Label the person 'interested' and the book 'interesting'. Elicit the difference before looking at the examples from the text.

> -ed adjectives describe a reaction to something. -ing adjectives describe the person/thing that causes the reaction.

3b When students have completed the exercise, ask them if they agree with sentences 1, 3, 5 and 7.

> 1 boring   2 disappointed   3 tiring   4 annoyed   5 terrifying
> 6 depressed   7 interested   8 amusing

3c Get students to discuss the questions in pairs or small groups. Then ask individual students to share their answers with the class.

4   Before students look for the phrasal verbs in the text, point out that *take place* is *not* a phrasal verb: although it looks and acts like one, it is just an idiom; phrasal verbs are usually verb + adverb/preposition, as in *turn on*.

> In the UK, the sport really **took off** after it was featured on television.

5   Get students to compare answers in pairs before checking with the class.

> 1 took up   2 took off   3 took over   4 took after   5 took to

6   Whichever way students record phrasal verbs, encourage them to record examples or notes on usage as well as the meaning. If time allows, use the following sentences to revise the grammar of phrasal verbs:

  1 Parkour **took off** *in the 1990s.* (intransitive)

  2 He **took off his tracksuit/took his tracksuit off** *before the race.* (transitive, separable)

  3 He **took up acting.***/He* **took it up**. (but NOT *He took up it.*) (pronoun in separable phrasal verbs goes between verb and particle)

  4 Damon Hill **took after his father**. (transitive, inseparable)

5 Discovery

Module 5 includes topics such as human science, the future and technology.

Lead-in p. 63

Ask students to briefly describe the photos before they discuss the lead-in questions in pairs or small groups.

5A The modern world

Photocopiable activity

Activity 5A (p. 101) can be used here. It is a quiz about the human body, designed to be an introduction to the module and will help to pre-teach some useful vocabulary.

Reading pp. 64–65

1 It would be a good idea to check the pronunciation of the fields of science before students do the exercise.

> **1** c **2** f **3** e **4** d **5** a **6** b

2 The title of the article makes it quite clear what students are going to read. The book titles might throw up a number of possibilities, which would generate interest in the text.

3 Point out to students that only when they have skimmed the article will they be able to predict which part to look in for each question. It would be useful to set a suitable time limit (e.g. 15 minutes) for the task so that students become aware of the time available in the exam, although you could give them a few minutes more at this stage if necessary. Remind students to highlight key words in the questions and if time allows, get them to compare answers in pairs before you check with the class.

> **1** D **2** D **3** B **4** A **5** D **6** B **7** C **8** A **9** C **10** B

4 Get students to discuss the questions in pairs or small groups.

> **1** In A, his earlier books were on other subjects and therefore this book doesn't follow on.
> **2–3** Students' own answers

5 Additional questions could include: *Have you ever studied any of these subjects? Would you like to?*

Language development 1 pp. 66–67

1a Look at the first sentence and elicit that *I don't feel well* is in the present and *I'm going to be sick* is the consequence in the future. See if students can think of any other possible situations for *I'm going to be sick* (e.g. someone on a roller coaster or someone who has seen/eaten something disgusting). There are a number of possible answers here, so you could ask students to compare answers in pairs before class feedback, or ask more than one student for their ideas for each item.

> **2** Two colleagues/friends are trying to arrange to meet tomorrow but the speaker can't because he/she has a driving test.
> **3** One friend to another. The speaker has bought something, e.g. a mobile phone, and has found that it doesn't work.
> **4** One friend to another. They have a secret and the speaker doesn't trust the third person not to reveal the secret if she is told about it.
> **5** Friends, or husband and wife. They are going to the cinema or theatre and the speaker is waiting for the other person who is still getting ready.
> **6** Two strangers at a supermarket or station. One is offering to carry the other's heavy bag.

1b Encourage students to look at the sentences in their contexts and not just identify future forms that they may already be familiar with.

> **1** 'm going to be   **2** 'm taking   **3** 'm going to take   **4** 'll tell
> **5** starts   **6** 'll carry

1c When students have completed the table, give examples of how a decision might become an arrangement (e.g. *You read a restaurant review and think it sounds good, so you decide: 'I think I'll take X there.' Later, when someone asks what your plans are for the weekend: 'I'm going to take X to … .' Then, after you ring and book the table, you could say: 'I'm taking X to … .'*).

a 3 b 6 c 2 d 1 e 5 f 4

1 planned, definite arrangement (e.g. in a diary)

2 I can't, I'm afraid. I'm taking my driving test tomorrow.

3 planned, fixed (e.g. a public timetable)

4 Hurry up! It starts at eight.

5 planned, decided earlier (intention)

6 Did I tell you it doesn't work? I'm going to take it back to the shop.

7 prediction: we notice something in the present that will make something happen

8 I don't feel well. I think I'm going to be sick.

9 unplanned, decided now (e.g. an offer, a promise)

10 That bag looks heavy. I'll carry it for you.

11 prediction: we expect something to happen (it is our opinion or we have experience of it)

12 I know what she's like. I'm sure she'll tell everyone, so don't tell her!

2a Give students time to study the grammar box and sentences and answer the question. Point out that although the present simple is used after the time words, the clause refers to the future.

3

2b Get students to compare and discuss their answers in pairs before checking with the class.

1 will be 2 I'm going to visit 3 we get 4 starts 5 I'll cook
6 I'm having 7 Tara's going to have 8 you go

3a Students read the quote and underline the examples of the future continuous and future perfect.

future continuous: will be having
future perfect: will have established

3b When students have matched the forms with their uses, it might be useful to compare the structures with those practised in earlier units:

The present continuous refers to an action in progress now. The past continuous refers to an action in progress at a point in the past. Hence the future continuous refers to an action in progress at a point in the future.

The present perfect refers to an action before now. The past perfect refers to an action before a point in the past. Hence the future perfect refers to an action before a point in the future.

1 future perfect 2 future continuous

3c Get students to compare answers in pairs before checking with the class.

1 will have found 2 will be travelling 3 will have discovered
4 will be living 5 will have taken over, will be providing
6 will be making, will be going

4a When students have completed the exercise, show how the language to express certainty is often stressed: *We may have found life on other planets but I doubt it.*

1 very certain 2 not certain 3 fairly certain 4 not certain
5 fairly certain

4b As students give their opinions on the predictions in Exercise 3c, encourage some discussion leading in to the questions in 4c.

4c If time allows, let students discuss the questions in pairs or small groups before sharing their ideas with the class.

5a–b Give students enough time to think about and complete the sentences before they discuss them in pairs or small groups.

6 Point out that the mistakes are all to do with verb forms. Checking through a piece of writing systematically, in this case just checking the tenses, is an important exam strategy. To help students, you could tell them that there are ten mistakes in the text.

After I **finish** the last year of university, I am definitely going to have a long holiday. I expect **I'll go** with my friend, Luis, to a place where we **will do** lots of sport and **relax** in the sun to recover from all our hard work.

But before that there is a lot of work. My exams **start** on 15 June and they **last** two weeks. The results will not **be** here before the end of August, so I **will have** a long time to wait. For the next month, I **will be studying** for two hours every evening and I **won't be going** out during the week.

Writing pp. 68–69

1 Before students look at the questions, get them to briefly describe the photos. Then ask them to discuss the questions in pairs and make notes.

2 Go through the task with the students. Refer them to page 177–178 in the Exam reference section and give them some time to think about the questions. Then discuss the answers as a class.

1 d (and possibly b) 2 all the points on page 177–178

3a In this exercise, students decide on the best idea for the third point in their essay. Discuss the questions as a whole class. For question 2, elicit ideas from different students.

3b Give students time to think about the questions here and make notes, then get them to discuss their ideas in pairs or small groups.

3c Students match the topics in the box with the paragraphs. Check answers with the class.

Paragraph 1: state the overall situation (a problem)
Paragraph 2: solution 1: television programmes
Paragraph 3: solution 2: interactive museums
Paragraph 4: solution 3: (your own idea)
Paragraph 5: explain why this is an important topic

3d This exercise highlights the main structure of an essay. Give students a couple of minutes to complete the task, then check answers with the class.

a paragraph 1 b paragraphs 2–4 c paragraph 5

3e Allow plenty of time for students to organise their notes into paragraphs. Go round monitoring and providing help as needed.

4a Remind students that the first sentence of a paragraph is the 'topic sentence' and will identify the topic of a paragraph. Give them time to expand the notes into complete sentences and get them to compare answers in pairs before checking with the class.

4b Before students do the exercise, point out that some sentences can go in more than one paragraph. Check answers with the class.

4a–b
a Another idea would be to set up interactive science museums in every town, where parents could take their children at the weekends. (paragraph 3 or 4)
b As the average scientist is not very well paid, many children are put off from entering science as a career. (paragraphs 2, 3 or 4)
c Although young people love gadgets, at school many see science as dull. (paragraph 1)
d Whatever we choose, it is vital that more young people are attracted into science. (paragraph 5)
e One way would be to have lively television programmes presented by celebrities. (paragraph 2)

4c Students now think about supporting points for each paragraph. Give them enough time to match the pairs of sentences and then complete them using their own ideas. Ask individual students to share some of their sentences with the class.

1 d   2 b   3 c   4 a   5 e
Example sentences:
1 The reason is that society's prosperity depends on continued scientific progress.
2 They think it means working in a badly paid job in a boring laboratory.
3 This worrying attitude has led to fewer young people pursuing a scientific career.
4 It's much better to teach children science by getting them to do hands-on experiments which they enjoy.
5 This is because we live in a celebrity culture and children identify with well-known actors and singers.

4d Go through the rubric with the class and elicit modal verbs that can be used when giving solutions (can/could, will/would, may/might). Also check that students know what a conditional sentence is. Give examples if necessary. Ask students to first complete the gaps in the sentence openings and then to complete the sentences using their own ideas.

Suggested answers:
1 One way in which science *could be made* more attractive would be to set up interactive museums.
2 Another idea *would be* to find more interesting ways of teaching science.
3 If more teachers *used/were to use* games in science classes, children would get more interested.
4 If scientists in general *were* better paid, science might be a more attractive subject for young people.

5 Students could write their essay in class or for homework. Suggest a time limit of 20–25 minutes.

Sample answer:
Although young people love gadgets and technology, some see science as uninteresting and 'uncool'. Over time, the number of young people, particularly girls, pursuing science and technology studies and careers has dropped.
One way in which science could be made more attractive would be to have lively television programmes presented by celebrities, with subjects which were relevant to the experience of the young. We live in a celebrity culture and children identify with well-known young people.
Another idea would be to set up interactive science museums in every town, where parents could take their children. It's much better to teach children the principles of science through hands-on experiments than to lecture them in a classroom.
Of course, there would be more incentives if the average scientist were better paid and young people were made aware of the range of jobs available. A lot of people are put off a scientific career because they think it means working in a badly paid job in a boring laboratory.
Whichever way we choose, it is vital that more young people are attracted into science, since society's prosperity depends largely on continuous scientific progress.

6 Without looking at the checklist on page 198, ask students to work in pairs and make a list of things they need to check when editing their work. Briefly discuss their answers, then refer them to the checklist on page 198 and ask them to check their work (and/or swap with a partner and check each other's).

Expert language: Avoiding over-generalisation

Ask students to look at the example sentence, then write the 'over-generalised' version on the board: *Women are more intelligent than men.* Ask students to compare and comment on the two sentences. Students then complete the task and compare answers in pairs before class feedback. There are a number of possible answers here, so if time allows, elicit different versions of each statement from different students.

Example answers:
2 On some occasions technology might do more harm than good.
3 For many people dogs can make wonderful pets.
4 Some people feel that children should not be allowed to take smartphones to school.
5 Generally speaking, I think Canada is one of the best places in the world to live.
6 In many situations it might be better to tell a lie than the truth.

5B Technology

As a lead-in, with books closed, ask students the difference between a discovery (something that existed but was not known before, such as penicillin) and an invention (something new that did not exist before, such as the telephone). Ask them what they consider the most important invention in human history.

Speaking pp. 70–71

I First ask students to briefly describe the two photos (left: teacher operating *smart board* with finger; right: *smart watch* with missed phone call icon). They then look at the spidergram and discuss the questions in pairs or small groups before sharing their ideas with the class.

2a–b Students first match the actions with their definitions and then the actions with the equipment. Check answers with the class.

> **2a**
> **I** d **2** e **3** g **4** f **5** c **6** a **7** h **8** b
> **2b**
> **Suggested answers:**
> digital camera: store
> laptop/tablet: download, log on, click on, cut and paste, telework, back up, word process, store
> MP3 player: download, store
> satnav: download, store, possibly click (on)
> smartphone: download, log on, store

2c Get students to discuss this in pairs or small groups, then share their ideas with the class. Elicit as many examples for each item as possible from different students.

> **Example answers:**
> **I** to listen to music
> **2** to word process/write an email
> **3** to click on icons/move the cursor around the screen
> **4** to telework/for videoconferencing
> **5** to store/back up data

3 You could also ask what students think computer technology might be used for in the future.

4a Get students to discuss the question in pairs, in preparation for the exam task that follows.

4b Once you have checked students' answers, tell students that it is important in Paper 4 that they know what to do in each part. If they have any doubts, they should check with the examiner. They will not be penalised for this at all. The candidate in the recording summarises the examiner's instructions, which is a good way to check you have understood.

> **I a** about something together for about two **b** have some time to look at the **c** what the benefits of these items might be
> **2** we have to discuss why each of these items might be useful

4c Before students listen, point out that in the exam, they can discuss the items in the spidergram in any order. Play the recording for students to complete the task, then check answers with the class.

> **I** portable gaming devices **2** driverless cars **3** robots
> **4** 3D television **5** ebook readers

> Yes, they both participate in the discussion.

4d Elicit the candidates' point of view, then get a few students to share their opinion with the class.

4e Before students answer the question here, ask them what the candidates had to do in this part of the task (decide which item might have the most benefits, in about a minute).

> driverless cars; reasons: would be good for older people/the disabled/people who don't like driving; would reduce accidents

4f After checking answers to question 1, ask students what other phrases they can use to express strong/tentative agreement (e.g. *You're absolutely right. I couldn't agree with you more. Absolutely. That's exactly how I feel. I take your point, but … . I see your point. However, …*).

> **I a** I completely agree with you. Good point. Of course. That's true. Yes, you're right.
> **b** I suppose so. Yes, I can see the advantage of … but … ; Yes, but … ; I guess so. Yes, possibly.
> **2** no

5a These are typical Part 4 questions, extending the topic from Part 3. Students could consider why some are easier to answer than others, e.g. is the language difficult or would they find it hard to come up with ideas and opinions?

5b Go through the rubric before students listen and if necessary, play the recording a second time.

> Students should tick questions 2 and 3.
> Yes, both candidates participate more or less equally. The interlocutor asks if the other candidate agrees.

6a–b If your class is not equally divisible by three, it would be better to have one or two groups of four, with an extra examiner/interlocutor.

7 Students should discuss their own and the others' performance.

Listening p. 72

I Before students discuss the questions, ask them to briefly describe the picture; elicit/pre-teach the items illustrated (MP3 player, portable games console, hands-free phone, portable DVD, mobile phone).

2 Emphasise the importance of studying the sentences as carefully as possible before listening. Explain to students that the more they are able to predict the type of words in each gap, the easier it will be to hear the missing information. Play the recording for students to complete the task but do not confirm answers yet.

1 (food) shopping 2 shoes 3 crossword 4 online banking
5 speed 6 (road) accidents 7 (extra) space 8 spellcheck
9 (online) research 10 1980s

3 Students should discuss whether their answers fit logically and grammatically and also compare the spelling of more difficult words. After the discussion, confirm answers to Exercise 2.

4 Remind or elicit from students what *collocation* means before they do the exercise. During feedback, highlight the *form* of the verbs used (e.g. gerund after the prepositions *from* and *to* in questions 2 and 3). Get students to highlight each collocation and encourage them to record them in their vocabulary notebooks.

1 taking 2 paying 3 booking 4 save 5 catch up 6 try

5 The discussion could be done in pairs or small groups, which then feed back to the whole class.

Use of English 1 p. 73

1 To remind students of how key word transformations work, you could start by putting the first sentence (*I can't speak Mandarin Chinese.*) on the board and eliciting an alternative way of saying it. Let students compare and discuss their answers in pairs before checking with the class.

1 how to speak; question forms/structures with question words
2 cleaned the house by herself; reflexives (and word order)
3 put off handing in; phrasal verbs (+ -ing)

2 Refer students to the strategy on pages 175–176 and elicit or remind them of essential points (e.g. use between two and five words; do *not* change the word given).

1 on my own 2 no point in Tania going 3 love each other
4 wasn't until she left 5 painted this room myself
6 couldn't/didn't carry on working

3 The task analysis highlights a number of areas that could be tested in the exam and that students might want to do more practice in if they had problems. If time allows, get them to discuss in pairs or small groups before checking with the class.

1 a 6 b 1, 3, 5 c 4 d 2 2 Students' own answers

Language development 2 p. 74

1a As you go through the grammar box with students, you could use simple drawings on the board to illustrate differences (e.g. *He hurt himself:* a man sitting on a chair with an arrow pointing down to indicate *fell off*. *He hurt his sister:* a man and a woman with an arrow pointing from the man towards the woman to indicate *bumped into*. They *talked to each other:* two people facing each other, with speech bubbles. *They talked to themselves:* two people with speech bubbles, but further apart, not facing each other, and with a line between to indicate that they are in separate rooms and talking to themselves!).

She cleaned the house **by herself** last week.
I live **on my own** in this house.
They love **each other** very much.

1b Students could discuss their answers in pairs, referring to the grammar summary, before class feedback.

1 I used to live **on** my own.
2 ✓
3 Can you help **me**?
4 Robots can't talk to **each other**/**one another**.
5 ✓
6 Have you enjoyed **yourself**?
7 ✓
8 Relax ~~yourself~~!
9 I built the model **on** my own.
10 Clare and Rob met **each other**/**one another** last year.

1c Point out that students will need to use object pronouns here, as well as language from the grammar box.

1 own 2 itself/themselves 3 myself 4 myself 5 each other/
one another/them 6 us 7 themselves 8 me 9 themselves

2 After question 1, as a contrast, you could ask: *What things do you prefer to do* **by** *yourself?*

3a Go through the grammar box with students before they do the exercise, pointing out that the word order in B (*question word + clause*) is as in a statement, not as in a question. Get students to compare answers in pairs before you check with the class.

1 know how to use 2 you've done what I 3 where to find/
where we can find 4 know who to/know who I should

3b If students can't think of anything true to write, encourage them to try to invent interesting sentences.

Use of English 2 p. 75

1 Set the questions as a quick competition in groups. Check that students know *penicillin* (today, a medicine known as an antibiotic because it kills bacteria and so helps cure infections).

1 Alexander Fleming 2 Isaac Newton 3 Archimedes

Background

1 Sir Alexander Fleming: see texts on p. 75 (Ex. 2a and 2b).
2 In the first century BC, Archimedes discovered that an object placed in water 'loses' an amount of weight equal to the weight of the water that it has displaced. He is said to have discovered this when he got into a full bath and it overflowed.
3 Sir Isaac Newton discovered gravity in 1687, stating that gravity is the force of attraction between two objects and that greater objects, such as the earth, pull smaller objects, such as people, towards them. He is said to have discovered this watching an apple fall from a tree to the ground.

2a Remind students not to focus on the gaps. They should only need a minute or so to do this exercise. Students might need help with the words *mould* and *germs*.

1 penicillin 2 mould 3 bacteria 4 important

2b Get students to do the exercise on their own and then compare answers in pairs before class feedback.

> **1** investigation **2** accidentally **3** unknown **4** delighted
> **5** excitement **6** effective **7** infections **8** successfully
> **Help:**
> **2** an adverb **7** plural

3a–b Repeat the process with the second text but this time you could introduce a suitable time limit (e.g. 8–10 minutes). When students have finished, ask them which of the three discoveries in Exercise 1 they think is the most important.

> **3a**
> Lucy's Baby was important because of the completeness of the remains and therefore the opportunities it gave for research.
> **3b**
> **1** careful **2** length **3** researchers **4** unusual **5** development
> **6** mixture **7** criticism **8** insufficient
> **Help:**
> **5** -ment **8** negative

Language development 3 p. 76

1 Explain to students that nouns can be formed from verbs or adjectives. This exercise focuses on nouns formed from verbs. Check that students know the meaning of the words in the table, then practise pronunciation/stress.

> -ment: excitement, development
> -ure: mixture
> -ence: evidence
> -tion/-sion: investigation, infection, conclusion
> -y: discovery
> -er: researchers
> -or: ancestors

2a Before students do the exercise, ask if they know of any famous explorers. Get them to compare answers in pairs, but do not confirm yet as students will read about the explorers in this quiz in Exercise 2b.

> **1** B **2** A **3** C **4** A

2b Get students to compare answers in pairs first, then check with the class. Finally, elicit the correct answers to the quiz questions in Exercise 2a.

> **1** assistance, organisation **2** existence, achievement
> **3** sailors, equipment **4** explorer, failure

3a This exercise focuses on nouns formed from adjectives. Again, check that students know the meaning of the words, then focus on pronunciation.

> -ness: illness, kindness, loneliness, sadness
> -th: strength, truth, width
> -ity: equality, generosity, popularity, reality

3b Get students to compare answers in pairs before checking with the class.

> **1** popularity **2** descriptions **3** ability, importance
> **4** observations, loneliness

4a Go through the sentence with the class. Encourage students to try to guess the meaning of the phrasal verb by looking at the words around it.

> C

4b Students could use their dictionaries to check their answers here. Encourage them to record the phrasal verbs in their vocabulary notebooks, with example sentences.

> **1** b **2** d **3** f **4** a **5** g **6** e **7** c

4c Remind students to put the verbs in the correct form. After checking answers, you could provide personalised practice by giving students sentence stems to complete, e.g.

> 1 The best idea I've come up with is/was …
> 2 I once tried … but it didn't come off.
> 3 Once when I was looking for … I came across …
> 4 Recently I came up with …

> **1** come up **2** came round **3** came out **4** came across
> **5** come about **6** come off **7** come up with

Photocopiable activity

Activity 5B (p. 102) can be used here. It is a game of dominoes in which students form nouns by joining suffixes to verbs.

6 Enjoying yourself

Module 6 includes topics such as favourite books and films, art and music.

Lead-in p. 77

With books closed, get students to compare *art* (painting, drawing, sculpture, etc.) and *the arts* (more general). Brainstorm different types of arts, e.g. music (classical, pop, folk, opera), theatre, musicals, dance (ballet, contemporary), cinema, art (modern, different periods/media), literature. Build up a spidergram on the board, then ask students what 'arts' are shown in the photos on page 77. Get them to discuss the lead-in questions. In the first question, *important to you* could be interpreted either as something that you personally spend time on or that you consider to be important in general.

6A Music

Reading pp. 78–79

Photocopiable activity

Activity 6A (p. 103) can be used either as a lead-in to the unit or as follow-up to the Reading section. It is a questionnaire designed to find out how ambitious students are.

Background

The title of the text comes from Nirvana's classic song *Smells Like Teen Spirit*, from their 1991 album *Nevermind*. Nirvana were one of the first grunge bands and the singer, Kurt Cobain, was referred to as 'the spokesman of a generation'. His girlfriend used a deodorant called *Teen Spirit* and the song came about from a reference to that.

1   Students talk about the types of music in question 1 and brainstorm more items for the list. Other genres of music could be: pop, soul, punk, indie, house, etc. For question 2, students need not mention every association; the exercise is just to process the new vocabulary.

2   Students skim the text to find out what type of music each person is known for. Remind them that skimming should take 60–90 seconds for a text of this length.

> Jamie Cullum: jazz   Michael Bublé: swing   Katie Melua: jazz, blues and folk   Marcella Puppini: 1940s music

3   Students do the exam task. Do not confirm answers yet, as students will discuss them in Exercise 4.

> 1 B   2 D   3 A   4 D   5 C   6 A   7 D   8 C   9 A   10 B

4   Comparing answers and giving reasons will help students to focus on the links between the text and the questions and help you see how well students have understood it. After the discussion, check/confirm answers with the class.

5   The exercise would work well with students working together in groups or as a whole class, sharing and justifying answers.

Language development 1 pp. 80–81

1a   Ask students if they know any music by the artists in the photos. Then give them time to complete the matching task.

> 1 A   2 C   3 D   4 B   5 F   6 E

1b   Students could also discuss the origins of each genre as a lead-in to the text in Exercise 2a.

2a   Ask students to ignore the clauses in italics for now. Students might be interested in the example of Jamaican English in the Bob Marley song, where *no cry* means 'don't cry'. Check answers with the class.

> 1 reggae and punk: in the 1970s and 80s; hip hop: in the 1990s and 2000s
> 2 New York

2b   It would be useful to find one example of each type of clause with the whole class and to highlight their structures before students look for the rest. Check answers with the class.

> **Defining relative clauses**
> 1 The bands which dominated Western popular music
> 2 the one singer who had the most influence   3 that first emerged in the 1970s   4 the records they made
> **Non-defining relative clauses**
> 1 Elton John, whose piano-based songs were hugely popular,
> 2 Bob Marley, who had a huge hit with *'No woman, no cry'*,
> 3 decades in which 'boy bands' and 'girl bands' became popular,
> 4 hip hop, which was an Afro-American musical movement

3 Before students do the exercise, review what each relative pronoun is used for (*who* for people, *whose* for possession, etc.). Check answers with the class, then follow up with a discussion about the artists mentioned in the exercise.

> **1** The singer Katy Perry, **whose** real name is Katheryn Hudson, ... ; Katy, **who** heard very little pop music as a child, ...
> **2** *The X-Factor* is a British television programme **where** members of the public **who** are ... It is the programme in **which** the popular ...
> **3** The rock band Snow Patrol was formed in 1994 in Scotland, **where** two of its original members ... ; ... the band (**which/that**) they admire most ...
> **4** Shakira, **which** means 'grateful' in Arabic, was born in Colombia, **where** she grew up ... ; ... every country in **which** it was sold.
> **5** ... one of several singers **who/that** were first discovered ... *The Mickey Mouse Club*, **which** first began ... ; Other Club singers **who/that** went on to ...
> **6** Oasis, **whose** major musical influence was the Beatles, was one of several bands in the 1990s to **which** the media ... Zak Starkey, **whose father,** Ringo Starr ...

4–5 These exercises require students to think a little more about both which type of clause to use and how to use it. You could ask students to compare answers in pairs before you check with the class.

> **4**
> **1** I saw a poster which/that was advertising a gig for a new rock band.
> **2** I phoned the box office, which was in London.
> **3** There was an answering machine which/that was telling me to call another number.
> **4** I spoke to a man on the other number who/that told me there were only expensive seats left.
> **5** I booked two tickets which/that cost 100 euros each.
> **6** I paid by credit card, which is a very convenient way to pay.
> **7** On the day, we went to the theatre, which overlooks the River Thames in London.
> **8** We couldn't get into the theatre, which had been closed because of technical problems.
> **9** I went home with my friend, who was very disappointed.
> **10** Next day I phoned the theatre, which was very helpful and offered replacement tickets.
> **5**
> **1** Salsa, which means 'sauce' in Spanish, is a mixture of Spanish Caribbean rhythms and styles.
> **2** The salsa band Sonora Carrusales, whose songs are played in salsa dance clubs everywhere, was formed in Colombia in 1995.
> **3** The singer Gloria Estefan, who was born in Cuba but now lives in the USA, uses salsa rhythms in many of her songs.
> **4** The Puerto Rican American Victor Manuelle, whose career began when he was discovered by salsa superstar Gilberto Santa Rosa, is often thought of as a romantic salsa singer.   **5** The album *Travesia*, on which Manuelle improvises vocals and lyrics within a salsa tune, was a huge success with fans.

6 It can be difficult for students to grasp that a participle clause can be used to refer to different times. Point out that the time reference is usually clear from the second part of the clause, e.g.: *The woman singing that song* **is** ... . *The car going round the corner* **was** ... . Give students enough time to study the grammar box before they do the exercise.

> **1** I saw a poster advertising a gig for a new rock band.
> **3** There was an answering machine telling me to call another number.
> **5** I booked two tickets costing 100 euros each.
> **7** On the day, we went to the theatre overlooking the River Thames in London.

7 This exercise will require some planning. It could be done in class or for homework, with students talking about their sentences in the next lesson.

Photocopiable activity

Activity 6B (p.104) can be used here. It is a game in which students use relative clauses to define vocabulary associated with the arts.

Writing pp. 82–83

1 Some discussion here on if, where and when students see bands live would be useful, to generate interest in the topic and some relevant vocabulary.

2 Students read the task and discuss the questions. They could do this as a whole class or in pairs, followed by class feedback.

> **1** to inform; to entertain
> **2** three: the band, their performance at the concert, whether you would recommend it
> **3** a description and explanation (e.g. facts) with opinion; opinion (recommendation) in the third part
> **4** a mix of neutral and informal

3 Students complete the paragraph plan. You could ask them to compare answers in pairs before you check with the class.

> **1** attention-grabbing introduction
> **2** brief description of the person/band and concert
> **3** what you liked
> **4** what you didn't like
> **5** recommendation, conclusion

4a–b Point out how a strong opening engages the reader and a strong ending has a positive effect on the reader. During class feedback, ask students to explain why the chosen paragraphs are better.

> **4a**
> B
> **4b**
> A

4c One way to look at the table would be to go through it first with the whole class, using a band that most students are familiar with as an example. Then students choose some sentences to complete about their favourite artist.

5 Review the outline and content of the review before students complete the writing task.

> **Sample answer:**
> **A gig to remember**
> Without doubt, the British rock band Arctic Monkeys have given this year's best live show. As teenagers a few years ago, they made the fastest-selling album ever but seemed shy and awkward on stage. Now they have matured and become an amazing live act. Since the frontman Alex decided to cut his hair and dress like a skinny rock star of the 1950s, he moves confidently around the stage, waving his arms and encouraging us to shake our hips. The crowd were ecstatic!
> The set began with their hit, *Do you wanna know*. The guitar playing was tight, as always, and the rhythm supported by Matt's powerful drumming. The band were on top form throughout, winning fans over with a list that combined older with new hits.
> My only reservation is that although the songs have clever lyrics and great melodies and sound fresh every time, some lack the emotional and poetic force of their best.
> But this is a minor criticism. Overall, it was a performance to remember and all fans should try and catch them while they're on tour.

6 Remind students to check their writing thoroughly. Focus their attention on the checklist here and also refer them to the full checklist on page 198 of the Expert writing section.

Expert language: Avoiding repetition

Start by giving students an example of language with a lot of repetition in it, to show them why it is important to avoid it, e.g. *Mike writes stories about a group of teenagers. The teenagers in Mike's stories live in a big city. The teenagers have a lot of problems in the city. Mike writes about the problems the teenagers have in the city and how the teenagers overcome the problems of city life.*

> **a**
> **1** good musicals   **2** the audience   **3** *We Will Rock You*   **4** the actors'   **5** *We Will Rock You*   **6** the actors   **7** actors   **8** the youngest actors'   **9** the youngest actors   **10** the acting and singing   **11** the plot   **12** the fact that the plot is unsatisfactory/can't be taken seriously   **13** the characters
> **b**
> **1** They   **2** It, there   **3** it   **4** then   **5** ones

6B Art and entertainment

As a lead-in, with books closed, ask students the difference between a gallery (a place where you can see (and sometimes buy) works of art) and a museum (a place where important cultural, historical or scientific objects are kept and shown to the public). In the USA, *museum* is also used for some public galleries, e.g. the Metropolitan Museum of Art.

Speaking pp. 84–85

1a Use the photos and opening questions to gauge students' interest in art.

> **1** classical: A; modern: B   **2** Students' own answers

1b Give students enough time to complete the exercise. You could get them to compare answers in pairs before checking with the class.

> **1** keen   **2** can't see the point   **3** fascinating   **4** appeal   **5** special   **6** absolutely   **7** into

1c Before students do the exercise, remind them of alternative ways to mark the stress on a word (e.g. *enjoyable*, *enjoyable*, *enJOYable*). Check answers with the class, then let students talk about a work of art they know. They could do this in pairs, small groups or as a whole class.

> stress on first syllable: awful, boring, brilliant, dreadful, moving, powerful, shocking
> stress on second syllable: amusing, depressing, enjoyable, exciting

2a–b If time allows, you could expand the exercise with examples of each and other people who work in the arts.

> **2a**
> **1** a painter   **2** a sculptor   **3** a dancer   **4** a producer   **5** a reviewer/a critic
> **2b**
> **1** the person who arranges how dancers should move during a performance
> **2** someone whose job is to tell jokes or make people laugh

3 After checking answers, you could follow up by eliciting other types of TV programme (e.g. sports, drama, magazine, detective series, lifestyle). Ask students which type of programme they most like watching.

> **1** quiz show   **2** soap opera   **3** documentary   **4** sitcom   **5** reality show   **6** current affairs   **7** chat show

4 You could get students to do this in pairs, comparing and discussing their answers.

> **1** viewers (others relate to theatre)   **2** final act (others relate to TV)   **3** cartoon (others relate to theatre)   **4** box office (others relate to TV)   **5** trailer (others are film genres)

5 Reassure students that in the exam they won't be required to have any expert knowledge but in Paper 4 they could be asked a question like this about their personal preferences.

6a Elicit the format of Paper 4 Part 2 (individual long turn followed by a short response from the other candidate), then play the recording for students to complete the instructions.

> these types of art might be interesting to people

6b Play the recording, then ask for the answers to the two questions.

> **1** yes **2** yes

6c Tell students that the expressions on the recording may not be heard in the same order as they are on the page. Play the recording, then check answers with the class.

> 1, 4

6d Students listen again and complete the candidate's response. Check answers with the class.

> **1** easier to understand than some **2** the painters wanted to say **3** easily learn something about **4** it's strange or funny

7 Point out to students that it is important that they are prepared for the interlocutor's question and listen to it carefully. Play the recording for students to complete the instructions and response, then check answers with the class.

> **1** young people are more interested in **2** definitely **3** more interesting for older people **4** are younger and more fashionable

8 Students complete two exam tasks. Point out the strategy box before they begin.

9 Allow enough time for students to discuss their performance in pairs and give each other constructive feedback.

Listening p. 86

1 This is the first time students look at Paper 3 Part 1 in detail. Look at the first question and key words with the students, then give them enough time to mark the key words in questions 2–8.

2 Go through the strategy box before students do the task. If there is time, after checking answers, students could have a discussion based on the arts. They should each choose one of the following topics and prepare to speak about it by making notes. Then put them in small groups for the discussion.

- *your favourite film of all time*
- *the type of music you most enjoy listening to*
- *a play you have enjoyed (at the theatre, on the radio, on TV)*
- *a novel you have read more than once*
- *the painting you would most like to have hanging on your bedroom wall*

> **1** B **2** C **3** B **4** A **5** B **6** A **7** B **8** C

3 Let students discuss their answers, then play the recording for them to note down the words that led them to each answer.

Use of English 1 p. 87

1 Students could discuss these lead-in questions in pairs, small groups or as a whole class.

2a Students skim the text before they attempt the exam task in Exercise 2b. Check answers with the class.

> **1** T **2** F **3** T

2b Start by reminding students that structural words (prepositions, auxiliaries, pronouns, determiners, etc.) are often gapped in this type of exercise. Look at the example with the class and point out that the gapped word is part of an adjective + noun collocation (*interested in*). Point out the Help notes that students can use if necessary.

> **1** there **2** which **3** at/by/about **4** any **5** are/is **6** to/before **7** in **8** at/by/with

3 Let students discuss the questions in pairs or small groups first. During class feedback, elicit answers to question 2 from different students.

> **1 a** 3, 8 **b** (3), 6, 7, (8) **c** 5 **2** Students' own answers

4 Remind students of the importance of learning dependent prepositions and find out if they have a particular method. Compare their methods with those given here.

Language development 2 p. 88

1a Go through the grammar summary with the class. Point out that these phrases are followed by nouns, pronouns or *-ing* forms. After checking answers, encourage students to record the prepositional phrases in their vocabulary notebooks.

> **1** of **2** for **3** for **4** between **5** by **6** in **7** in **8** to **9** with **10** of

1b You could ask students to compare answers in pairs before you check with the class.

> **1** for **2** for **3** from **4** for **5** of **6** at **7** for **8** in **9** with **10** in **11** by/about/at **12** about

2 Students could discuss these personalised questions in pairs or small groups.

3 Go through the grammar box with the class. Highlight the difference between the state, expressed by *be used to*, and the action, expressed by *get used to*. You could ask students to compare answers in pairs before you check with the class.

> **1** used, live **2** get used, living **3** wasn't used, filming **4** get used, hearing **5** didn't use, print **6** aren't used, watching **7** get used, staring **8** 'm not used, going

4 Students should do this in pairs or small groups before class feedback. You could ask each group to discuss just one of the points, then report back to the class.

Use of English 2 p. 89

1 Discuss the questions in open class. Possible further questions: *Do you and your friends find the same things funny? Is humour different in different countries?*

2a Elicit the advice as a means of reminding students of the strategy for this type of exercise.

2b Before students do the task, ask if they have heard of Ricky Gervais (see Background below). Also point out the Help notes.

> **1** embarrassment **2** fantastically **3** employees **4** conclusion
> **5** attractively **6** underestimate **7** ability **8** similarity

Background

Ricky Gervais was born in Reading in 1961. In his early working life he was in a band, he managed a band and was a radio DJ. He started out in TV comedy with bit parts on various shows before his sudden success in the sitcom *The Office*, which he co-wrote, directed and starred in. He has won numerous awards, including Emmies, Golden Globes and BAFTAs.

3 Get students to look at the photo and ask what they know about Penelope Cruz (see Background below). Again, point out the Help notes.

> **1** recognition **2** glamorous **3** believable **4** unable
> **5** disappointing **6** performance **7** strength **8** organisations
> **Help:**
> prefix: question 4 (*unable*); nouns: questions 1, 6, 7, 8

Background

Penelope Cruz was born in Madrid in 1974. She studied classical ballet at a young age and later moved to California to pursue acting. She has appeared in both Spanish and Hollywood films. In 2009, she won an Oscar, becoming the first Spanish actress to do so, for her performance in *Vicky Cristina Barcelona*.

4 Let students discuss the question in pairs or small groups, then elicit answers from different students.

5 Students could discuss these in pairs or small groups. Possible further question: *Which actor/actress would you choose to play your life?*

Language development 3 p. 90

1a Discuss the questions with the class. Elicit examples of awards ceremonies that students know of.

1b Give students enough time to complete the article, then get them to compare answers in pairs before checking with the class. During feedback, highlight the endings used to form nouns (e.g. *-ment*, *-ician*, *-ist*, *-or*).

> **1** entertainment **2** musicians **3** singers **4** director
> **5** actor(s) **6** dramatist **7** presenter **8** comedians
> **9** surprising **10** performers

2a Students find examples of adjectives with negative prefixes in the two articles on page 89. Get students to copy the table in their vocabulary notebooks and ask them to make it big enough to add other negative adjectives in the future. Check answers with the class.

> unable, incredible, disappointing

2b Students add the adjectives in the box to their table from Exercise 2a. You could get them to compare answers in pairs before checking with the class.

> un-: unfair, unfit, unsatisfactory, untidy
> in-: inexperienced, insecure
> dis-: dishonest, disloyal
> im-: impatient, impolite, impractical
> il-: illiterate, illogical

2c Give students enough time to match the adjectives from Exercise 2b with the descriptions. Check answers with the class.

> **1** untidy **2** impractical **3** dissatisfied/insecure **4** unsatisfactory
> **5** illiterate **6** inexperienced **7** unfit

2d Encourage students to answer honestly! If they know each other well, they could be asked to agree or disagree with what people say about themselves.

3a The verbs *say*, *speak*, *tell* and *talk* are often confused. Go through the grammar box with the students and give them enough time to complete the exercise. After feedback, encourage them to record the collocations in their vocabulary notebooks.

> **1** The teacher **told** us a horror story.
> **2** I can't stand it when artists **talk** politics.
> **3** We all **said** a prayer together.
> **4** My little sister is just learning to **tell** the time.
> **5** My brother **speaks** three languages.
> **6** **Say** hello to Rosie for me.
> **7** Mike **told** the police what he had seen.
> **8** Don't trust him. He's always **telling** lies.

3b Remind students to use the correct form of each verb. If time allows, get them to compare answers in pairs before you check with the class.

> **1** speak **2** say **3** say **4** talks **5** told **6** telling **7** say
> **8** speak **9** tell

4 After students have written their sentences, get them to discuss them in pairs. Encourage them to ask questions about each other's sentences and explain them further if necessary.

7 In fashion

Module 7 includes topics such as food and restaurants, describing clothes and changing hairstyles.

Lead-in p. 91

Ask students to look at the photos in pairs and briefly describe each one. Then go on to the lead-in questions. If students need help with ideas for question 1, give them prompts such as where we eat, what we eat, who we eat with, who prepares the food; what people wear, level of formality of clothes, what clothes are/aren't acceptable in different situations, where we get our clothes. In question 2, the quote means that no fashion is really new – it's just the return of an old fashion.

Background

Geoffrey Chaucer (c.1343–1400) was the greatest English writer before Shakespeare's time. His most famous work, *The Canterbury Tales*, was written in the last ten years of his life.

7A Fast food

Reading pp. 92–93

1   This would work well as a class discussion. You could also ask students if they have heard of any competitive eating events. Ask them to note down the three things they would like to know, so they can refer to their lists when they do Exercise 2.

2   Ask students to look at their notes and skim the text to see if they can find answers to their questions.

3   Use the task strategy in Module 2, page 22 to remind students of good exam technique for multiple-choice questions. You could do question 1 as an example, following the procedure in the strategy box, if you think it necessary. Point out the Help notes for questions 1 and 2.

> 1 B   2 A   3 C   4 B   5 D   6 D

4   Students could discuss the questions in pairs, small groups or as a whole class. You could also ask about celebrity chefs in their country/-ies or the use of celebrities to promote (unhealthy) food.

Language development 1 pp. 94–95

1a   With books closed, ask students how often they eat in restaurants, what type they most enjoy going to and on what occasions. Or ask them to talk briefly about the last time they went to a restaurant (who with, why, where, who paid, etc.). Then get students to open their books and do Exercise 1a, individually or in pairs. Check answers with the class.

> 1 W   2 C   3 W   4 W   5 W   6 C   7 W   8 C   9 W   10 C

1b   First check students' understanding of the terminology in the table. When students have completed the table, ask: *What verb form are the verbs in the table followed by?* (infinitive). It may be necessary to highlight the fact that while *must* and *have to* both express obligation, the negative forms are quite different.

> Giving permission: 1 are allowed to; 2 can
> Expressing prohibition: 3 are not allowed to; 4 can't; 5 mustn't; 6 are not supposed to
> Expressing obligation: 7 must; 8 have to; 9 are supposed to
> Expressing lack of necessity: 10 don't have to

2a   Do question 1 as an example, then give students enough time to complete the rest of the sentences. Check answers with the class.

> 1 must book   2 can't wear   3 is allowed to come
> 4 are supposed to wait   5 don't have to have   6 mustn't bring
> 7 aren't allowed to play   8 can pay

2b   Students could do this in pairs, small groups or as a whole class. They could go on to describe school rules or rules in a job that they do (or once did).

3a   Ask students to skim the email and answer the two questions. Tell them not to worry about the sentences in italics yet.

> 1 no
> 2 Using a mobile phone was not allowed.

3b   During feedback, check understanding of *needn't have* with concept questions: *Did he wear a suit?* (yes) *Was it necessary?* (no). You could add further examples, such as *I needn't have taken any money to the restaurant.* Concept questions: *Did I take it?* (yes) *Was it necessary?* (no) *Why?* (Maybe someone else paid the bill.) *Did I know that before I went?* (no).

> It was permitted: They were allowed to use the play area.
> It was prohibited: The children couldn't play in the restaurant.
> It was necessary: We had to pay by credit card.
> It wasn't necessary: We didn't have to book a table.
> It was done but it wasn't necessary: He needn't have dressed so smartly.

4a   Students could do this exercise individually or in pairs. Encourage them to think about what the two options express each time.

> 1 didn't have to pay   2 were allowed to   3 had to   4 could
> 5 couldn't keep   6 had to   7 have to cook   8 needn't have worried   9 didn't have to

4b If students find it hard to think of food and eating rules, ask them to think of any rules they had in other areas, such as clothes, going out, use of the bathroom, tidying up, etc.

5 Before students do the exercise, point out that the mistakes are all to do with form and that all these forms express advice and recommendations. You could ask students to compare answers in pairs before you check with the class.

> **1** You ought **to** complain about that soup – it's cold.
> **2** You shouldn't **have** a dessert if you're full up.
> **3** If you don't like pasta, you'd better ~~to~~ have a pizza.
> **4** You must ~~have~~ try that new restaurant in Castle Street.

6 You could ask students to skim the email first and answer the following two questions: *Who is writing to who?* (Louise to Melanie) *Why?* (to give her instructions for looking after her house while she's away). They can then read the email again and replace the words in italics with the correct form of the verbs in the box.

> **1** You have to **2** you mustn't **3** can **4** You don't have to
> **5** can **6** You must **7** You'd better

7 Give students time to think and write, then get them to compare and discuss their sentences in pairs or small groups.

Photocopiable activity

Activity 7A (p. 105) can be used here. It is a pairwork activity that gives further practice of the language covered in this section.

Writing pp. 96–97

1 First get students to look at and briefly describe the two photos. They then discuss the questions in pairs, small groups or as a whole class.

2 This exercise focuses on task completion, style and effect on the reader, which all contribute towards the general impression mark in the exam. If time allows, students could discuss the questions in pairs before class feedback.

> **1** three: description of the situation (views of visitors and local people), comments on trends/dissatisfaction, recommendation
> **2** semi-formal and impersonal (It is for your teacher, who will expect it to sound like a report.)
> **3** good organisation (with headings), clear analysis, sensible comments/suggestions/recommendations

3a Get students to look at the examples under the headings and give them time to make notes, adding as many points as they can think of. They should then choose the two most important points under each heading.

3b Point out to students that some pieces of advice can go with more than one paragraph. You could get them to discuss their answers in pairs before checking with the class.

> Paragraph 1: b, d
> Paragraph 2: a, e, g
> Paragraph 3: a, e, g
> Paragraph 4: c, f

3c Once students have matched their notes with the paragraphs, point out that they now have the basic structure of their report. Explain that they don't have to come up with a lot of complex ideas in the exam – just clear, well-organised points.

3d Students could do this in pairs or small groups. Encourage them to discuss the strengths and weaknesses of each of the three headings before deciding on the best one.

> C is the best. It is short and clear and tells the reader immediately what the report is about. A is too vague and B sounds as if it's from a travel guide.

4a Elicit what a topic sentence is (a sentence, usually the first one, which summarises or identifies the main point of a paragraph). Give students time to complete their sentences, then get them to discuss and compare them in pairs.

4b Point out that the sentence openings in the table are useful for any report but obviously, it is important to use them correctly. If time allows, go through the table with the students before they do the matching exercise.

> The main aim/purpose of this report is to ... 9
> To prepare for this report ... 5
> We are fortunate to have ... 7
> These are very popular with ... 4
> Since they want to ... 10
> A cause of dissatisfaction was that ... 8
> As a consequence,/Consequently, ... 1
> It was commented upon by ... 2
> All things considered ... 6
> It is recommended that ... 3

4c Do this with the whole class, as a quick check.

> passive, more, less

5 Give students 20 minutes to write their report.

> **Sample answer:**
> Local eating places
> The main purpose of this report is to give an overview of the town's eating facilities. As part of the survey, both tourists and local residents were asked their views.
> Cafés, pubs and restaurants
> There are a number of good quality restaurants in the area, which cater for most tastes: pizza houses, sushi bars, exclusive French restaurants and gastro pubs. We are also fortunate to have several cafés and sandwich bars, which are very popular in the mornings with young mothers and children and with office workers at lunchtime.

Recent trends/Dissatisfaction

It was reported that in recent years most of the fast food restaurants had extended their hours, with most open until midnight. It was also stated that prices had gone up dramatically in some of the better restaurants and, as a consequence, people are going out less than they used to or eating at cheaper restaurants.

Room for improvement/Recommendation

The main area of concern among a number of people interviewed was the lack of vegetarian meals available in many of the restaurants and it is recommended that restaurants are made aware of this view.

6 Give students another 10 minutes to check their work. They could then work in pairs and check each other's reports, to see if they find it easier to spot other people's mistakes than their own. This may help them to look at their own writing more objectively.

Expert language: Passive report structures

These exercises focus on different ways of using passive structures to add emphasis when writing a report. Point out that *be supposed to* here means 'be generally said to'.

a
1 (that) the Principal is in favour of extending the lunch break
2 (that) about 20 students will take part in the research
3 (that) many residents have written a letter of protest
4 (that) some of the shopkeepers are also not happy
b
1 is supposed to be getting more and more expensive
2 are supposed to be eating out less than we used to
3 is supposed to be something we do, not watch on TV
4 are supposed to be taking business away from restaurants

7B How do I look?

As a lead-in, with books closed, ask students to brainstorm items of clothing in pairs or groups for two minutes. Alternatively, you could ask them to talk about their favourite item of clothing, saying why they like it, where they got it and when they wear it.

Speaking pp. 98–99

1 Students could discuss the differences in pairs, small groups or as a whole class.

In the photo on the left, both interviewers and interviewee look very smart. The interviewers are dressed formally in suits and ties, whereas in the other photo they are wearing more casual fashionable clothes – open-necked checked shirts.

2 It might help students to think about *when* as well as *where* people wear these items.

Example answers:

flip flops: on the beach, at a pool   fur coat: in the winter
high heels: at work   jumper: in the winter   open-neck shirt: on holiday   parka: on a scooter   pyjamas: in bed   sandals: in the summer   shorts: on the beach, in the summer   slippers: at home tracksuit: at the gym   trainers: at the gym   trouser suit: at work vest top: in the summer

3 The phrases and phrasal verbs here might need explanation if the exercise is done with the whole class. Alternatively, students could use dictionaries if working alone. Students might be familiar with 'dress-down Fridays', where office workers wear less formal clothes at the start of the weekend. Elicit the opposites of *tuck in* (untuck) and *taken in* (let out).

Example answers:
1 for an informal party; some offices on a Friday
2 a special occasion   3 to change what you are wearing
4 to put an item of clothing on to check if it fits properly
5 to look smarter
6 to put something on a peg or on a clothes hanger to keep it clean and tidy
7 when your clothes are too small
8 if a piece of clothing is too big, e.g. when you buy it or after losing weight

4 Again, you might need to explain some of the words in the box or ask students to check in a dictionary. Look for examples of the styles and fabrics in the class.

Example answers:
bootleg jeans   cashmere scarf/sweater/coat   chunky sweater cotton dress/T-shirt   denim jacket   moleskin trousers   roll-neck sweater   suede jacket/boots   three-quarter length skirt/boots/trousers

5a Check understanding of the adjectives in the box before students complete the table. You could get them to compare answers in pairs before checking with the class.

opinion: elegant, old-fashioned
size/shape: fitted, short-sleeved, straight, tight
colour: khaki, navy
pattern: checked, patterned, striped
origin: French, Italian
material: linen, silk, viscose, woollen

5b Students might be tempted to use an adjective from each category, so point out that it would be very unusual/unnatural to use more than three or four before each noun.

Example answers:

Photo 1: The woman between the two men is wearing a plain cream suit and white shirt. The woman opposite her is wearing a plain, white short-sleeved shirt. The man on the right is wearing a grey suit and a striped, navy silk tie.
Photo 2: The man facing the camera is wearing a blue and white checked, long-sleeved cotton shirt. The woman on his left is wearing a plain, long-sleeved shirt. It may be cotton or silk.

6a–b Students could discuss this in pairs or groups first, then share their ideas with the class.

7a Elicit the format of Paper 4 Part 2, then play the recording for students to listen to the candidates and answer the questions.

> **1** Each candidate is given two photographs. He/She has to talk on his/her own for about a minute, answering a question about his/her photographs. He/She then has to answer a short question about his/her partner's photographs.
> **2** The first answer is better. The candidate compares the two photos well, rather than just describing the two separately. They also say why they think the people are dressed in that way, as the interlocutor asked.
> The second candidate describes some aspects of the pictures but doesn't really describe them, and doesn't say why they might be wearing those clothes, so doesn't give a complete answer to the task.

7b Students listen again and tick the phrases the candidate uses to check she has understood the question. Check answers with the class.

> 3

8a–b Refer students to Tasks 1 and 2 in the Expert speaking section and give them enough time to read the instructions. Check that students know what they have to do before they begin each task. If your class is not divisible by three, it would be better to have one or two groups of four, with an extra examiner/interlocutor.

9 Students discuss their performance in their groups.

Listening p. 100

1 This would work well in small groups. Emphasise that students should give examples and/or add details, as in the example.

2 Remind students of the strategy for this task and point out the Help notes that they can use if necessary. Check answers with the class.

> **1** G **2** H **3** E **4** C **5** B
> **Help:**
> Speaker 1: She 'doesn't feel right' in them.
> Speaker 2: 'feeling relaxed and not having to worry about what you look like'

3 After checking answers, ask students which of the five speakers they are most similar to.

4 This would work well as a whole class discussion. For question 2, ask students what *fashion victim* means (someone who wears what is fashionable even if it doesn't look good on them). Ask them if they know any fashion victims.

Language development 2 p. 101

1a Go through the table with the class. Point out or elicit that being modals, all the verbs in the table are followed by the infinitive. You could get students to compare answers in pairs before checking with the class.

> **1** Marlie's in her pyjamas. She **must** be going to bed.
> **2** It **can't** be his jacket – it's too small.
> **3** That **must** be Kate. I recognise that voice.
> **4** I think that's John's case, so he **may/might/could** be here.
> **5** She's decided not to buy those shoes. She **may not/might not** have enough money.
> **6** Mike **can't** work in a clothes shop – he knows nothing about fashion!

1b As students look at the pictures, encourage them to think about what is certain and what is possible.

> **Suggested answers:**
> A must belong to a woman. She might be rich because she has a number of credit cards. She must like to look nice because she's got a mirror, a lipstick and perfume in her bag.
> B could belong to either a man or a woman because there's nothing like make-up or aftershave. I think he/she works in a high-powered job because of the computer and calculator.
> C could belong to someone on holiday or a working tour because there is a map in the rucksack.

2 From the examples in the table, highlight the past modal form (modal + *have* + past participle) and point out that *have* here is weak and contracted in spoken English. Practise pronunciation of the contracted forms such as *must've* before students do the exercise.

> **1** can't have left **2** may/might/could have been stolen **3** must have cost **4** may/might/could have been, may/might/could have bought **5** can't have been/can't be **6** must have had

3 First elicit what type of word students should use after *looks/feels/seems* (an adjective). Encourage students to use both present and past modals. When they have completed their sentences, get them to compare in pairs or groups.

Photocopiable activity

Activity 7B (p. 106) can be used here. It is a mingling activity where students use modals of deduction to correct or respond to other students.

Use of English 1 p. 102

1a–b The aim here is to revise the strategy for key word transformations. Make sure that students are clear about why the answers are wrong, then elicit the correct answers.

> **1a–b**
> **1** The candidate has changed the key word *been* to *be* and therefore incorrectly changed the tense. Correct answer: *must have been pleased*
> **2** The candidate has written more than five words. Correct answer: *wish I could go to*

2 Students complete the exam task. Point out the Help notes that they can use if necessary. Check answers with the class.

1 must be tired   2 haven't eaten for   3 must have just been on
4 too unfit to   5 may have been in the/may have been having a
6 can't have left

3 Let students discuss the questions in pairs first, then check answers with the class.

1 questions 1, 3, 5, 6; 1 is in the present; 3, 5, and 6 are in the past.
2 question 2: present perfect simple; question 4 too/enough + infinitive

Use of English 2 p. 103

1 You could start by asking students if they can think of anyone that has an unusual hairstyle. They could discuss the questions in pairs or small groups, then as a whole class.

2a Point out to students that the idea here is to find the answers in the text, not to give their own opinions to the questions. Check answers with the class.

1 to make statements, to shock, to copy icons
2 1960s: Beatles style, 1970s: long hair, skinhead and dreadlocks; recently: copying fashion icons

2b Students do the exam task. Set a time limit of about 15 minutes and also point out the Help notes for questions 3 and 8.

1 D   2 B   3 B   4 D   5 C   6 A   7 B   8 C

3 Students could do this in pairs, small groups or as a whole class. Encourage them to record the collocations in their vocabulary notebooks.

2 (in the hope), 6 (in fashion)

4 Students could discuss in pairs or small groups, then share their ideas with the class.

Language development 3 p. 104

1a Students complete the examples, then check their answers with the text on page 103.

A in   B on   C in

1b Point out that all the phrases in this exercise are correct in themselves, but that they aren't all correct in this context. As you check answers, make sure students understand both phrases in each pair.

1 at all times   2 in danger of   3 from bad to worse
4 at first   5 by mistake   6 to my surprise   7 by that time
8 in an extremely bad mood   9 From then on   10 without fail

Background

Fashion weeks are when a number of designers come together to show their latest collections to other people in the fashion industry. They usually take place twice a year in places like Paris, New York, London, Milan and Tokyo.

1c One way to learn these phrases is by preposition. Check that students know the meaning of all the phrases listed and can provide the correct preposition for the phrase they cross out in each group (given in brackets in the answer key below).

1 the beginning (in)   2 conclusion (in)   3 time to time (from)
4 purpose (on)

1d Get students to compare answers in pairs before you check with the class.

1 in the end   2 in fashion   3 out of date   4 on purpose
5 for a change   6 in luck

2a Let students choose the correct options and then get them to check their answers with the text on page 103.

A make   B spend

2b Ultimately, the choice between make and do is down to collocation but students might notice that expressions with do emphasise an activity or process, whereas expressions with make emphasise the creation or production of something new. Check answers with the class, then encourage students to record the collocations in their vocabulary notebooks.

1 do   2 make   3 make   4 do   5 do   6 make   7 make
8 do   9 make   10 do   11 make   12 make

2c Give students time to complete the text, then check answers with the class.

1 an Armani suit   2 a lot of money on it   3 in cash   4 trying it on
5 it would be comfortable   6 feel so good   7 to show my friends

2d As you check answers, point out or elicit the difference in meaning between the verbs.

1 rise   2 became   3 earned   4 damaged   5 resign   6 healed

2e Before students begin, point out that they may need to change the form of the verbs. Give them time to complete the text, then check answers with the class.

1 retired   2 spend   3 expect   4 made   5 do/try   6 bought
7 make   8 made

Background

Royal Ascot is a four-day horse-racing festival which takes place in June each year in Ascot, near Windsor. Members of the Royal Family always go and it is a big social event with a strict dress code. Women have to wear dresses and hats – the hats are famously lavish and outrageous – and men have to wear morning suits – a jacket with long 'tails' at the back and striped trousers.

Module 8 includes topics such as love, relationships, family, living alone or with others, hobbies and free time.

Lead-in p. 105

Get students to look at the photos in pairs and briefly describe each one. They then discuss the lead-in questions in their pairs before they share their ideas with the rest of the class. The quote means that if you are alone, you are independent and can make all your own decisions – you don't have to compromise with a companion.

Background

The American essayist, poet and philosopher Henry David Thoreau (1817–1862) lived by the doctrines of Transcendentalism as recorded in his masterwork *Walden* (1854). He was a vigorous advocate of civil liberties, as evidenced in the essay *Civil Disobedience* (1849). He once spent a night in jail for refusing to pay his taxes, which he had done in protest at the American government's support of slavery and its war on Mexico.

8A Relationships

As a lead-in, you could ask students, in pairs or groups, to brainstorm different types of relationship (father–son, teacher–student, husband–wife, etc.).

Reading pp. 106–107

1   This would work well as a class discussion. Depending on your teaching situation, you could also ask if any students would like to tell the class where and how they met their partner.

2a Get students to look at the photo, title and introduction to the article, then discuss the questions with the whole class.

> 1 on the Tube (the London Underground), by chance
> 2 *Meant to be* means 'destined or fated to happen'.

2b Instead of giving students a time limit for this exercise, you could get them to give you a signal when they have finished, such as putting their pen down, so you can get an idea how long it is taking them.

3   Point out the Help notes that students can use if necessary and give them a time limit of 10 minutes to complete the reading task. Do not confirm answers yet.

> 1 G   2 F   3 B   4 D   5 E   6 A
> **Help:**
> Gap 1: G ('It was Dennis, who had …')
> Gap 2: F ('gave the man's briefcase a kick')
> Gap 3: B ('as she stepped onto the platform')

4   Let students compare and discuss in pairs, then check answers with the class.

5   Before students discuss the questions, check that they know what *soul mate* means (someone you are naturally close to, as you share the same emotions and interests and understand each other). During feedback, you could confirm to students that the story of Wendy and Dennis is actually true.

6a–b Both exercises focus on vocabulary from the text. You could ask students to compare answers in pairs before checking with the class.

> **6a**
> with
> **6b**
> 1 packed   2 dropped off (to sleep)   3 got to her feet
> 4 scribbled (down)   5 flustered   6 dashed

Language development 1 pp. 108–109

1a Students read the sentences in the box and discuss the questions. If they need prompting, get them to think about the problems of going out with someone from another country, e.g. language barriers, cultural differences, family, acceptance.

1b You could get students to try to guess the answers first, then read the blog and check.

> 1 He approached her in the National Art museum.
> 2 Yes, very.

1c Explain to students that they need to read the reported statements and work out what was actually said each time. You could do the first one or two with the class, as examples. Get students to compare answers in pairs before you check with the class.

> 1 don't talk   2 'm just trying   3 've seen   4 've been looking
> 5 Leave me   6 Join me   7 Do you like   8 's   9 Do you regret
> 10 'm, 've ever been

1d Discuss the questions with the class. For question 1, first point out that in examples 1–8, there is the usual change of tense for reported speech. Then ask students to discuss the question. If they find it hard, prompt with clues (e.g. for example 10: *Was she happy when she was asked? Is she happy now?*). For question 3, explain that these changes depend on context (e.g. *I'll do it this afternoon,* reported a few minutes later, would be *He said he would do it this afternoon.* Reported the next day, it would be *He said he would do it yesterday afternoon.*).

1 Because what is being reported is still true in the present.
2 past perfect simple
3 today → that day, tomorrow → the next/following day, yesterday → the day before/the previous day, last week → the week before/the previous week, next month → the following month, this → that, here → there, come→ go, bring → take

2 Before students begin, point out that they will also need to change pronouns. You could do the first one or two items with them, as examples. Check answers with the class.

1 what I was 2 was studying 3 that was 4 to go out 5 had nearly 6 he had 7 had been 8 was 9 if/whether he could pick me/to pick me 10 would be 11 had to be

3a This exercise provides freer, more personalised practice. Give students a little preparation time, then get them to complete the exercise in pairs.

3b This would work well in groups of four. Students should report what their partner said (e.g. *She told me her favourite place is the beach.*) and also any questions they asked (e.g. *I asked her when she had first gone there.*).

4a Demonstrate the effect of reporting someone's exact words using only *said* or *told*: *I said ... and he said ... so I said ... then he told me ... .* Explain that sometimes the exact words are not important, so we can use reporting verbs to summarise and add variety. Check meaning and pronunciation of the verbs in the box before students complete the sentences.

1 accused 2 invited 3 agreed 4 suggested 5 explained

4b It may be a good idea to do this exercise with the class, so that students can clearly see how each of the verbs fits into the table.

4c Get students to do this in pairs, using a dictionary if necessary. Point out that some verbs can go in more than one category. When students have completed the table, elicit the negative construction for each verb, e.g. verb + object + *not* + *to*-infinitive; verb + *not* + *-ing*. Also point out that the structure verb (+ object) + *that* + clause is very common but not possible for all verbs.

4b–c
Verb + *to*-infinitive: agree, admit, decide, offer, refuse
Verb + object + *to*-infinitive: invite, advise, remind, warn
Verb + *-ing*: suggest, admit, deny, recommend
Verb (+object) + prep + *-ing*: accuse, apologise, insist
Verb (+ object) + *that* + clause: advise, explain, admit, decide, deny, insist, remind, warn

5 Transformations from direct to reported speech are common in Paper 1 Part 4. Encourage students to look at the table in Exercise 4b for help and remind them to think about pronoun changes.

1 advised her not to get married yet/advised her that she shouldn't get married yet
2 admitted starting the argument/admitted that she had started the argument

3 insisted on talking to the manager
4 warned her sister not to go out with Mike/warned her sister that she shouldn't go out with Mike
5 apologised to his girlfriend for hurting her feelings
6 suggested staying in that weekend/suggested that they (should) stay in that weekend
7 offered to carry the bag for her mother
8 refused to help him

6 Give students a little time to prepare their sentences, then ask them to compare and discuss them in pairs or groups. You could get them started by giving some examples about yourself.

7 Point out that here the verbs are being used to report general statements about the present and so the present simple is used. After class feedback, students could discuss them in pairs, groups or as a whole class, saying whether they agree with each one and giving their personal opinion.

1 Sometimes people suggest that marriage is an old-fashioned idea.
2 Parents often persuade their children to get married.
3 Some people insist on getting married while they are still teenagers.
4 One couple admits/admitted getting married for financial reasons.
5 Some women decide not to change their surname.

Photocopiable activity

Activity 8A (p. 107) can be used here. It uses quotes to practise reported speech and reporting verbs.

Writing pp. 110–111

1 Get students to do this in pairs or small groups, followed by class discussion. Point out that they should make notes in question 2.

2 Give students time to read the task, then discuss the questions as a whole class.

1 It is possible to argue one point of view, as long as you bear in mind the other point of view and back up your points, but it is probably easier to have a balanced discussion comparing the advantages and disadvantages.
2 fairly formal

3a In their pairs/small groups, students brainstorm ideas for the third point in the essay, using their notes from Exercise 1. You could then elicit a few ideas from different pairs/ groups.

3b This is a standard format for an essay of this type. Point out that there is no fixed number of paragraphs but essays of this length and type usually have four or five paragraphs. Also tell students that each point should be backed up with a reason. Students may also decide to include one or more specific examples for each point.

4a After checking answers, point out or elicit that for pairs A, C and D, style is the important issue; for pair B, it is more a question of which is a more 'open' and interesting introduction to the essay.

A 1 B 2 C 2 D 2

4b Give students time to match the statements with the paragraphs, then check answers with the class.

A paragraph 4/5 **B** paragraph 1 **C** paragraph 3/4
D paragraph 2/3

4c Go through the sentence openings in the table with the class. Then give them time to write the headings in the correct column, individually or in pairs, and check answers with the class.

1 The first part of the argument **2** Another reason **3** General introduction **4** Conclusion **5** The second part of the argument

5 Give students 20–25 minutes to write their essay.

Sample answer:
Nowadays more people are deciding to live by themselves. Some people claim this is more enjoyable and in young people it develops a sense of responsibility, whereas others disagree.
The main advantage of living alone is that there is nobody to tell you what to do, so you can live your life in your own way. What is more, you can organise or decorate your house as you want. There is no one else to disagree with.
On the other hand, it can be quite lonely for some people. By nature, we are social animals. Secondly, it is more expensive because you have to pay all the rent and bills yourself, so you have less money to enjoy yourself. Last but not least, it can be quite hard to find a nice flat for one person, so you might not be able to live in the best area.
To sum up, there are strong arguments on both sides. In conclusion, I believe that living alone is better for older people who have more money and like privacy but not for young people who need to share the costs.

6 Students check their work and tick the statements that are true about their essay.

Expert language: Linking expressions

This exercise focuses on linking expressions which would be useful in Paper 2 Part 1 and are also often tested in Paper 1.

1 In fact **2** In addition **3** For instance **4** Moreover **5** Besides
6 Nevertheless **7** Even so **8** On the other hand

8B Hobbies

As a lead-in, with books closed, get students, in groups, to think of two popular hobbies and two more unusual ones. Then compare and vote on which group has thought of the most unusual hobbies.

Speaking pp. 112–113

1a First ask students if they have heard of the people in the photos. Then check that they understand the meaning of the hobbies listed here, as well as their pronunciation. Let students match the hobbies with the people, in pairs or small groups, but do not confirm answers yet.

1b Refer students to page 210 to check their answers to Exercise 1a. Then discuss the questions here with the whole class.

2a You could extend the activity by eliciting other ideas for each verb in box A.

collect rare coins, E do amateur dramatics, D go waterskiing, B
learn how to draw, A make models, F play Monopoly, C

2b–c The exercise extends the vocabulary in 2a. Check the verbs of the odd ones out (*play darts*, *play pool*), then elicit more examples for each verb. Point out how the use of *a bit of/some* makes the language sound more natural. Find out what things students collect or used to collect when they were younger.

2b
1 darts (play darts) **2** pool (play pool)
2c
collect: stamps, autographs;
do gymnastics, athletics, body-building, yoga, archery, crossword puzzles, origami
go: jogging, windsurfing, horse-riding, cycling, skiing, swimming, fishing make: jewellery, clothes play: tennis, football, badminton, table-tennis, violin,. Guitar

3a Remind students that with all new vocabulary, they need to record the word stress. You could get them to compare answers in pairs before checking with the class.

Photography is stressed on the second syllable. The others are all stressed on the first.

3b There are no fixed answers here. Students may disagree. The point is to practise the vocabulary and to talk about different aspects of a hobby.

4 Explain or elicit the meaning of *dabble in something* (do it in a way that is not serious or fanatical) before students discuss the questions. You could get them to discuss in pairs or small groups first, then elicit a few ideas from different pairs/groups.

5a Help students with their questions by asking what they like to know about someone that they have just met. Emphasise that they should just make notes for the answers and not write full sentences.

5b This could be done in pairs or with the whole class mingling, each student moving on to a different partner after they have answered a question.

6a Before students listen, elicit what you would need to do to create a good first impression (e.g. be positive and attentive, speak clearly and with reasonable accuracy and fluency, give extended answers but not go on for too long, listen carefully to the interlocutor and the other candidate).

1 Anna: home town, free-time activities, favourite TV programme; Giorgio: home town, special occasions, family, favourite TV programmes
2 They both create a good first impression. They are positive, they speak accurately and fluently, they extend their answers and they listen carefully.

6b You could ask students to shout *Stop!* or raise their hands each time they hear a candidate describe a word they don't know.

> Anna: colleague ('it's another person who works with me')
> Giorgio: regular (customers) ('we go there often')

7 Before students begin, refer them to the strategy box on pages 179–180 of the Exam reference section. Give them time to read the strategies or go through them as a class. Finally, give the assessors some guidance on things to look for, such as accuracy, fluency, expanding answers appropriately, making a good first impression.

8 You could do this after each turn if you have plenty of time available. If time is short, it will probably be more efficient to do it when everybody has had their turn.

Listening p.114

1 Before students listen, point out the Help notes that they can use if necessary. Play the recording for them to complete the exam task but do not confirm answers yet.

> **1** B   **2** A   **3** A   **4** C   **5** C   **6** B   **7** C
> **Help:**
> **2** It means 'outside'.
> **4** mending things
> **6** In this context, it means 'become an obsession'.

2 Let students compare and discuss answers in pairs, then play the recording again for them to check. Finally, check answers with the class.

3 Students could discuss the questions in pairs or small groups. If time allows, get different students to share their ideas with the class.

Photocopiable activity

Activity 8B (p. 109) can be used here or later in the unit, whenever you feel a speaking activity is needed for a change of pace. It is a Paper 4 Part 3 type discussion, in which students have to choose a leisure activity.

Use of English 1 p. 115

1 Students discuss the questions in pairs or small groups before brief class feedback.

Background

In Britain fishing is said to be one of the most popular participant hobbies. Football is more popular as a spectator activity but more people fish than play football.

2a Give students a minute to read the text and answer the questions.

> **1** Angling is fishing with a rod, line and bait (as opposed to with trailing lines, nets, etc.).
> **2** More women are doing it.

2b Allow about 10 minutes for the task. If time allows, you could get students to compare answers in pairs before checking with the class.

> **1** on   **2** being   **3** why   **4** did   **5** of   **6** However   **7** in   **8** as

3 Get students do to this in pairs, then check answers with the class.

> **1** 2, 4   **2** 1, 7

4 The discussion is a chance to react to the topic; it could include students' experiences of fishing or other 'cruel' sports.

Language development 2 p. 116

1a Give students time to read through the grammar box before doing the exercise. Check that they understand the distinction made in B between general ability (i.e. long-term) and specific ability (i.e. on one occasion). Also highlight the grammar of the verbs in D: *know how* + *to*-infinitive, *manage* + *to*-infinitive, *succeed in* + *-ing*. Explain to students that for each question, they need to think about the time (past, present or future) and whether it is about general or specific ability.

> **1** can   **2** was able to   **3** could, have been able to   **4** couldn't, wasn't able to   **5** have managed to   **6** will be able to, can   **7** managed to   **8** managed to find, succeeded in finding

1b Give students some time to look at and think about the sentences on their own before they discuss with their partner.

2 Students can refer back to the grammar box to either help them do the exercise or to check their answers after they have finished.

> **1** won't be able to finish   **2** manage to stay   **3** succeeded in passing   **4** can't come   **5** couldn't win   **6** don't know how to play   **7** wasn't able to stay   **8** couldn't swim

3 Point out that students need to think about both meaning and form and that more than one answer may be possible for some items.

> **1** can use   **2** could/was able to put together   **3** succeeded in building/managed to build   **4** could/was able to reach   **5** couldn't/wasn't able to fly   **6** succeeded in winning   **7** can/will be able to carry on

Background

Lego®, the construction toy using interlocking plastic bricks, started in Denmark in the 1940s. The name is derived from the Danish words *leg godt*, meaning 'play well'. Such is the success of Lego® that it has been estimated that on average, there are 62 Lego® bricks for every person on earth!

Use of English 2 p. 117

I The aim here is to focus on some of the more lexical areas frequently tested in Paper I Part 4. Students could answer the questions in pairs or on their own before class feedback.

> **a** 3   **b** I   **c** 2

2a Ask students to look at the questions and decide what language point is tested in each. Identifying the type of language being tested will help them towards the right answers.

2b Students complete the exam task. Point out the Help notes that they can use if necessary. After feedback, encourage students to record the phrasal verbs, fixed phrases and collocations in their vocabulary notebooks.

> **2a–b**
> **I** get away with cheating (a phrasal verb)
> **2** in case we want to (a fixed phrase)
> **3** 's unlikely (that) there will (a fixed phrase)
> **4** had to be called off (a phrasal verb)
> **5** didn't succeed in persuading (verb + preposition)
> **6** had trouble (in) writing (noun + preposition)

3 In pairs, students compare answers and discuss the questions about the exam task.

Language development 3 p. 118

Ia Start by getting students to read the posts and match them with the pictures. Do not focus on the meaning of the phrasal verbs in italics here, as these are dealt with in the following exercises, but clear up any other vocabulary difficulties.

> **I** C   **2** B   **3** A

Ib The *True/False* statements here are intended as a guide to what the phrasal verbs mean. Elicit meanings or get students to check in a dictionary.

> **I** T   **2** T   **3** T   **4** T   **5** F   **6** T   **7** T   **8** F   **9** T   **I0** F

Ic Students could discuss this in pairs, small groups or as a whole class.

2 This exercise introduces more phrasal verbs with *get*. Again, if the meaning is not clear, get students to check in a dictionary.

> **I** A   **2** B   **3** B   **4** A   **5** A   **6** B

3a This exercise practises the verbs introduced in Exercises Ia and 2. Point out that students may need to change the form of some verbs and if time allows, get them to compare answers in pairs before checking with the class.

> **I** get together   **2** get, down   **3** got away with   **4** get on with
> **5** get by   **6** getting up to   **7** get off

3b Encourage students to expand their answers and develop them into a conversation.

9 The consumer society

Module 9 includes topics such as giving money to charity, shopping, customer relations and banking.

Lead-in p. 119

With books closed, write *consume* on the board and ask students what it means (use time, energy, goods, etc.). Elicit related words and write them on the board, e.g. *consumer* (someone who buys and uses products and services), *consumer goods* (goods that people buy for their own use, rather than goods bought by businesses and organisations), *consumer society* (a society in which buying products and services is considered to be very important), *consumerism* (the belief that it is good to buy and use a lot of products and services), *consumption* (the amount of something that is used; the act of buying and using products and services). Then get students to look at the photos and ask how each one represents consumerism. Finally, students discuss the lead-in questions in pairs, groups or as a whole class.

9A A matter of conscience?

Ask students if they prefer making, spending, saving or giving away money, and why.

Reading pp. 120–121

1a–b You could start by getting students to look at the logos and asking if they have heard of/what they know about these charities (see Background below). You could also get students to brainstorm local or international charities that they know of before discussing the questions. Draw their attention to the use of *the* with an adjective (e.g. *the homeless*, *the elderly*) to refer to a group of people and elicit other examples.

Background

WWF, founded in 1961, is the world's largest independent conservation organisation operating in over 90 countries. Oxfam, started in 1942 as 'The Oxford Committee for Famine relief' in response to food shortages caused by the war, is a world leader in Emergency relief, promotes health and education, and campaigns for debt relief, Fair Trade and conflict resolution. Age Concern campaigns for the fair treatment and well-being of elderly people in society. Shelter, a domestic UK charity, was set up in 1966 to ensure that everyone has a suitable, decent and affordable home.

2 You could do the first question with the class, as an example, to remind students how to do the task, then set a time limit of 10–15 minutes. Do not confirm answers yet.

| 1 C | 2 E | 3 A | 4 D | 5 B | 6 B | 7 E | 8 A | 9 D | 10 C |

3 Get students to compare and discuss their answers in pairs, then check with the class.

4 This would work well in groups of three or four students.

5 Encourage students to use the context to guess the meaning of any unknown words. Get them to compare answers in pairs before checking with the class.

| 1 do my fair share | 2 applaud | 3 moved | 4 brings it home to you |
| 5 make donations | 6 ashamed | 7 rough | 8 make a point of |

Language development 1 pp. 122–123

1a Ask students what they know about Warren Buffet and Bill Gates before they discuss the question.

Background

Warren Buffet, consistently ranked among the world's wealthiest people, made his money through successful long-term investment. His simple strategy has been to spot strong undervalued businesses and improve them. He is said to have modest tastes and still lives in the same house he bought in a suburb of his hometown of Omaha, Nebraska, in 1957. In 2012, *Time* magazine named Buffet one of the most influential people in the world.

The aims of the Bill and Melinda Gates Foundation are: reducing poverty and improving health and access to education. It funds research and medical care for sufferers of the most serious conditions in the developing world such as malaria, tuberculosis and AIDS.

1b Students read the statements and answer the concept questions. You could get them to discuss and justify their answers in pairs before you check with the class.

| 1 no | 2 yes | 3 yes | 4 no |

1c–d Point out to students that they should look carefully at the context. Before feedback, refer them to the Expert grammar section (pages 194–195) and ask them to check their answers.

> Zero conditional: If someone from a charity comes ... I nearly always give ... ; if/when + present simple + present simple
>
> First conditional: If I see ... I'll probably give ... ; if + present simple + will
>
> Second conditional: If I had ... , I'd leave ... ; if + past simple + would
>
> Third conditional: If I had been ... , I wouldn't have left ... ; if + past perfect + would have + past participle

2a This exercise practises the zero, first and second conditionals and shows how the choice of structure is a personal one, depending on how likely the speaker thinks the if part is to happen. Do the first question with the class and discuss the difference in meaning between a first and second conditional question here: first conditional: possible and likely, e.g. addressing someone who has entered a competition and believes he/she has a good chance of winning; second conditional: unlikely or imaginary, e.g. a conversation between two people who are just imagining the situation – they do not actually believe they have a good chance of winning a lot of money.

> **1** If you won a lot of money, what would you spend it on?/If you win a lot of money, what will you spend it on?
>
> **2** If a classmate asks you to lend him/her a small amount of money, what will you do?/If a classmate asked you to lend him/her a small amount of money, what would you do?
>
> **3** If a classmate asks you to lend him/her a large amount of money, what will you do?/If a classmate asked you to lend him/her a large amount of money, what would you do?
>
> **4** What do you do when you need change for a vending machine?/What will you do if you need change for a vending machine?
>
> **5** If you found a lot of money, what would you do?/If you find a lot of money, what will you do?
>
> **6** What would you do if you lost a/your wallet or purse?
>
> **7** What would you say if you received a present you didn't like?/What do you say if you receive a present you don't like?
>
> **8** What will you buy if you go shopping this weekend?

2b Encourage students to expand their answers, giving reasons.

3 This exercise practises the third conditional. Do the first question with the class and ask: Did he set his alarm? (no) Did he oversleep? (yes)

> **2** If he hadn't been late for work, he wouldn't have got the sack.
>
> **3** If he had been able to find another job, he wouldn't have started his own business.
>
> **4** The business wouldn't have been a great success if it hadn't been such a good idea.
>
> **5** If James hadn't worked very hard he wouldn't have become a millionaire.
>
> **6** So, he wouldn't have become very rich if he had set his alarm!

4a Get students to do the exercise in pairs, then check answers with the class. Explain that in 1, at the moment is not just 'at this precise second of speaking' – it is a present situation that was also true at the time of the past action.

> **1** at the moment, yesterday **2** last week, now

4b Give students time to match the statements with the explanations, then check answers with the class. If necessary, give two more examples about yourself:
1 I trained to be a teacher in the past. I am a teacher now. If I hadn't trained to be a teacher (in the past), I wouldn't be a teacher (now).
2 I am your teacher now. I marked your homework last week. If I weren't your teacher (now), I wouldn't have marked your homework (last week).

> **a** 2 **b** 1

5 Before students begin, ask them to think about the time in each part of each sentence: is it in the past or now/generally true? Do the first question with the class, as an example, and ask: Do I earn more money? (no) Did I go for a job interview? (yes).

> **1** earned, wouldn't have gone **2** would be able to, hadn't spent
> **3** had invested, would be **4** weren't, would have been **5** were, would have reduced **6** would be, hadn't missed **7** couldn't have bought, weren't

6 Point out that these conjunctions are alternatives to if in certain situations. You could get students to look at the Expert grammar notes (pages 194–195) before or while they do the exercise.

> **1** provided that **2** Unless **3** Even if **4** as long as

7 Get students to check answers in pairs before you check with the class. Ask students to justify their answers.

> **1** Unless, hurry up, will miss
> **2** gives, as long as/if/provided that, spend
> **3** If, hadn't lent, would have
> **4** will come, as long as/if/provided that, pay
> **5** If, didn't run, would have
> **6** Even if, had asked, wouldn't have been
> **7** If, didn't work, wouldn't feel
> **8** If, were/was, wouldn't have spent

Photocopiable activity

Activity 9A (p. 110) can be used here. It is a game in which students ask and answer questions about real, imaginary and past situations.

Writing pp. 124–125

1a This would work well as a class discussion.

1b Get students to discuss the question in pairs, making notes under the headings. When they have finished, ask different students to share their ideas with the class.

2 Ask students to read the task and mark the key words. They then discuss the questions in pairs or small groups before class feedback. Remind them to think about the purpose of their article, what they have been asked to include and what style would be suitable.

> **1** saying what you would do with the money and giving your reasons
> **2** to be informed, entertained and engaged
> **3** by using colourful language, a range of vocabulary and structures, expressing your opinion/commenting

3a Before students start planning their article, you could refer them to the article in the Expert writing section (page 201) and ask them to read through the tips in the callout boxes. Then give them some time to go through their notes from Exercise 1b and choose three or four points for their article.

3b–c Students make a paragraph plan for their article and then check it using the questions in Exercise 3c.

3d Students now think about possible titles for their article. If time allows, you could elicit a few ideas from different students, write them on the board and get the class to vote on the best title.

4a Give students time to read the extracts, then discuss with the class. Get them to justify their answers.

> **A** main body   **B** conclusion   **C** introduction or conclusion

4b Check answers to the matching task first, then give students time to complete the sentences. If time allows, you could get them to swap with a partner, read and comment on each other's sentences.

> **Example answers:**
> **1** (C) Have you ever dreamt what life would be like if you became rich unexpectedly? What a thought! Everything would be dramatically different/turned upside down!
> **2** (A) Of course, money can't buy happiness. Suddenly, you discover you have a lot of 'friends' who ask you for money and if you spend the whole lot without a great deal of careful thought, you'll end up poor and miserable.
> **3** (B) If you want to know what I'd do with the rest of the money, I can't tell you right now because I'm not sure. I'll decide when I have to/when the time is right but you can rest assured that I won't be wasting any money on luxury cars.

4c Remind students that in the exam, it is important that they use a range of structures in their writing. Give them time to complete the sentences, then check answers with the class.

> **1** would do, start, putting, saving
> **2** would buy, deserve, provide/have provided, want/have wanted, means/meant, have to/had to
> **3** wouldn't be, just to spend, would give, struggle/are struggling

4d Elicit the meaning of *colour* here, and remind students that adjectives always help to make a piece of writing more interesting and engaging. During feedback, elicit as many adjectives for each item as possible.

> **Example answers:**
> **1** hard-working   **2** gorgeous   **3** needy/unfortunate   **4** great
> **5** run-down

4e Go through the phrases in the table with the class, then let them complete as many as they think necessary for their article.

5 Give students 20 minutes to write their article.

> **Sample answer:**
> **Don't throw it all away!**
> Have you ever dreamt of becoming rich unexpectedly? Just imagine what your life would be like! However, some people who get rich quickly are very careless with their money and end up being poorer than they were before.
> That's why I'd be very careful. I wouldn't want a completely different kind of life, so I'd start by putting some of it away, in case everything went wrong – set up a kind of 'emergency fund'. Then I would buy my hard-working parents a new home. They deserve it because they have always provided me with everything I've always wanted, even if it meant they had to go without. I would also give some money away to needy people who are struggling in the world and have no food. It would not be right to just spend the money on myself. Then I think I would take a year off from studying and travel round the world in great comfort. I've spent most of my life travelling on a limited budget and sleeping in hostels.
> After that, who knows? I'll see, but I certainly won't be buying any luxury cars!

6 Remind students of the importance of checking their work and how best to do it systematically.

Expert language: Intensifying adverbs

Explain to students that they can use intensifying adverbs in their writing to emphasise the degree or intensity of something. Get them to check the meaning of all the adverbs in italics in a dictionary before they do the exercise. During feedback, elicit or explain that they are normally used *before* adjectives and *after* verbs.

> **1** dramatically   **2** ridiculously   **3** bitterly   **4** clearly   **5** deeply
> **6** greatly   **7** fully   **8** hugely

9B Spending money

As a lead-in, with books closed, put a line on the board with a smiley face at one end and a sad one at the other and ask students where they would put shopping on it and why. They could draw their own line and put different types of shopping on it as you call them out, e.g. shopping for clothes, shoes, presents; shopping in traditional shops, supermarkets, online; Sunday shopping, late-night shopping. They then work in pairs and explain their line to a partner.

Speaking pp. 126–127

1a Start by asking students to briefly describe the photos. Then get them to match phrases 1–7 with the different places in the spidergram. During feedback, ask them to give reasons for their answers.

Possible answers:
1 boutique **2** department store **3** boutique **4** supermarket/department store **5** boutique **6** shopping mall **7** street market

1b Get students to practise the pronunciation of the different words in pairs or chorally, as a whole class.

shopping malls   street markets   department stores   boutiques
supermarkets

1c Get students to check the meaning of any unknown words in a dictionary. During feedback, check pronunciation of *aisle*, *organic* and *escalators*.

Suggested answers:
aisle: supermarket   changing rooms: boutique   escalators: shopping mall/department store   organic food: supermarket/street market   trolley: supermarket

1d After feedback, you could teach/revise vocabulary for other types of shops (e.g. antique shop, bookshop, fishmonger's, greengrocer's, jeweller's, pet shop, sports shop, toy shop).

1 butcher's **2** chemist's **3** florist's **4** newsagent's
5 stationer's **6** shoe shop

2 Get students to compare answers in pairs before checking with the class. After feedback, encourage students to record the collocations in their vocabulary notebooks.

1 price, costs **2** price **3** cost, pricey **4** cost **5** price

3 After students have completed the sentences, elicit ideas from different students about the situation in each item. After feedback, encourage them to record the collocations and phrases in their vocabulary notebooks.

(Possible answers are given in brackets.)
1 out of (shop assistant to customer – item has sold out)
2 pay (customer to shop assistant – not certain where to pay)
3 offer (customer to shop assistant – looking for a bargain)
4 put (customer on the phone to department store)
5 hang on (shop assistant on phone to customer who has asked if something is in stock)
6 just (customer browsing in a shop – to shop assistant)
7 keep (shop assistant to customer – customer has been serving someone else)
8 return (shop assistant on the phone to customer making a complaint about an item which is not working)

4 Before students begin, ask a student for a brief description of the task in Paper 4 Part 3. Refer the interlocutors to page 211 of the Expert speaking section and the candidates to the spidergram on page 126, and give them a few minutes to complete the task.

5 Refer students to the strategy on pages 179–180 and get them to discuss their performance in pairs.

6a Again, ask a student for a brief description of the task in Part 4. Let them compare answers in pairs, then check answers with the class.

a 5 **b** 6 **c** 1 **d** 3 **e** 4 **f** 2

6b Students listen to the sample answer and discuss the questions as a whole class.

4

6c Get students to discuss the questions in pairs before checking with the class.

3, 4

7 Encourage students to use the phrases in Exercise 6c to add to their own opinions and agree or disagree with the other candidate. If your class is not divisible by three, it would be better to have an extra candidate in some groups than pairs with only one candidate, so that the candidates get to agree or disagree with each other.

8 Encourage students to discuss their own and their partner's performance, and not to be too critical!

Listening p. 128

1 Remind students of the type of task and elicit the strategy. You could do question 1 with the class, as an example.

1 what advertised? key words: television, computer, board game
2 what doing? faulty goods, money back, goods delivered
3 what doing? blaming, advice, suggestion
4 where? bus station, shop, library
5 what complaining about? attitude of staff, accuracy of information, arrangements changed
6 who talking to? hotel receptionist, conference organiser, secretary
7 which sector successful? travel, health, entertainment
8 what about? disadvantages e-commerce, new idea, research into success

2 You could let students compare and discuss their answers in pairs, both between the first and second listening of each extract and after the second listening.

1 C **2** B **3** B **4** A **5** B **6** C **7** A **8** B

3 First check that students understand *faulty*, *cash refund*, *credit note*, *ripped off* and *compensation*. All the words are from the recording, which you could use to help with context and examples. Then students discuss the questions in pairs or groups and if time allows, share their answers with the class.

Use of English 1 p. 129

1 Students could discuss the questions in pairs, small groups or as a whole class. You could introduce some useful vocabulary here, such as *shop around*, *wait for the sales*, *buy in bulk* and *get good value for money*.

2a Encourage students to recall as much of the strategy as possible before checking on page 175.

2b This would work well as a whole class activity.

2c Give students a time limit for the task (e.g. 12–15 minutes). Point out the Help notes that students can use if necessary.

> **1** one **2** is **3** of **4** what **5** is **6** to **7** are **8** there
> **Help:**
> 2, 5: singular   7 plural

3 Students could discuss the questions in pairs, small groups or as a whole class.

Language development 2 p. 130

1 Go through the grammar box with the students before they do the exercise. When they have finished, you could get them to compare answers in pairs before class feedback.

> **1** Everyone **thinks** it's a good idea.
> **2** The majority of us **agree**.
> **3** ✓
> **4** Neither of them **knows** what to buy.
> **5** These jeans **don't** fit.
> **6** ✓
> **7** Ten euros **isn't** very much.
> **8** ✓
> **9** These scissors **don't** cut very well.
> **10** The United States **has** a new President.

2 Tell students that they don't need to choose a tense (all the verbs are in the present simple) but they need to decide which verbs are singular and which are plural. Students could have further practice by conducting a class/group survey into shopping habits/opinions and then reporting back to the class using quantity expressions such as *a large number of*, *the majority of* and *hardly anyone*.

> **1** sells   **2** feel   **3** causes   **4** wants   **5** seem   **6** is   **7** say
> **8** admit   **9** confess   **10** wanted/want

3 Although this is a relatively basic grammar point, it can still cause difficulty for some students and is often tested in the exam. Give students time to study the grammar box before they do the exercise.

> **1** There are   **2** it is   **3** there is   **4** It is   **5** there are   **6** it is

4 This exercise gives further practice of the impersonal *it* and *there*. It would work well in pairs or small groups.

Use of English 2 p. 131

1 You could give your own answers to the questions as an example. Get students to give examples in their discussion. You could also ask them to name their favourite and least favourite shops.

2 Elicit the strategy for Paper 1 Part 3 before students do the task and point out the Help notes that they can use if necessary. You could get them to compare answers in pairs before checking with the class.

> **1** exhaustion   **2** impatient   **3** service   **4** friendliness
> **5** satisfaction   **6** ensure   **7** flight   **8** personally
> **Help:**
> 2 both

3 Students could discuss this in pairs, small groups or as a whole class. Possible further question: *Is it worth paying more to go shopping where the staff are knowledgeable and helpful?*

4 Point out the Help notes and get students to compare answers in pairs before checking with the class.

> **1** intentions   **2** employment   **3** retirement   **4** entertainment
> **5** financial   **6** investment   **7** unaffordable   **8** assistance
> **Help:**
> 6 a suffix   7 an adjective

5 This would work well in pairs or small groups. Ask students to give reasons for their answers.

Language development 3 p. 132

1 Students complete the quiz in pairs, using a dictionary if necessary. You could get them to do one section at a time so that you can check answers and focus on differences in meaning within each section.

> **1** a ✗   b ✗, ✗   c ✓   d ✗, ✗   e ✓   f ✗   g ✓
> **2** a from   b to   c to   d on   e on   f into   g into   h from
> i on   j to
> **3** a the tickets, a big profit, a discount   b a refund, a receipt, a loan
> **4** a discount   b profit   c refund   d interest   e bill   f salary
> g fine   h loan

2 Discuss how this topic vocabulary could be recorded and what other things students will need to note (e.g. prepositions, which verb to use with the word, whether it is formal or informal).

3 First check that students understand all the statements. They should discuss them in pairs or small groups, giving reasons for their answers and examples from their own experience if possible.

4a Students looked at forming adjectives in Module 2B and nouns in Module 5B. Here they look at forming verbs. Point out the change in word stress in the verb/noun forms of *record*: <u>record</u> (n), re<u>cord</u> (v). Before students categorise the verbs in the box, check pronunciation of *blood*, *bleed*, *choice*, *choose*, <u>import</u> (n) and im<u>port</u> (v).

> No change: calm, dry, import, name
> Internal change: bleed, choose
> Prefix: endanger
> Suffix: criticise, fatten, lengthen, strengthen, widen

4b–c Give students a couple of minutes for each matching task, then check answers with the class.

> **4b**
> **1** criticise   **2** import   **3** endanger   **4** choose
> **4c**
> **1** widen   **2** modernise   **3** calm   **4** strengthen

Photocopiable activity

Activity 9B (p. 111) can be used here. It is a split crossword which practises money vocabulary and word formation.

10 Out and about

Module 10 includes topics such as travel, holidays, public transport and space tourism.

Lead-in p. 133

With books closed, write *Out and about* on the board and ask students what they understand by it. It can mean both 'not home and busy' and 'away travelling'. Then get students to identify the means of transport in the photos and discuss the questions and quote.

Background

The American novelist and travel writer Paul Theroux (b.1941) taught English in Malawi, Uganda and Singapore for eight years before settling down in England and beginning a career as a writer. His novels include *The Family Arsenal* (1976), about a group of terrorists in the London slums, and *The Mosquito Coast* (1982), about an American inventor who attempts to create an ideal community in the Honduran jungle. He first achieved commercial success with a best-selling travel book, *The Great Railway Bazaar* (1975), describing his four-month train journey through Asia. Other travel books include *The Old Patagonian Express* (1979), *The Happy Isles of Oceania* (1992) and *The Last Train to Zona Verde* (2013).

10A Travel

With books closed, get students to write the word *travel* vertically on a piece of paper and then write words across it that they associate with the topic. Demonstrate on the board how to start, e.g.

```
        t  i  m  e
     t  r  a  i  n
        a
a  d  v  e  n  t  u  r  e
        e
     p  l  a  n  e
```

In pairs, students then explain the significance of their words, e.g. *time: you need a lot of time to really enjoy foreign travel; train: my favourite way to travel.*

Photocopiable activity

Activity 10A (p. 112) can be used here or as a follow-up after the reading section. It is a questionnaire to discover what students consider important when travelling.

Reading pp. 134–135

1 This exercise is designed to reinforce the habit of predicting. Students could discuss the question in pairs, small groups or as a whole class.

2 Students skim the text and answer the question. Set a time limit of 1–2 minutes.

> Toronto, New York, Miami, Los Angeles

3 Elicit the strategy for this task. Then, at this stage, leave students to do the task without further help.

> **1** B **2** C **3** A **4** C **5** D **6** B

4 This exercise looks at collocation. After feedback, encourage students to record the phrases in their vocabulary notebooks.

> **1** c **2** e **3** b **4** d **5** a

5 You could also ask students: *In what ways is travel becoming easier or harder?'*

Language development 1 pp. 136–137

1a With books closed, brainstorm places to stay while on holiday. Pre-teach *self-catering* (when you arrange your own food and cooking, e.g. staying in an apartment rather than a hotel). Then get students to discuss the question, giving reasons for their preferences.

1b Students read the text and answer the question. Explain that the answers to question 1 are in the text, whereas they will have to think of the answers to question 2 themselves.

> **1** They stay cool in summer, they are well decorated, there is a buffet breakfast, a barbecue area is being constructed.
> **2** You have to share facilities with others, the shops are not very close, breakfast is not included (and it could get too hot), there is some building work going on.

1c Elicit the form of the passive (*be* + past participle). During feedback, point out that not stating who has done something has the effect of making the statements more impersonal and so more formal. Highlight the use of *by* when we want to say who has done something: *They were built ... **by** a team of highly skilled workers ... .*

> Examples: are grouped, were built, have been designed, have (all) been decorated, is served, is (now) being constructed, will (soon) be completed, can be found
> The passive is used here because the actions described are more important than who does them.

1d During feedback, elicit why each tense is used. Explain that the passive is not a tense and the rules of tense use are exactly the same as for active verb forms.

> **1** are grouped   **2** is served   **3** is being constructed
> **4** have been designed   **5** have been decorated   **6** were built
> **7** will be completed   **8** can be found

2a This exercise focuses mainly on form. Get students to work in pairs to identify the correct tense in each case and establish how to form that tense correctly. Check answers with the class.

> **1** are situated   **2** were redecorated   **3** can be accessed
> **4** will have been installed   **5** are being built   **6** has been given
> **7** must be checked   **8** will be asked

2b Here, students have to think about both form and use, changing the sentences from active to passive to make them more formal. You could do the first one or two items with the class, as examples.

> **1** Our facilities are always being improved.
> **2** All our flats have been modernised in the last two years.
> **3** Our kitchens have been equipped to the highest standards.
> **4** The beds will be made daily.
> **5** The holiday village can be found two kilometres outside the town.
> **6** A full programme of sports activities is offered.
> **7** Very few complaints were received last year.
> **8** Extra people may be accommodated on the sofa beds.
> **9** The maximum number of people allowed in each caravan is indicated in/by our brochure.
> **10** Keys must be returned to reception on departure.

3 Start by writing the following sentences on the board: *Fleming discovered penicillin. It is an important medicine.* Ask students to rewrite the sentences, emphasising the medicine (*Penicillin is an important medicine. It was discovered by Fleming.*). Students then study the grammar box and answer the questions.

> **A** by   **B** 1   **C** 1 thought; 2 said   **D** to cheer, to empty

4 Students complete the conversations with the correct passive form of the verbs. You could get them to compare answers in pairs before checking with the class.

> **1** it was composed by Schubert   **2** were given   **3** was seen
> **4** is believed (that)   **5** has been promised   **6** it was discovered by Fleming   **7** is thought to have hidden   **8** will be made to pay

5a Students read the text and rewrite it using the passive, to make it more formal. Check answers with the class.

> **Suggested answer:**
> The town has changed a lot in the last 30 years. All the old factories have been pulled down and replaced with hi-tech science parks. It's felt to be unfortunate that one of the older schools was also demolished, as children will have to be sent by bus to the next town. It is said that a brand new school will be built in the town in the next few years when extra funding is provided by the Government. That will be appreciated by the newer residents in particular.

5b Students could either talk or write about the changes in their own town. Before they do, you could get them to talk about the two photos here, encouraging them to use the passive where possible.

Photocopiable activity

Activity 10B (p. 113) can be used here. Students write travel-related news stories based on notes.

Writing pp. 138–139

1 Start by asking students what kind of things people complain about or apologise for. These ideas could act as prompts when students discuss the questions. Ask them to look at and discuss the questions in pairs, small groups or as a whole class. Accept any reasonable answers.

> **1**
> **Example answers:**
> To make a complaint:
> • to a law firm about the way they handled a family matter (formal)
> • to a company for sending the wrong item a second time (semi-formal)
> • to another student about what they have been saying about you in public (informal)
> To apologise:
> • on behalf of a company to apologise to a customer about their poor service (formal)
> • to a teacher about your bad behaviour (semi-formal)
> • to a friend for forgetting their birthday (informal)
> **2**
> a very formal = a; b semi-formal = b; c informal = b

2a–b Get students to read the task and discuss the questions. They could do this in pairs, small groups or as a whole class.

> **2a**
> to apologise to the parent and explain what happened (semi-formal)
> **2b**
> **Suggested answers:**
> ski slopes poor, lessons fewer than promised, accommodation inadequate

3a Students can now start planning their email. Get them to brainstorm ideas in pairs or groups and make notes under the headings given.

3b This exercise focuses on paragraph organisation, which students should find quite easy by this stage.

3c Students could brainstorm ideas for the final paragraph in pairs or small groups, then complete their paragraph plan individually.

> **Example answer:**
> You could say that you take the complaint seriously and explain what you will do as a result (e.g. change the arrangements next year, offer a partial refund).

4a Before students do the exercise, clear up any vocabulary difficulties. Check that they understand *insufficient*, *unsatisfactory*, *in advance*, *tuition* and *inconvenience*.

> **I** weren't enough   **2** not good enough   **3** told beforehand
> **4** unhappy about   **5** point out   **6** get in touch
> **7** couldn't get   **8** if we put you out in any way   **9** a pity

4b Again, clear up any vocabulary difficulties (e.g. *enquiry*, *astonishment*) before students begin. Point out that there may be more than one way to rewrite each sentence and if time allows, elicit answers from different students for each item during feedback.

> **Suggested answers:**
> **I** We were very worried when you told us ...   **2** After I asked the company, ...   **3** I was amazed that this turned out not to be true and ...   **4** I'm sorry that single rooms were extra ...
> **5** I hope your son will carry on ...

4c–d Students could work on these individually or in pairs. For Exercise 4c, point out that there may be more than one way to rewrite each sentence and during feedback, elicit different versions from different students if time allows.

> **4c**
> **Suggested answers:**
> **I** I would like to thank you for contacting us.
> **2** It is unfortunate that the beginners' slopes were unsatisfactory.
> **3** Extra lessons were not included in the price.
> **4** I apologise but he should have informed us of that in advance.
> **5** We were extremely concerned about the lack of snow.
> **4d**
> 2, 3, 5

4e Go through the sentence openings in the table with the class, then give them time to write complete sentences for their emails.

5 Give students 15–20 minutes to write their email.

> **Sample answer:**
> Dear Ms White,
> First, let me apologise for any disappointment your son experienced on our ski trip. It is true that there were several concerns. Since we had been led to believe by the company that there would be sufficient slopes for both beginners and advanced skiers, we were extremely upset when this turned out not to be the case. It was also unfortunate that lack of snow meant that artificial snow had to be used instead.
> As for the question of lessons, if you look at the letter we sent out, you will see that only five one-hour ski-lessons were included in the price and that extra hours would have to be paid for separately.
> In relation to accommodation, I am not quite sure what you are referring to. I know that in one room there were not enough beds but this was not the case in your son's room.
> We would like to assure you that we take all complaints seriously. We have already decided that next year we will change the company and the location for our trip and we hope that your son will consider joining us again.
> Yours sincerely,

6 Remind students to use the checklist in the Expert writing section to check their work.

10B Getting around

As a lead-in, with books closed, get students to think of the differences in meaning between the following nouns: *travel* (uncountable: the activity of travelling; countable, usually plural: journeys for pleasure to places far away), *trip* (a short journey or one that is not usually made) and *transport* (a system or method for carrying passengers or goods from one place to another).

Speaking pp. 140–141

Ia Before students discuss the question, ask them to name the forms of transport in the photos (bus, scooter, van, (sail)boat, train, plane).

Ib Clear up any vocabulary difficulties before students do the exercise. Get them to discuss their answers in pairs before class feedback. They should justify their choices.

> **I** the tube (The others are on water.)
> **2** delivery van (The others have two wheels and are ridden.)
> **3** tram (The others are air transport.)
> **4** handlebars (On a bicycle – the others are from a car.)
> **5** carriage (The others are parts of boats.)
> **6** sidecar (On a motorbike – the others are cars.)

Ic Remind students of ways of marking stress and if you think it necessary, model pronunciation of the words, getting students to repeat them.

> **I** ca<u>noe</u>, yacht, the tube, <u>row</u>ing boat
> **2** <u>mo</u>ped, <u>scoo</u>ter, <u>mo</u>torbike, de<u>liv</u>ery van
> **3** tram, <u>heli</u>copter, <u>gli</u>der, <u>space</u>ship
> **4** clutch, <u>hand</u>lebars, ac<u>cel</u>erator, <u>steer</u>ing wheel
> **5** deck, oars, <u>carr</u>iage, mast
> **6** <u>hatch</u>back, sa<u>loon</u>, <u>side</u>car, es<u>tate</u>

2a Students could use gerunds (e.g. driving) or means of transport (e.g. car, bus) to answer. If using the latter, get them to think of as many forms as possible for each as this will extend and reinforce the vocabulary.

> be forced to land: plane
> confirm your flight: plane
> disembark: boat
> fasten your seatbelt: plane/car/delivery van
> get clamped: car
> get low on petrol: car/moped/scooter/motorbike/delivery van
> get points on your licence: car/moped/scooter/motorbike/
> delivery van
> go on a cruise: boat
> it's two stops on the Northern Line: the tube
> stop in a lay-by: car moped/scooter/motorbike/delivery van
> take a driving test: car
> take on as hand luggage: plane

2b This exercise looks at common vocabulary mistakes connected with transport. Get students to compare answers in pairs before you check with the class.

1 I'm tired. Let's **get** (**into**)/**take**/**catch** a taxi.
2 I think we get **off** the bus ...
3 Oh no! We've **missed** the last train! ...
4 'Have you ever **ridden** a horse?' ...
5 Our ship **docks**/**stops** in Cairo ...
6 What's the **price**/**cost** of the ticket? ...
7 It's a long **journey** there ...
8 Wonderful! The train's exactly **on** time!

3 The discussion could be in groups, with the whole class or as a debate, with the class divided into two groups, each presenting one side.

4a This is a review of the format of Paper 4 Part 2. Get students to discuss the statements in pairs before you go through them with the class.

1 T
2 F (You must compare the photos.)
3 T (But you must give a personal opinion about the photos)
4 F
5 F (The second candidate has to answer a question and there are two parts to the first part: Compare and ...)
6 T

4b Before students do the exercise, remind them of the meaning of *speculate* (talk about possibilities) and *paraphrase* (explain a word in another way). Check answers with the class.

1 g   2 c   3 a   4 f   5 b   6 d   7 e

4c Keep this fairly brief to avoid creating endless lists!

5a–b Divide the class into groups of three. If your class is not equally divisible by three, have one or two groups of four with an extra assessor. Give the interlocutors time to check the instructions and prepare the material.

6 Encourage everyone in each group to discuss the candidates' performance.

Listening p. 142

1 Recap various forms of public transport if not following on immediately after the Speaking section. Remind students to give reasons for their answers in the discussion.

2 Remind students of the best strategy for this task type. Get them to look at the rubric and ask what type or types of transport will be discussed (different types of bikes). Then play the recording for students to complete the task but do not confirm answers yet.

1 F   2 C   3 H   4 E   5 D

3 Get students to compare answers in pairs and remind them to give reasons for their choices. Then check answers with the class.

4 Before students discuss the questions, check that they understand *look down on* and *status symbol*.

5 Students could use dictionaries to check the vocabulary before discussing the questions.

Language development 2 p. 143

1 Explain that in question 1, students need to think of the time referred to in each case, rather than the verb forms. Verb forms are focused on in question 2. During feedback, remind students that, as with conditionals, the wish contrasts with reality, so we use a positive verb form for a negative situation and vice versa, e.g. *I wish I could afford this car* (but I can't); *I wish we hadn't moved here* (but we have).

1 the present: 1, 3; the past: 2; the future: 4, 5
2 the present: *wish* + past simple, *if only* + *could*; the past: *wish* + past perfect; the future: *wish* + *would*; *if only* + *would*
3 *If only* is stronger/more emphatic.

2 Point out to students that they will need to think about the time reference and a possible change/regret in each situation.

Suggested answers
2 I wish/If only I hadn't dyed my hair bright red. I wish/If only I'd kept it blonde.
3 I wish/If only he didn't/wouldn't borrow my car./I wish/If only he would stop borrowing my car.
4 I wish/If only I could afford a taxi./I wish/If only I didn't have to take the bus.
5 I wish/If only I hadn't come to see this./I wish/ If only I were/ was watching something else.
6 I wish/If only he/she would hurry up./I wish/If only he/she didn't/wouldn't take so long in the bathroom.

3 This exercise provides personalised practice of the grammar covered in this section. Look at the first two questions and get students to think about what would fit. If time allows, you could get students to discuss their answers in pairs before sharing them with the class.

4 Before students do the exercise, go through the grammar box with them, pointing out how these expressions use the tense shift backwards to express hypothetical situations.

1 A   2 B   3 B

5 Remind students to think carefully about the time (present or past) and the choice of verb form (present or past).

1 learnt   2 was/were   3 phoned   4 had met   5 had bought

6 Get students to compare their answers in pairs before sharing them with the class. If time allows, elicit different sentence endings for each item from different students.

Use of English 1 p. 144

1 This exercise aims to revise some of the strategies for key word transformations tasks. Begin with a quick review of the task: ask: *How many questions are there?* (six); *How many words should you write?* (between two and five); *Can you change the key word?* (no). Then ask students to look at the statements in the speech bubbles. Get them to discuss in pairs first, then check with the class.

Suggested answers:
1 Leave it and come back to it when you've done the ones you can do.
2 Make sure you write something for every question. Don't leave any gaps.

2 Point out that students shouldn't rush key word transformations. They should work slowly and carefully to avoid unnecessary mistakes. If time allows, you could get them to compare answers in pairs before checking with the class.

1 wish I'd gone   **2** would rather you phoned   **3** hardly anyone/anybody at/in   **4** is supposed to be   **5** (high/about) time you stopped going   **6** you mind not using

3 Students could discuss these in pairs first. During class feedback, remind them that in the exam, the questions test a wide range of structures and vocabulary.

1 1, 2 and 5
2 change 1: *I'd rather* → *Would you mind*; change 2: *didn't use* → *not using*

Use of English 2 p. 145

1 Students could discuss these in pairs or small groups, or share their experiences with the whole class.

2a This is a review of the task strategies for Paper 1 Part 2. You could also ask: *Can you use contracted forms, like 'don't'?* (No, they count as two words.).

1 after (You should read the text right through first for a general understanding.)
2 short (If you get stuck with one answer, you will have less time for the rest of the task and the rest of the paper.)
3 word (If you put more than one word, it will be marked as incorrect, even if one of the words is correct. If you can't decide between two possible answers, you should always choose one rather than put both.)

2b Remind students that skimming the text will not only give them a general understanding, it will also help them identify the style, time frame and possible source of the text, all of which could help them complete the task. Check answers with the class.

1 He had an unusual accident after he couldn't stop his car.
2 For dangerous driving.

2c Students complete the exam task. Get them to compare answers in pairs before you check with the class.

1 off   **2** down   **3** through   **4** could   **5** on   **6** by   **7** no   **8** of

3 During feedback, remind students that verb + preposition collocations and phrasal verbs are often tested in Paper 1 Part 2.

1 0, 5, 6   **2** 1, 2, 3

4 Get students to reread the text before the discussion. For question 1, if they don't think the man was telling the truth, ask them to suggest what really happened.

Language development 3 p. 146

1a With books closed, read out the examples in the box, missing out each preposition and eliciting it from students. Then get students to look at the sentences and underline the verb + preposition collocations.

trapped in, concentrate on, followed by

1b Encourage students to use their dictionaries to check their answers. After class feedback, encourage them to record the collocations in their vocabulary notebooks.

1 about   **2** from   **3** about   **4** to   **5** with   **6** in

2 The exercise looks at verbs that have different meanings when followed by different prepositions. You could get students to compare answers in pairs before checking with the class.

1 for, on   **2** about, of   **3** to, from   **4** as, for   **5** of, from
6 to, for

3 You could start by asking students if they have ever considered a trip into space as tourists. Before they do the exercise, point out that some of the verbs can be followed by more than one preposition, so they should think carefully which one is correct in the context.

1 from   **2** of/about   **3** about   **4** at   **5** for   **6** on   **7** to/with
8 in   **9** to   **10** to   **11** with   **12** at

4 Verbs of perception can be easily confused because two different verbs in English may translate as just one verb in the students' language. Encourage students to use dictionaries to check their answers and during feedback, check that they understand the differences:
• *look*: a deliberate action; *see*: not deliberate; *watch*: a deliberate action over a period, e.g. a football match or TV programme
• *gaze*: look at something for a long time because it is so interesting; *peer*: try to look at something but with difficulty; *stare*: look in a very fixed way for some time
• *hear*: could be deliberate or not; *listen*: a deliberate action

1 a looked, seen;   **b** watch
2 a stare;   **b** peered;   **c** gazed
3 a listened, hear;   **b** listen;   **c** heard
4 a feel, touching;   **b** Feel;   **c** touch

11 Well-being

Module 11 includes topics such as happiness, relaxation, avoiding stress, diet, health and retail therapy.

Lead-in p. 147

With books closed, ask students what they do to make themselves feel good. You could give one or two examples of your own to get them started (e.g. go for a walk, go to the gym, have a big cream cake!). Ask students to look at the module title and elicit its meaning (a feeling of being healthy, happy and comfortable with life). Then get students to discuss the lead-in questions.

11A Happiness

Reading pp. 148–149

Photocopiable activity

Activity 11A (p. 115) can be used at the start of the unit to introduce the topic or as a follow-up to the reading section. It is a group discussion on factors in life that affect happiness.

1a Students discuss the questions in pairs. It is usually said that an optimist will describe the glass as half full, whereas a pessimist will describe it as half empty.

1b If students have already done the photocopiable activity, their answers from it would be relevant to question 1. Question 2 implies that when you know the secrets, it is possible to control happiness.

2 Pre-teach *temperament* (the emotional part of someone's character, how likely they are to be happy, angry, etc.). Give students about 15 minutes to do the task. Then get them to compare answers in pairs, saying which parts of the text helped them. Check answers with the class.

> 1 E   2 G   3 D   4 C   5 A   6 F

3a Point out that these words are all used in the text, either as nouns or adjectives. Check answers with the class.

> 1 contented   2 satisfied   3 frustrated   4 anxious   5 depressed
> 6 stressed   7 miserable

3b Give one or two examples of your own to get students started. Let them choose which emotions they want to discuss, as they may not want to discuss unhappy experiences.

4 Students could discuss the questions in pairs, small groups or as a whole class.

Language development 1 pp. 150–151

1 With books closed, divide the class into groups and see which group is first to come up with a specified number of ways to relax (e.g. five to ten). Then ask students to open their books and discuss the question in Exercise 1: *What do you do to relax?* Give prompts if necessary to encourage ideas: *How do you relax at the weekend? At home? With friends? After a long day at work?*

2a Ask students if they recognise the woman in the photo (see Background below). If so, what do they know about her? They then read the extracts and answer the questions.

> 1 being happy   2 due to her close family upbringing

Background

Catherine, Duchess of Cambridge (Catherine Elizabeth Middleton), was born in 1982 in Reading, Berkshire, England, the eldest of three children. She is the wife of Prince William, Duke of Cambridge, second in line to the British throne.

Catherine grew up in Chapel Row, a small village near Newbury, Berkshire, England. She studied art history at the University of St Andrews in Scotland, where she met Prince William in 2001. Their engagement was announced in November 2010 and their wedding took place on 29 April 2011 at Westminster Abbey in London. On 22 July 2013, Catherine gave birth to the couple's first son, Prince George of Cambridge.

Her hobbies include tennis, swimming, sailing, photography and painting. She has been said to have had a major impact on British fashion, known by some as 'the Kate Middleton effect', while in 2012, she was named one of the *100 Most Influential People in the World* by *Time* magazine.

2b Begin by eliciting the function of the words and phrases in italics. Ask: *What do the words and phrases explain?* (the reason for something). Then look at sentence 1 as an example and ask: *What did Mark do?* (He left his job.); *Why?* (Because it was stressful.). During feedback, make sure that students understand that *as*, *because* and *since* all operate in the same way, and so do *because of*, *due to* and *owing to*. But these last three can operate in two different ways: followed by a noun or *the fact that* + subject + verb.

> 1 as, since, because
> 2 owing to, due to, because of
> 3 owing to, due to, because of

2c Point out that there are three possible answers for each sentence and that students should list them all.

> **1** as/because/since
> **2** because of/due to/owing to
> **3** because of/due to/owing to
> **4** as/because/since
> **5** Because of/Due to/Owing to
> **6** because of/due to/owing to

2d Here students need to think about the form that follows each word/phrase. Get them to compare answers in pairs before checking with the class.

> **1 a** was snowing; **b** the snow/the fact that it was snowing;
> **c** the snow/the fact that it was snowing
> **2 a** was raining; **b** the rain/the fact that it was raining;
> **c** it was raining

3a Go through the table with the students before they do the exercise. Point out that *in order that* and *so that* operate in the same way, as do *in order to*, *so as to* and *to*. Highlight the use of *in case* to describe precautions, a way of being safe from something that might happen, and how it is followed by the present simple when referring to the future (e.g. *I'll take an umbrella in case it rains.*).

> **1** in order to/so as to/to **2** in order that/so that **3** in case

3b Remind students to look at what follows the options in italics, as that tells them what fits grammatically.

> **1** to **2** in case **3** so that **4** in order to **5** In order that
> **6** in case **7** so as to **8** so as not to

4 Go through the table with the students before they do the exercise. Draw their attention to *despite* (one word) and *in spite of* (three words), which are often confused. If time allows, you could get students to write alternative sentence endings for 1–8.

> **1** e **2** c **3** h **4** a **5** g **6** b **7** f **8** d

5 This exercise practises all three types of clause: reason, purpose and contrast. Tell students that for each one, they should identify the type of clause first, then think of a logical ending.

> **Example answers:**
> **1** ... I have tried many times.
> **2** ... the noise of the cats outside.
> **3** ... he knows where to pick me up.
> **4** ... the glorious spring sunshine ...
> **5** ... find out whether they open on Sundays.
> **6** ... the fact that we reminded him to take it.

Photocopiable activity

Activity 11B (p. 116) can be used here. It is a game in which students use clauses of reason, purpose and contrast to make sentences about themselves.

Writing pp. 152–153

1 First ask students to look at the photo and tell you what they think it represents. Then ask them to discuss the questions in pairs, small groups or as a whole class.

2 Give students time to read the task and briefly discuss the questions in pairs. Then check with the class, asking students to explain/justify their answers. During feedback, point out that while the task doesn't say that you should recognise other points of view, in an opinion essay, it is best to acknowledge another point of view for balance.

> **1** F **2** T **3** F **4** F **5** T

3a Let students discuss these in pairs or groups. They could add their own ideas to the list. Ask them to choose which point they will use in their essay.

3b Students complete their own paragraph plan. They could do this on their own or in pairs, before discussing ideas as a class.

3c As including another point of view was discussed in Exercise 2, students may have already thought about this and included it in their paragraph plan. Discuss the question as a whole class.

3d Check that students remember what a topic sentence is before they do the exercise. You could write the list of phrases given here on the board, elicit a few more from different students and add them to the list.

3e Students now make notes for supporting points for each topic sentence. Weaker students may benefit from working in pairs to discuss ideas first.

4a–c Students could do these on their own or in pairs. Point out that in Exercise 4b there are a number of possible answers.

> **4a**
> Adding a point of view: in addition, in fact, just as, similarly
> Making a contrast: but, however, on the other hand, whereas, yet
> **4b**
> **Example answers:**
> **1** Money doesn't automatically make us happy. In fact, it makes some people very unhappy.
> **2** It is very stressful to lose money but if we are careful with it, it gives us security.
> **3** We should relax and laugh whenever possible. Similarly, being with friends can give pleasure. However, spending time alone is important.
> **4** Getting too little sleep can cause unhappiness just as eating badly can affect our moods for the worse, whereas going for long walks can have a beneficial effect.
> **4c**
> **1** that, we **2** they, it, these **3** This/It **4** themselves, This/That, us

4d Discuss the odd one out first, then let students choose a phrase and write a sentence for their essay.

> **4** (The other expressions refer to other people.)

5 Give students 20 minutes to write their essay.

Sample answer:
Some people claim they are naturally cheerful. However, in my view, how we lead our lives is the main reason we are either happy or unhappy.
Take money, for example. Money doesn't automatically make us happy. In fact, it makes some people very unhappy because they are frightened of losing what they've got. On the other hand, if we're not greedy and don't spend it foolishly, it can reduce stress and give us security.
Then consider health. If we eat badly, get too little sleep and don't exercise, our health will decline and make us miserable. Eating well and going for lovely long walks in the countryside can make us feel better generally.
The third thing I think is important is to have a positive outlook on life. We should all enjoy things like music and being with our friends. At the same time, it's important to spend time alone and live as simply as possible, which is not easy in the 21st century!
All of these make a big difference to our happiness, no matter what our natural temperament.

6 Give students approximately 10 minutes to check their work.

Expert language: Spelling

a Tell students that as a general principle, if they are unsure of the spelling of a word, they should avoid using it in the exam. But knowing which words they commonly misspell will help when they check their work.

b These are all common students' spelling errors. Students could check answers with a partner or in a dictionary before class feedback.

c You could follow this up in a later lesson with a short dictation of the words, either in isolation, in these sentences, or in different sentences.

b
1 immediately **2** separate **3** unnecessary **4** truly **5** religious **6** therefore **7** neither **8** responsible **9** until **10** definitely **11** generally **12** receive **13** apparently
c
1 likely, happiness **2** forty, piece, advice **3** government, definitely, knowledge, happened **4** Unfortunately, occasion, medicine, effect **5** principle, politicians, independent

11B Health and fitness

As a lead-in, with books closed, ask students how healthy they think their lifestyle is on a scale of 1–10. Ask them how healthy they were a few years ago and how healthy they think they will be in ten years' time. What has changed and what do they think will change?

Listening pp. 154–155

1 Students describe their exercise habits in small groups. You could also ask if they take as much exercise as they would like to or think they should.

2a Clear up any vocabulary difficulties before students do the quiz in pairs.

(Health quiz)
3a flu: headache, aching muscles, fever, cough, sneezing; food poisoning: feeling sick, vomiting, diarrhoea, stomach cramps
3b arthritis: joints; migraine: head; bronchitis: chest; tonsillitis: throat
4 a T **b** F (but there are very few) **c** T **d** F **e** T

2b Pairs now compare their answers, either in groups or as a whole class. They then record words they want to remember in their vocabulary notebooks.

3 This exercise practises prepositions. Students may need help with some of the vocabulary here; you could explain (see answer key below for definitions) or let them check in their dictionaries. During feedback, establish why the preposition is needed in each case (1 after a comparative; 2 adj + prep collocation; 3 phrasal verb; 4 verb + prep collocation).

1 for (Unsaturated fats usually come from plants rather than animals and are better for your health. Saturated fats usually come from animals and an excess of these in your diet is very bad for your health.)
2 to (allergic: having a medical condition in which you become ill or in which your skin becomes red and painful because you have eaten or touched a particular substance)
3 without (dehydrated: having lost too much water from your body)
4 from (virus: a very small living thing that causes infectious illnesses; antibiotic: a drug that is used to kill bacteria and cure infections)

4 This would work well as a class discussion. You could also ask students if they consider their diet to be balanced and why.

5a This would work well as a class discussion. For question 2, the diseases don't have to be the most deadly (e.g. malaria) but can include those that are widespread (e.g. cholera, hepatitis, sleeping sickness, influenza, pneumonia).

5b Remind students that before they listen, they should try and guess what type of information might be missing, based on the context.

1 noun **2** (plural) noun **3** (plural) noun **4** (adjective +) noun **5** (plural) noun **6** adjective + noun **7** (plural) noun **8** noun (phrase) **9** adjective + noun **10** noun

6 Get students to compare their answers in pairs before checking with the class.

> **I** health care **2** advertisements **3** prisoners **4** sugar
> **5** snacks **6** main meal **7** carbohydrates **8** heart disease
> **9** mental health **10** memory

7 Students could discuss the questions in pairs, small groups or as a whole class.

8 If students need help with ideas, ask them to think of foods that are popular in different countries (e.g. for *Carbohydrates*: pasta, rice, bread, potato, couscous).

Speaking p. 156

1a First ask students what they remember about Paper 4 Parts 3 and 4, then get them to look at the statements and decide whether they are true or false.

> **a** F (2 minutes) **b** T **c** F **d** T **e** F **f** T

1b During feedback, elicit what form/pattern follows the unfinished phrases (*Why don't we start by* + *-ing*; *Do you think we should* + infinitive; *Yes, but* + clause; *We could also* + infinitive; *So are we agreed that* + clause).

> **I** b **2** c **3** d **4** a **5** f **6** e

2 Divide the class into suitable groups. If possible, it would be good to record one or more of the groups doing the task now that they are more familiar with the format and the exam is getting closer, then play it back when students do the task analysis at the end.

3a To ensure that all students have an opportunity to practise, you could ask students to change roles after every two questions.

3b Students should discuss their own performance and that of other members of their group. Encourage them to be constructive.

Language development 2 p. 157

1a–b To introduce the language point, write the following on the board: *My problem is that I eat _____ much chocolate. It's _____ nice that I can't say no! I don't have _____ willpower to stop and it's costing me _____ a lot of money!* Invite different students to complete each gap with a suitable word. Then give them time to study the grammar boxes and complete the exercises. Highlight the fact that *enough* is used before nouns and after adjectives, as confusing them is a common mistake with some students at B2 level.

> **Ia**
> **I** so **2** such **3** such a
> **Ib**
> **I** noun, adjective, adverb
> **2 I** c **2** a **3** b

2 Students should do this in pairs, then refer back to the grammar boxes to check their answers before class feedback.

> **I** Jim's **such a** good doctor that everybody likes him.
> **2** My yoga class is great – I'm always **so/very** relaxed afterwards.
> **3** Paul has bought such ~~an~~ expensive fitness equipment!
> **4** The food is too ~~much~~ spicy for me to eat.
> **5** I think my diet's **healthy enough** overall.
> **6** I'm **too** tired to go jogging now.
> **7** John is so unfit **that** he can't even run for a bus.
> **8 There aren't enough** rooms in this hotel for everyone.
> **9** You should be pleased with yourself for losing so **much** weight.
> **10** I'm not **old enough** to join that club.

3 *As* and *like* are commonly confused by some students, partly because they both translate as the same word in some languages and partly because of the number of different uses of *like*. Go through the examples in the box with the class, then ask them to complete the sentences.

> **I** like/such as **2** as **3** like **4** like/such as **5** as if/as though
> **6** As

4 After feedback, ask students if they would like to do something similar.

> **I** as **2** like **3** As **4** like/such as **5** like **6** as

Use of English 1 p. 158

1a Get students to discuss the question in pairs first, then share their ideas with the class.

1b Students discuss this in pairs. During feedback, elicit what has led to the mistakes in each case and how they could have been avoided by following the instructions and checking carefully.

> **I** meeting my wife for the **2** in case the tickets are
> **3** was so tired (that) he **4** as long as we arrive

2 Students should be able to do this without too much help from the task strategy. Do not confirm answers yet.

> **I** put you up **2** such a delicious **3** Judy whether she wanted
> **4** isn't enough room/space **5** unlike/not like Tom to be
> **6** is not as/so popular now as

3 Let students compare and discuss their answers in pairs, then check as a class.

Use of English 2 p. 159

1 Ask: *How do you think the person in the photo is feeling?* Elicit answers from a couple of students, then ask: *Do you feel the same way about shopping?* Students then look at the questions and discuss them in pairs, small groups or as a whole class.

2a Remind students that they should always read the text for a general understanding first and tell them that these questions are to help focus their reading.

> **1** shopping for fun
> **2** It can be good because it gives exercise. It can be bad if it becomes an addiction.

2b Give students a time limit of 8–10 minutes to do the exam task, then check answers with the class.

> **1** B **2** D **3** A **4** D **5** C **6** A **7** D **8** B

3 The discussion brings in other domestic activities/chores that might be beneficial such as gardening, taking a dog for a walk, vacuuming and ironing. Students could discuss in pairs, small groups or as a whole class.

Language development 3 p. 160

1a The topic of health is rich in idiomatic expressions and phrasal verbs. You could begin with books closed, brainstorming any words or phrases students already know. Students then look at the sentence and choose the correct meaning for *under the weather*.

> b

1b First get students to read the text and answer the following question: *Is George now more or less healthy than he used to be?* (more). Then you could do the first item with the class, as an example, so that they can see how the exercise works.

> **1** felt older and less energetic **2** unwell **3** didn't want to eat
> **4** was very tired **5** get back his energy **6** was physically fit
> **7** healthy **8** fit and healthy

1c If possible, show students how to find expressions in a dictionary and point out that if they look up an expression under one word, they might be directed to another word where the expression is listed.

2a–b If students are unsure of any of the phrasal verbs, get them to check in their dictionaries.

> **2a**
> **1** put on **2** give up **3** picked up **4** cut down on, cut out
> **5** coming down with, get over **6** take up
> **2b**
> **a** 6 **b** 2 **c** 5 **d** 4 **e** 1 **f** 3

3 This is an opportunity for personalised discussion. When students have finished, you could get them to think of more questions to ask each other, using both the idiomatic expressions and the phrasal verbs on the page.

12 Making a point

Module 12 includes an extract from a novel and topics such as the media, advertising, communicating ideas and celebrities.

Lead-in p. 161

With books closed, brainstorm ways in which we receive information (e.g. newspapers, magazines, TV, radio, websites, books, post, email, phone, text messages, advertising).

Get students to look at the photos and discuss the questions. Tell them that there are no hard and fast answers to questions 2 and 3. You might want to discuss one or two of the photos with the class, to give them an idea of the kind of answers required. Some examples of what students might come up with: newspapers: to inform; TV: to inform and entertain; email: to communicate about work and with friends; billboard advertising: to advertise and promote products.

> 1 newspapers, TV, email, billboards (US) / hoardings (UK),

12A Bookworm

As a lead-in, with books closed, you could put students in groups and see how many types of book they can think of in three minutes or get them to draw a table with two columns headed *Fiction* and *Non-fiction* and write the genres into the correct column as you dictate them from the table below. They then discuss the differences between the genres.

Fiction	Non-fiction
novel, horror, fantasy, crime/thriller, mystery, adventure, poetry, children's, mythology, science fiction	biography, autobiography, history, science, travel, sport, art, food and drink, health, philosophy, home and garden

Reading pp. 162–163

1a Students could discuss this in pairs, small groups or as a whole class. Get them to expand with examples of what they have read recently or what they are reading at the moment.

1b Elicit as much as you can from the photo and ask if anyone has read the book or seen the film.

> It's a crime thriller.

Background

Patricia Highsmith's crime thriller *The Talented Mr Ripley* was first published in 1955. The 1999 film was directed by Anthony Minghella. Tom Ripley, a poor young man, pretends that he is a friend of Dickie Greenleaf, a spoilt millionaire playboy who has gone to Italy. Dickie's father offers Tom money to convince Dickie to come home but when the errand fails, Tom kills Dickie and assumes his privileged life.

2 Give students 15 minutes to complete the task. Do not confirm answers yet.

> 1 B   2 A   3 D   4 C   5 C   6 B

3 Let students compare their answers in pairs, explaining where they found them in the text, then check with the class.

4a Get students to discuss their answers in pairs before you check with the class.

> nouns: impatience, frustration, anger, disappointment, impulse, shame, friendship, companionship, respect, ingratitude, hostility, irritation, attention, rudeness
> adjectives: arrogant, crazy, ashamed, amused

4b If students can't guess what the expressions mean, get them to look them up in their dictionaries, deciding each time what the key word is and where to look for the expression.

> *It crossed Tom's mind*: he thought; the idea came into his mind suddenly for a short time
> *shoving him out in the cold*: rejecting/abandoning him
> *step right into Dickie's shoes*: become Dickie; adopt the life and position Dickie had
> *eating out of his hand*: having control over; getting him to do exactly as he wanted

5a Get students to discuss the questions in groups. Ask anyone that has read the book or seen the film not to 'give the game away' until others have expressed their opinions. Encourage students to give reasons for their answers.

5b Again, ask students to work in groups. You could specify a number of advantages and disadvantages that each group should think of or get some groups to think of just the advantages and others to think of just the disadvantages and then compare their ideas. Remind students to give examples of films that they have seen which were based on books.

Language development 1 pp. 164–165

1a Give students time to read the sentences, then ask them to discuss the questions in pairs or groups. Check answers with the class.

> 1 to find out more about the American way of life
> 2 the humour; not knowing anything about the USA before reading it
> 3 because they're too tired to look for a hotel

1b This revises different ways of connecting ideas covered earlier in the book. Get students to compare their answers in pairs before you check with the class.

> Students should underline:
> **a** in order to **b** As **c** before **d** If **e** who **f** While **g** and **h** Because **i** When **j** so ... that **k** However
>
> Relative pronoun: who
> Conjunction + clause: while, when
> Conjunction + -ing: before
> Clause of result: so ... that
> Conditional: If
> Linking conjunction: and, however
> Clause of purpose: in order to
> Clause of reason: as, because

2 Students should discuss the sentences in pairs and then use the table in Exercise 1b to check their answers before class feedback.

> **1** The part that/which I liked/The part I liked best was the ending.
> **2** The main character is an old man who ~~he~~ has never left his home town.
> **3** It was **such a** good book that I couldn't stop reading it.
> **4** **While** the police look for/During the police **search** for the main suspect, Holmes makes other enquiries.
> **5** It is set in a town where there are a lot of factories ~~in~~.
> **6** It can be helpful to see the film before **reading/you read** the book in English.
> **7** If you ~~will~~ like science fiction, you'll probably like this book.
> **8** It is a good story **but** the main character is not very realistic.
> **9** The police are called in **to** investigate the theft of a painting.
> **10** I didn't like the ending because ~~of~~ I thought it was disappointing.

3 Give students time to read through the information in the grammar box. Then elicit why it might be useful to make sentences shorter (e.g. to make your writing more interesting, to give it more impact, to avoid repetition). For each sentence, students need to identify whether both parts of it occur at the same time or one occurs earlier, and whether the sentence is active or passive. Do the first item with the class, as an example.

> **1** Being **2** Writing **3** Having experienced **4** criticised
> **5** having had **6** Having read **7** completely satisfied

4 For each group of sentences, students should produce one longer sentence using the connecting devices given in brackets. Look at the example with the class and explain/ elicit how it has been constructed: the first sentence is reduced to a participle clause (*Written by a woman*) and combined with the second using a relative pronoun (*who has lived in India for many years*), resulting in some small changes to the third sentence (*the book tells us a lot about life there*). If you think students are not too confident with this, do question 2 with them, then get them to work in pairs, and check their answers as they complete each one.

> **Suggested answers:**
> **2** It is about a young English woman who goes to India with her child because she wants to find out the true story of her grandmother.
> **3** Her English grandparents lived in India together, but her grandmother fell in love with an Indian man.

4 Having arrived there, she starts to follow the same life path as her grandmother when she falls in love with an Indian.
5 Being set in two periods and telling two women's similar stories, it shows that lifestyles and attitudes change a lot over two generations, but love and relationships never change.

Background

The author of *Heat and Dust*, Ruth Prawer Jhabvala (1927–2013), was born in Germany. She emigrated to England and went to university in London. She moved to India in 1951 after marrying an Indian architect and wrote a number of novels set in India. She wrote *Heat and Dust* in 1975 and in 1983 the famous producer–director partnership of Ismail Merchant and James Ivory made it into a film with Prawer Jhabvala writing the screenplay.

Photocopiable activity

Activity 12A (p. 117) can be used here. Students use a variety of connecting words and phrases to tell a story, working towards a specified ending.

Writing pp. 166–167

1 Get students to discuss the questions in pairs or small groups. Then ask a few students to share their answers with the class.

2 When students have read the task, you could ask them whether they read book reviews themselves and if so, whether they tend to read them before or after they have read a book. Then discuss the task and questions as a class.

3a Let students decide which book they are going to review. Then put them in pairs and ask them to answer the questions, telling their partner about their book. Remind them to read the task again.

3b–c Having discussed their ideas with their partners, students now organise them under the headings. Give them 2–4 minutes to do this. When they have finished, ask them to number the events they have listed in the order they occur.

3d–e These exercises encourage students to think about the key points to include in their review, along with how it will be organised into paragraphs. If time allows, you could get them to compare answers in pairs.

> **3e**
> **Suggested answers:**
> 3, 5, 1, 4, 2

4a–b Deal with any vocabulary difficulties before students categorise the words. You could explain the meanings yourself or ask students to check in their dictionaries. Give them time to write the words under the correct heading, then ask them to think about connotation: are the words positive or negative?

Suggested answers:
Characters: lifelike (P), weak (N), passionate (P), moving (P), imaginative (P), brave (P), lovely (P), original (P), successful (P), entertaining (P), unconvincing (N), appealing (P), clever (P), attractive (P), boring (N), sensitive (P), awful (N), impressive (P)
Events: unexpected (P), moving (P), predictable (N), imaginative (P), disappointing (N) , original (P), successful (P), entertaining (P), unconvincing (N), clever (P), attractive (P), boring (N), awful (N), impressive (P)
Setting: imaginative (P), lovely (P), original (P), unconvincing (N), attractive (P), boring (N), awful (N), impressive (P)

4c Limit this activity, either by specifying how long students have to think of other adjectives or how many they should think of in each category. Once they have thought of some words, they could ask other students to decide if they are positive or negative.

4d Give students time to complete the exercise, then check answers with the class.

> **I** ones   **2** it is/so   **3** do so   **4** not

4e Go through the sentence openings with the class, focusing on what type of word or clause could come next (e.g. *This is a story about* + a person/time/place + *who/when/where* ... ; *It is set in* + time/place).

5 Give students 15 minutes to write their review.

Sample answer:
***Animal Farm*, by George Orwell**
This is an unusual book, set on a farm. The characters, led by the pigs, are mainly animals, who get rid of the cruel, drunken human owner and take over the farm. They set up a government of their own.
The story isn't exciting but it's clever. At first, after the revolution, the animals are equal but later the pigs become more powerful and start to change everything. By the end of the novel, the animals realise they have gone back to where they started.
In one way, the story is obviously not a true story but in another way, it is meant to tell the story of communism from a satirical point of view.
The characters are very convincing. Napoleon, the leader of the pigs, is strong and corrupt. Other animals are honest but weak. They all represent people and events in Russia in the 1920s and 30s.
Although I enjoyed this book, I can imagine older people who were brought up when communism was still strong in the world and have probably read a lot about the Russian Revolution, would enjoy it even more.

6 Draw students' attention to the list given here and also refer them to the full checklist on page 198.

Expert language: Attitude phrases

This exercise practises a number of phrases that can be used in this type of writing. As you check answers, make sure students know the meaning of the alternatives.

> **I** To be honest   **2** Generally speaking   **3** As far as I'm concerned
> **4** It goes without saying   **5** Without doubt   **6** Quite honestly

12B The media

If your students are from the same country, ask them if they think you can tell what type of person reads what type of paper or if you can say what someone is like from the paper they read. If your students are from different countries, get them to talk about newspapers in their countries with questions such as: *Are there different types of newspaper? Which types are most popular? Do people buy a lot of newspapers? What type of news stories do they mostly contain?* You might need to pre-teach words such as *national*, *local*, *domestic*, *international*, *tabloid* and *broadsheet*.

Speaking pp. 168–169

Here, students practise a complete Paper 4, although they will have to rotate the role of interlocutor at each stage. If they know who their partner will be for the exam and they are in the class, it would obviously be sensible for them to work together. If possible, it would be useful to record some of the students at each stage and use the recording for whole class feedback.

Ia Check understanding of *red-top newspaper* and *broadsheet*, which refer as much to editorial policy as to the size of the paper.

> **I** Essex Courier   **2** BBC website on the iPad   **3** The Mirror
> **4** The Times

Ib You could use the photos or a real paper for this exercise. Get students to compare answers in pairs before you check with the class.

> **Example answers:**
> **I** 'Tax blow for UK families'   **2** text below 'Tax blow for UK families' headline   **3** 'Real-life exclusive' story in The Mirror
> **4** The Times Sport section underneath iPad   **5** Luxury Homes

Ic Check answers with the class. Note that if students don't read newspapers, it can be hard for them to distinguish between the three types of writer.

> **I** lives in the country and reports with specialised in-depth local knowledge
> **2** researches and writes facts of the incident
> **3** writes regular articles (for a newspaper/magazine), especially about a particular subject or with personal opinion

Id Clear up any vocabulary difficulties before students complete the exercise. After feedback, encourage students to record the collocations in their vocabulary notebooks.

> **I** hit   **2** press   **3** meet, press   **4** features, forecasts
> **5** glossy, names, promote, launch, grab

2a Get students to check any unknown words in their dictionaries. Before they begin, point out that they may need to change the form of some words.

> **I** daily, circulation, readership   **2** journalism, editorial
> **3** commercials, advertising

2b Encourage students to build a lexical set of newspaper-related words with word families developed as fully as possible, with pronunciation and stress marked (e.g. _journalist, journalism, journalistic_).

3 Students could discuss the statements in pairs, small groups or as a whole class. You could also assign different statements to different pairs/groups, then ask students to share their ideas with the class.

4 Give the interlocutors a moment to look at the questions first.

5a–b Remind students to keep an eye on the time while their partner is speaking and stop them after approximately one minute.

6 Again, students need to watch the time. They should stop after approximately three minutes.

7 Remind students to expand their answers.

Listening p. 170

1a You could also ask: _Which is the most important part of the paper for you?_ or _Which part do you read first?_

1b Remind students of the importance of reading only the questions first. The discussion questions here help focus students on that.

2 You could elicit the strategy before students complete the task and, if time allows, get them to compare answers in pairs before you check with the class.

> **1** C **2** B **3** A **4** C **5** A **6** B **7** B

3 You could also ask: _Do you know any journalists? What qualities do they have?_

Use of English 1 p. 171

1a–b These exercises should serve as a reminder of the task format and strategy. Get students to discuss in pairs and give reasons for their answers.

> **1a**
> **1** T (The answer might depend on the small differences in meanings between the words.)
> **2** F (Understanding of the whole text is vital.)
> **3** T (The correct word might depend on the collocations.)

2 As always, students should skim the text first. Give them no more than 30 seconds, then check answers with the class.

> **1** a confident, masculine, attractive young man
> **2** The man is unmasculine and bookish.

3 Give students no more than 10 minutes to do the task and then some time to compare their answers in pairs before class feedback.

> **1** B **2** C **3** B **4** A **5** D **6** A **7** C **8** C

4 You could also ask: _Should advertising be aimed at children? Why/Why not?_

Language development 2 p. 172

1a With books closed, write on the board: _The board/classroom is messy._ Elicit _Someone needs to clean it_ and write it on the board. Then move _it_ to the start of a new sentence, to elicit _It needs cleaning./It needs to be cleaned._ Students then read the grammar box and complete the task.

> **1** The advert's too long. It needs shortening./It needs to be shortened.
> **2** Those posters are out of date. They need replacing./They need to be replaced.

1b You could elicit what needs doing just from the picture, before students look at the prompt sentences. After completing the exercise, students could talk about what needs doing in the room/building where they are studying.

> **1** It needs tidying up.
> **2** It needs cutting.
> **3** They need watering.
> **4** It needs rebuilding.
> **5** They need cleaning.
> **6** They need repainting.

1c If time is short, this exercise can be set for homework.

> **1** First money needs to be raised.
> **2** Then the advert needs to be written.
> **3** A script needs to be prepared and brought to life.
> **4** A good production company needs to be found.
> **5** An experienced director needs to be hired.
> **6** Well-known actors need to be recruited.
> **7** The advert needs to be shot in a studio you can afford.

2a It might be necessary to check some of the vocabulary here (e.g. _install, blunt, sharpen_) before students begin the exercise. Check answers with the class.

> **2** have had it stolen
> **3** let's have/get it repaired
> **4** I've had them checked/I'll have/get them checked/I'll have to have/get them checked/I'm going to have/get them checked
> **5** lets have/get it installed/we'll have/get it installed
> **6** I'll have/get them sharpened/we have/need to have/get them sharpened/let's have/get them sharpened

2b After feedback, ask students to think of other examples of people/places we go to in order to have something done.

> **Suggested answers:**
> **1** to have/get our teeth checked/a tooth removed
> **2** to have/get our eyes tested/some glasses made
> **3** to have/get our clothes cleaned
> **4** to have/get our hair cut
> **5** to have/get our nails done
> **6** to have/get our photo taken
> **7** to have/get a picture framed
> **8** to have/get clothes made

2c Introduce the expression *DIY* (*Do It Yourself*) and ask students if they are keen on it. Then get them to discuss the points, giving reasons for their answers and saying where they have something done/who they have it done by.

3 Give students a few minutes' preparation time before they discuss the questions in pairs or groups. The discussion could be extended by asking what other things they would like to have done for them.

Use of English 2 p. 173

1 This is a reminder of the basic strategy for Paper 1 Part 3. Get students to discuss the questions in pairs first, giving reasons for their answers.

> **1** Sentence by sentence, to get the complete sense of what is both before and after the gap.
> **2** Leave any you can't do and come back to them. When you have completed the text, you may have a better idea of what is needed.

2 Give students 30–40 seconds to skim the text, then check answers with the class.

> **1** Because they can then sell them to the press and earn a lot of money.
> **2** By saying the stars don't deserve privacy, as their jobs involve being in the public eye.

Background

Paparazzi are photographers (and writers) that follow celebrities in the hope of getting a story. The word comes from a character called Paparazzo, a photographer in Fellini's 1960 Italian film *La Dolce Vita*, which is all about celebrities, rich people and their parties.

3 Remind students that as well as making grammatical changes, they may need to alter the word to fit the meaning of the sentence.

> **1** sales   **2** unbelievable   **3** determination   **4** disapproval
> **5** complaints   **6** privacy   **7** action   **8** doubtful

4 Again, students skim the text and answer the questions. When they have finished, you could ask them if they are aware of the role of special advisers in their country and if they think they have too much power/influence. In the UK, they are also known as 'spin doctors' as one of their roles is to put a *positive spin* (a positive/favourable appearance) onto news and information.

> **1** the government
> **2** by influencing how newspaper stories are presented; by having an influence on how speeches are written

5 If students are interested in politics, give them some questions to discuss, such as: *Do you think politicians should present information in the best possible light? Do you believe what politicians in your country/other countries say? Should journalists be free to say what they like?* Introduce ideas such as censorship, privacy, security and sensitivity.

> **1** dramatic   **2** powerful   **3** responsibility   **4** editors   **5** freedom
> **6** memorable   **7** variety   **8** imaginatively

Photocopiable activity

Activity 12B (p. 118) can be used here or at the end of the unit. It is a grammar auction revising common mistakes at B2 level.

Language development 3 p. 174

1a When students have completed the table, ask them to highlight the endings that are used to form the various words. You could get students to check answers in pairs or in their dictionaries before class feedback.

responsible	responsibly	responsibility	–
believable	believably	*belief*	believe
worrying/worried	*worryingly*	worry	worry
embarrassing	embarrassingly	embarrassment	*embarrass*
recognisable/ recognised	recognisably	recognition	*recognise*
variable	variably	variety/variability	vary
decisive/decided	decisively/decidedly	*decision*	decide
imaginative	imaginatively	imagination	*imagine*
legal	legally	legality/law	legalise
satisfactory	*satisfactorily*	satisfaction	satisfy
approving/approved	approvingly	approval	*approve*
amazing/amazed	amazingly	*amazement*	amaze

1b Remind students that Use of English word formation texts are likely to include a number of negative prefixes. When they have completed the exercise, get them to identify patterns (e.g. *il-* before adjectives starting with *l*, *ir-* before *r*, *im-* before *p*, *un-* for adjectives ending in *-ic*, *in-* for adjectives ending in *-ate*) but point out that there are always exceptions!

> **1** illegal   **2** irresponsible   **3** unromantic   **4** disappear
> **5** inaccurately   **6** immoral   **7** improbable   **8** illogical
> **9** irregular   **10** imperfectly

1c In each sentence, students first need to identify which word is needed, then the form. Do the first item with the class, as an example.

> **1** irresponsible   **2** embarrassment   **3** illogical   **4** illegal
> **5** amazement   **6** decisive   **7** inaccurate

2 Again, students should think about both the word needed and the form. Start by checking that they know the form of the words given (*fashion* (n), *relation* (n), *survive* (v), *use* (n, v)).

> **1** better relationship   **2** absolutely useless   **3** became fashionable
> **4** chance of survival

3a Get students to focus on the clues that tell them what type of word is needed in each case.

> **1** professionally   **2** entertaining, unreadable   **3** generalise, stimulating   **4** admiration, creative, criticise, unreliable
> **5** intelligence, relationships, boring, offensive

3b Students could discuss the questions in pairs, small groups or as a whole class.

Teacher's notes for photocopiable activities

Pre-course quiz

Use: At the start of the course, before Module 1
Aim: To raise awareness of various aspects of the
Cambridge English: First exam and to answer some common
questions
Time: 15–20 minutes
Activity type: Pairwork/Groupwork. Students find out how
much they know about the exam by doing a quiz.
Preparation: Make one copy of the quiz (p. 87) per student.

Procedure

1 Tell students that they are going to do a quick quiz to learn
   more about the exam.

2 Give out a copy of the quiz to each student and set a time
   limit (5 minutes) to complete it. Students should first have
   a go on their own and then compare answers in pairs or
   groups.

3 Refer students to the Exam overview on page 6 of the
   Coursebook so they can check some of their answers.

4 Discuss answers with the class and answer any other
   questions about the exam that students have.

Follow-up

Refer students to the Exam reference section in the
Coursebook (p. 175) and explain that they can find more
detailed information about the exam there.

> 1 A   2 A   3 C   4 C   5 A   6 B   7 C   8 B   9 B   10 C
> 11 T   12 F (149–190 words)
> 13 F (contracted words count as the number of words they would
> be if they were not contracted, e.g. *isn't* = *is not* = 2 words)
> 14 F (as long as the examiner can recognise the word; words spelt
> out loud must be correct)
> 15 F (in pairs or a group of three, where there is an odd number)

1A: Lifestyle and families

Use: After Reading Exercise 6 (p. 8), or as an introduction
to Module 1
Aim: To practise giving and exchanging personal information
Time: 20–25 minutes
Activity type: Groupwork. Students play a board game
answering questions about themselves and their families.
Preparation: Make one copy of the activity (p. 88) per
group of four students, enlarged to A3 size if possible. You
will also need one dice per group and counters of different
colours.

Procedure

1 Divide the class into groups of four and give each group a
   copy of the board game, a dice and counters.

2 Quickly explain how to play the game: each student starts
   from a different corner of the board. They take it in turns
   to roll the dice and move around the board. When they
   land on a square, they read out the question (or another
   student reads it out to them) and answer it. The other
   students can ask a follow-up question. The next student
   then has a turn.

3 If anyone lands on a square with a question that they have
   already answered, they move forward to the next square.
   In squares with a slash (e.g. *house/flat*) students should
   choose the most appropriate word for their situation
   when reading out the question.

4 As students are discussing the answers, make a note of
   common mistakes. As there is no 'start' or 'finish', there
   are no winners and the game can be played for as long or
   short a time as is available.

5 Tell students to expand on their answers if they wish.

Follow-up

Spend 5–10 minutes giving students feedback on their
performance and correct any common mistakes noted. You
could write students' incorrect sentences on the board and, in
pairs, get students to correct them.

1B: Adjective + noun collocations

Use: After Language development 3 Exercise 3b (p. 20)
Aim: To practise common adjective + noun collocations
Time: 20–25 minutes
Activity type: Groupwork. Students match adjectives with nouns and then use the collocations to complete a text.
Preparation: Make one copy of the Part 1 cards (p. 89) per group of three or four students and one copy of Part 2 (p. 90) per student. Cut up the adjective and noun cards.

Procedure

Part 1

1   Write the following nouns on the board and ask students if they can remember which of them collocate with *sour*: *milk, tea, look, sound, banana, grapes*.

2   Divide the class into groups of three or four. Give each group a set of adjective cards (grey) and one set of noun cards (white).

3   Students match the cards to make collocations. Check answers with the class before they go on to do Part 2 of the activity. (The answers are the same as for Part 2, but in no particular order.)

Part 2

4   Now give each student a copy of the text and ask them to work individually to complete it using the adjective + noun collocations they formed in Part 1.

5   Check answers with the class.

1 guided tour	2 unique opportunity	3 domestic life
4 high speed	5 slight change	6 exact date	7 wide gap
8 hard work	9 quick breakfast	10 central heating
11 strong influence	12 memorable experience	13 natural light
14 valuable paintings	15 final destination	

Follow-up

Ask students to write a short paragraph using at least five of the collocations. They can write about anything they like.

2A: Work

Use: After Reading Exercise 5 (p. 22)
Aim: To practise giving and exchanging opinions and reaching a consensus; To revise and extend jobs vocabulary
Time: 25–30 minutes
Activity type: Groupwork. Students discuss a number of jobs in different categories and reach a consensus.
Preparation: Make one copy of the activity (p. 91) per group of three or four students and cut up into cards.

Procedure

1   Pre-teach some of the more difficult vocabulary (e.g. *miner, surgeon, chef, midwife, traffic warden, civil servant*) by putting the words on the board and getting students to check in their dictionaries.

2   Divide the class into groups of three or four and give each group a set of cards. Explain that students should discuss each question, giving reasons to support their opinions.

3   Students choose a card at random from the set and discuss the question. When/If they reach a consensus, they choose another card. Set a time limit (e.g. 5 minutes per card) and signal when time is up.

4   While students are discussing the questions, check that they are supporting their opinions with reasons and encouraging turn-taking. Stop after the first round and give feedback on their use of functional language.

5   Conduct feedback with the class, correcting common mistakes. Compare answers between the groups.

Variation

Use the cards one at a time for five-minute speaking activities at different times during the module.

Follow-up

In their groups, students think of a job in each category that beats those listed.

Suggested answers:
1 Some surveys suggest being a miner is the most stressful because of the physical dangers; others say that being a prison officer is.
2 Although some company directors and musicians are very highly paid, on average, the answer is more likely to be a lawyer or a surgeon.
3 In the UK, the answer is a judge because in addition to formal legal training, you need many years courtroom experience as a lawyer before becoming a judge.
4, 5 and 6 are a matter of opinion.

2B: Articles

Use: After Language development 2 Exercise 2 (p. 32)
Aim: To practise use of articles (*a/an*, *the* and zero article)
Time: 25–30 minutes
Activity type: Pairwork. Students complete a story by adding articles where necessary and then retell it to a partner.
Preparation: Make enough copies (pp. 92–93) so that half the students have Story A and half B. Cut up into sections.

Procedure

Explain that some stories have a moral and elicit what that means (a practical lesson about what to do or how to behave which you learn from the story). Tell students that they are going to read and tell two stories with a moral.

Part 1

1   Divide the class in two. Give students in one half a copy of story A and students in the other half story B. Do not give them the answer keys.

2   Give them five minutes to read the stories and complete them with *a*, *the* or − .

3   Get them to compare their answers in pairs or small groups, explaining choices.

4   Give out the answer keys and help with any problems or questions.

Part 2

1   Now divide students into pairs with an A and a B in each.

2   They should tell each other their story. Stronger students could retell the story from memory, paying attention to the use of articles; weaker students can read the text. Their partner has to try to guess what the moral of the story is before they confirm.

Follow-up

Ask students which story they prefer and why.

3A: Adjectives and adverbs

Use: After Language development 1 Exercise 6 (p. 39)
Aim: To practise adverbs of degree and adjectives studied in Module 5
Time: 25–30 minutes
Activity type: Groupwork. Students play a game of pelmanism, matching adjectives and adverbs with gapped sentences.
Preparation: Make one copy of both pages of the activity (pp. 94–95) per group of four or five students and cut up into cards.

Procedure

1   Divide the class into groups of four or five.

2   Place the cards face down on the table, in their two sets (grey and white). Students take it in turns to turn over a card from each set – one sentence card and one adjective/adverb card. If they match, the student keeps the pair and has another turn. If they don't match, the student turns them face down again, puts them back and the next student has a turn.

3   Groups can discuss whether a pair matches or not and ask for help where necessary. As they play, go round the groups, monitoring the pairs of cards collected. If any are wrong, explain why and return the cards to their piles. Some words can be used in more than one sentence.

4   The winner is the student with the most pairs.

1 surprisingly/remarkably   2 hardly   3 bleak   4 lively   5 well
6 hard   7 friendly   8 fast   9 rather/pretty   10 extremely
11 practically   12 absolutely   13 a bit/quite
14 pretty/rather/quite   15 quite a   16 actually   17 as well
18 seriously   19 remarkably/surprisingly
20 rather/pretty/extremely

3B: *-ing* forms and infinitives

Use: After Language development 2 Exercise 4b (p. 46)
Aim: To practise *-ing* forms and infinitives
Time: 20–25 minutes
Activity type: Groupwork. Students play a game, combining A cards and B cards to make correct sentences.
Preparation: Make one copy of both pages of the activity (pp. 96–97) per group of four students and cut up into cards.

Procedure

1   Hold up a set of A cards (white) and explain to students that the words on these cards are followed either by the *-ing* form or the infinitive (with or without *to*) and that in some cases, both are possible. Then hold up a set of B cards (grey) and explain that they are a set of verbs.

2   Tell students that they are going to play a game where they will need to combine A and B cards, making a logical sentence, either positive or negative, in any tense. Demonstrate with two cards, e.g. *think of* + *learn*: *I'm thinking of learning Spanish next year.*

3   Shuffle the A cards, deal out three to each player and place the remaining cards face down on the table. Turn the top card over and place it next to the pile. Do the same with the B cards.

4   Students take turns to combine an A card and a B card in their hand to make a sentence, placing the cards on the table in front of them as they do so. After making a sentence, they replace the two cards by taking one from each of the face-down piles.

5   If students cannot make a sentence, they can use their turn to change one of their cards, taking either the face-up card or the next face-down card from the corresponding pile. The card they put down goes on the face-up pile. Players should always have six cards (three from each set) in their hand.

6   Other players in the group accept or contest sentences. As students play, monitor their use of the structures, if necessary checking by asking students to repeat the pairs in front of them, returning the cards to the pile if they are not correct.

7   The student with the most pairs is the winner.

4A: Raising money

Use: After Writing Exercise 6 (p. 55)
Aim: To practise giving and exchanging opinions and reaching a consensus
Time: 20–30 minutes
Activity type: Groupwork. Students discuss possible ways of raising money for a club that they belong to and reach a consensus on the best way of raising the money.
Preparation: Make one copy of the activity (p. 98) per group of three or four students.

Procedure

1   Check that students are familiar with the concept of a charity. Ask them to name some charities that they have heard of and how charities raise money. Tell them that in some countries individuals often raise money for charities and elicit possible ways of doing so.

2   Pre-teach *bungee jump, busking* and *raffle*.

3   Divide the class into groups of three or four and explain that for this activity, they are all members of a club or society that needs to buy some new equipment.

4   Give each group a copy of the activity and tell them that they must work together to decide on the best method to raise some money.

5   Model the activity using *run a marathon* as an example, using the language in the speech bubbles and referring to the four prompt questions.

6   Give students a time limit (e.g. 10 minutes) to discuss and agree on the best method.

7   Different groups should report back to the class and explain their choice.

Follow-up

Ask students if any of them have ever done anything like this before for charity.

4B: Confusing adjectives

Use: After Language development 3, Exercise 2 (p. 62)
Aim: To extend work on comparing and contrasting commonly confused adjectives
Time: 30–45 minutes. Note that this activity is in two parts, which can be done on separate occasions.
Activity type: Part 1: whole class. Students mingle, teaching each other the difference between confusing adjectives.
Part 2: groupwork. Students play a board game asking and answering questions using the adjectives.
Preparation: For Part 1, make one copy of the first page (p. 99) and cut up into cards. For Part 2, make one copy of the second page (p. 100) per group of four or five students, enlarged to A3 size if possible. You will also need dice and counters.

Procedure

Part 1 (10–15 minutes)

1   Distribute the Part 1 vocabulary cards. If there are more students than cards, some can share.

2   Students check the difference between the words in a dictionary and think of or look up examples to explain the meanings.

3   Students mingle and each time they meet another student, they ask them to explain the difference between the words on their card (without showing it to them). Students help/teach each other where necessary.

Part 2 (15–25 minutes)

1   Divide the class into groups of four or five and give each group a copy of the board, dice and counters.

2   Students take it in turns to roll the dice and move around the board.

3   At each square, they read the question and decide who in the group to ask, choosing the correct word from the alternatives each time.

4   Go round monitoring and noting errors for feedback at the end.

Part 2
1 alone   2 classical   3 classic   4 imaginative   5 convenient
6 skinny   7 invaluable   8 tall   9 similar   10 alike   11 sensible
12 economical   13 sensitive   14 nervous   15 fun   16 terrific
17 terrifying   18 foreign   19 injured   20 old-fashioned

5A: The human body quiz

Use: After Lead-in (p. 63)
Aim: To generate interest in the topic of the human body and to pre-teach some important vocabulary for the Reading section in Module 5
Time: 15–20 minutes
Preparation: Make one copy of the activity (p. 101) per student.

Procedure

1   Tell students that they are going to do a general knowledge quiz on the subject of the human body. Ask them how much they know about the subject and if they study/studied biology at school.

2   Give each student a copy of the quiz and a time limit of five to six minutes to complete it.

3   Students then compare their answers in pairs.

4   Check answers with the class.

1 C   2 C   3 B (In an adult; the male brain is slightly heavier than the female brain.)   4 B (It's in the centre but the left side is bigger, so it leans that way.)   5 B (in a reasonably fit young adult)
6 C   7 A (The study of mental illness is psychiatry.)   8 B
9 B (*DNA* stands for 'deoxyribonucleic acid'.)
10 C (The skin is considered an organ as it has some very specific functions.)   11 B   12 A (hand: 27 bones; foot: 26 bones)

Follow-up

Ask students what surprised them most in the quiz.

5B: Forming nouns

Use: After Language development 3 Exercise 6 (p. 76)
Aim: To practise forming nouns from verbs
Time: 15–20 minutes
Activity type: Students play a game of dominoes, joining suffixes to verbs to make nouns.
Preparation: Make one copy of the activity (p. 102) per group of four or five students and cut up into dominoes.

Procedure

1 Review the concept of forming nouns from verbs by adding a suffix. Use the following verbs and elicit the nouns: *develop* (*development*), *accept* (*acceptance*), *discuss* (*discussion*).

2 Divide the class into groups of four or five and give each group a set of dominoes. Demonstrate how the final -e that is dropped is shown in brackets, e.g. *combin*(e) *–combination*.

3 One student deals four dominoes to each player. The rest of the dominoes remain face down on the desk in a pile.

4 Students take turns to place a domino, building a chain, (using either end). As they place each domino, they should say the word they have formed.

5 After placing a domino, students take another from the pile. If they are unable to place a domino to make a word, they take one from the pile and the next student has a turn.

6 As the students are playing, monitor that they have placed their dominoes correctly.

7 The winner is the first to get rid of all their dominoes.

6A: Ambition

Use: After Lead-in (p. 77) or after Reading Exercise 5 (p. 79)
Aim: To raise interest in the topic of ambition
Time: 15–20 minutes
Activity type: Individual and whole class. Students complete a questionnaire to find out how ambitious they are.
Preparation: Make one copy of the activity (p. 103) per student.

Procedure

1 Write the word *ambition* on the board and elicit its meaning (determination to be successful, rich, powerful, etc.; a strong desire to achieve something) and the adjective form (*ambitious*). Then elicit different types of ambition (work, money, family, spiritual, health, etc.).

2 Pre-teach *community*, *put off* and *mix with someone*.

3 Give each student a copy of the questionnaire.

4 Give students around 5 minutes to answer the questions, working individually.

5 Explain the scoring system: odd questions: 2 points for *yes*, 1 point for *maybe*, no points for *no*; even questions: 2 points for *no*, 1 for *maybe*, no points for *yes*.

6 Check totals: the higher the score, the more ambitious the person is. 12 is the average. Compare scores within the class and see who is the most/least ambitious person in the class.

Follow-up

In pairs, students ask their partner what their ambitions are and then report back to the class.

6B: The arts

Use: After Language development I Exercise 7 (p. 81)
Aim: To practise relative clauses and arts vocabulary
Time: 20–25 minutes
Activity type: Groupwork. Students play a game defining words for their team members to guess.
Preparation: Make one copy of the activity (p. 104) per group of four or five students and cut up into cards.

Procedure

1   Ask students if they are interested in the arts (music, dance, theatre, etc.), how often they go to performances and if they have ever performed in public.

2   Divide the class into groups of four or five. Give each group a set of cards and get them to sort them into words they know and words they don't. Get students to explain the words they know to the class. Teach any that no one knows.

3   Each group collects up all their cards and shuffles them well.

4   Write the useful phrases below on the board: *He/She is a person who ... They're people who ... It's a thing which ... It's a place where ... It's a time/occasion when ...* Explain that students are going to play a game in which they have to define the words on their cards for their team to guess, using the phrases on the board.

5   The first player in the team takes a card from the pile and without showing it to their team, defines the word. When the team guess it, the player puts it down on the table and defines the next word. If the player can't define the word or the team can't guess it, the player puts it to the bottom of the pile and continues.

6   After every minute or so, shout *Change!* The player has to pass the pile to the next person in the team, who has a go at defining words.

7   Stop the game after ten minutes. The winning team is the one with the most cards on the table.

7A: Cultural guide

Use: After Language development I Exercise 7 (p. 95)
Aim: To practise modals and expressions of permission, necessity, advice and recommendation
Time: 15–20 minutes
Activity type: Pairwork. Students complete a cultural guide.
Preparation: Make one copy of the activity (p. 105) per student.

Procedure

1   Ask students when they give flowers to someone (e.g. birthdays, anniversaries, to people in hospital) and if there are any 'rules' that they follow.

2   Put the following table on the board:

You	should(n't)/ought (not) to are(n't) supposed to are(n't) allowed to/must(n't) (don't) have to	give	an even number of flowers. an odd number of flowers./white flowers. /a single flower.

Get students to make sentences that show various ways of saying the same thing, e.g. *In some countries you are supposed to give an odd number/you aren't supposed to give an even number of flowers.*

3   Divide the class into pairs and give each student a copy of the activity. Students work together to make ten sentences that they think are true. Check answers with the class.

1 not supposed to, red (Red is only used for names of the dead.)
2 aren't supposed to, teacher's (Use the title *Teacher*.)
3 must, before (The bath is for soaking/relaxing.)
4 ought to, perfume
5 mustn't, coin (It shows disrespect to the king, whose head is on the coins.)
6 are supposed to, on the right
7 must, to an older person (It shows respect.)
8 ought to, lift
9 shouldn't, gifts
10 are supposed to, hands

Follow-up

Students write more sentences for their country/-ies and share them with the class.

7B: Modals of deduction

Use: After Language development 2 Exercise 3 (p. 101)
Aim: To practise modals of deduction
Time: 15–20 minutes
Activity type: Whole class, mingle. Students respond to or correct remarks made by other students.
Preparation: Make one copy of the activity (p. 106) per 14 students and cut up into cards.

Procedure

1 On the board, write a sentence containing a factual mistake, e.g. *I'm [number] years old – I was born in [year].* (where the age and date don't add up) and ask students what is wrong with it. Elicit possible corrections, e.g. *You can't be … years old if you were born in … . You must be …* or *You can't have been born in … if you're … years old. You must have been born in … .*

2 Now give each student a card. They should read it and decide on the answer or spot what is wrong with it. If students don't know what the correction should be, they could check with you.

3 Students stand up and mingle, telling students the information on their card.

4 Each student they meet listens and responds or 'corrects' it. If they don't know what the correction should be, they can ask the other student to explain. If students can give the correct response, they score a point before moving on to speak to another student.

5 The winner could be the first one to win a set number of points or the one with the most points after a set time.

Notes/Corrections

1 Penguins live in the Antarctic, not the Arctic.
2 Brazilians speak Portuguese.
3 Mobile phones were invented in the 1970s.
4 Edgar Allan Poe was a writer. *Girl with a pearl earring* was painted by Johannes Vermeer.
5 There are no kangaroos in South Africa.
6 The first moon landing was in 1969.
7 In Japan people drive on the left.
8 The Berlin Wall came down in 1989.
9 The famous leaning tower is in Pisa.
10 The minimum driving age is usually 17 or 18 (16 in some countries).
11 The euro was introduced in 2002.
12 People didn't watch TV in the 1920s.
13 The Louvre Museum is in Paris, France.
14 There are no snakes in New Zealand.

8A: Reported speech

Use: After Language development 1 Exercise 7 (p. 109)
Aim: To practise reported speech and reporting verbs
Time: 20–25 minutes
Activity type: Pairwork. Students put quotes into reported speech and guess who said them.
Preparation: Make one copy of both pages of the activity (pp. 107–108) per pair of students.

Procedure

1 Write the following quote on the board: *I want to live because there are a few things I want to do.* Then ask students: *Who said that he wanted to live because there were a few things he wanted to do before he died?* (Aneurin Bevan, 1897–1960, British politician).

2 Divide the class into pairs and give each student worksheet A or B. Explain that students are now going to do the same: they are going to look at last words from famous people and report them to their partner using *Who … ?* for him/her to guess.

3 Elicit different reporting verbs (e.g. *warn, advise, promise, suggest*) and write them on the board, telling students to try to use them in the activity.

4 Give students a few minutes to think about how they will put the quotes into reported speech.

5 Students take it in turns to report a quote. If their partner doesn't know the answer, they can guess from the choices at the bottom of their worksheet.

Follow-up

In pairs, students think of their own favourite quotes from famous people, films or books to ask the rest of the class.

8B: Leisure activities

Use: After Listening Exercise 3 (p. 114)
Aim: To discuss leisure interests and to practise giving and exchanging opinions and reaching a consensus
Time: 20–25 minutes
Activity type: Groupwork. Students choose a leisure activity to do together.
Preparation: Make one copy of the activity (p. 109) per group of three or four students.

Procedure

1 Ask students how they usually spend their weekends. What influences their choice (hobbies/interests, money, time available, friends)?

2 Introduce the activity: students are going to work in groups to choose a way to spend a weekend together doing something special (maybe before one goes off to study/join the army/get married, etc.).

3 Divide the class into groups and give each group a copy of the activity.

4 Remind students that they will need to discuss, suggest, agree, disagree and reach a consensus. Elicit some functional language they could use and write it on the board.

5 Students have 10 minutes to discuss and choose a trip.

6 Groups feed back to the class on which trip they chose and why.

Follow-up

Find out if any of the students have ever done any of the activities given and if they enjoyed them.

9A: Conditionals

Use: After Language development 1 Exercise 7 (p. 123)
Aim: To practise forming conditional sentences and recognising which is required in a given situation
Time: 20–40 minutes (see Variations below)
Activity type: Groupwork. Students form, ask and answer questions on real and hypothetical situations.
Preparation: Make one copy of the activity (p. 110) per group of three or four students and cut up into cards.

Procedure

1 Write on the board: *If you (stop / be) a teacher, what you (do)?* Ask students to make questions from it and elicit the three conditional forms possible: *If you stop/ stopped/had stopped being a teacher, what will you do/ would you do/would you have done?* Demonstrate how time expressions (*next year, last year*) would affect your choice of conditional.

2 Divide the class into groups of three or four and give each group a set of cards. Students shuffle the cards and place them face down on the desk.

3 Students take it in turns to take a card from the pile, make a question in an appropriate form and choose which of the people in the group they would like to answer it. Demonstrate with one of the cards. Point out that the conditional form they choose depends on either how likely they see the event or which time phrase they choose.

4 Students ask each other the questions and discuss answers, refusing to answer if they don't think the question is formed correctly.

5 Monitor closely and check that students are forming the questions correctly.

Variations

1 For a quicker activity, select fewer cards.

2 Use the cards a few at a time as 5-minute fillers over the next few lessons.

Follow-up

Discuss any interesting or amusing answers given.

9B: Money vocabulary

Use: After Language development 3 Exercise 4c (p. 132)
Aim: To revise money vocabulary from Module 9 and practise word formation
Time: 15–20 minutes
Activity type: Pairwork. Students work together to complete a crossword.
Preparation: Make one copy of the activity (p. 111) per pair of students and cut up into two sections.

Procedure

I   Write the word *tax* on the board and get students to think of all the words formed from it (*taxes*, *taxable*, *untaxable*, *taxation*).

2   Explain that they will work together to complete a crossword which contains nouns and adjectives related to money. They will have to form clues using the roots of the words, so they will need to think what type of word it is and what the root is.

3   Demonstrate with examples: *It's the noun of the verb 'to tax'* (= *taxation*). *It's the adjective of the noun 'price'* (*priceless*).

4   Divide the class into pairs and give students in each pair either a Student A or a Student B crossword.

5   Students check the form and meaning of the words on their half of the crossword.

6   Students take it in turns to ask for clues (e.g. *What's 3 across?*) with their partner giving a word formation clue (e.g. *It's the noun of ... It's the (negative) adjective of ...*).

7   When students have finished, they check answers by showing each other their completed crosswords, which should be identical.

10A: Travel

Use: After Lead-in (p. 133) or after Reading Exercise 5 (p.135)
Aim: To pre-teach some vocabulary and generate interest in the topic of travel
Time: 20–30 minutes
Activity type: Individual, then whole class. Students complete a travel survey and find a travelling companion.
Preparation: Make one copy of the activity (p. 112) per student.

Procedure

I   In pairs, students have a minute to tell a partner about their most recent holiday.

2   Discuss the difference between going on holiday and travelling. Explain the purpose of the activity: to find the most suitable travelling partner in the class.

3   Pre-teach difficult vocabulary, e.g. *exotic*, *basics*, *racy novel*.

4   Give out a copy of the activity to each student and give them five minutes to choose their answers individually.

5   Students now mingle and ask questions in order to find out who in the class has the most similar answers to them.

6   Students select a travelling companion with similar likes and interests to themselves.

Follow-up

Companions plan a trip together and report their plans back to the class.

10B: The passive

Use: After Language development 1 Exercise 5b (p. 137)
Aim: To review the passive
Time: 15–20 minutes
Activity type: Groupwork. Students prepare extracts of travel news.
Preparation: Make one copy of both pages of the activity (pp. 113–114) and cut up into cards.

Procedure

1   Ask students what type of news might be included in *Travel news* feature of a newspaper or magazine (e.g. strikes, delays, new ideas/companies, special offers).

2   Tell students that they are going to prepare a travel news feature for a local magazine/newspaper.

3   Divide the class into six groups (or fewer with a smaller class) and give each group one card.

4   Each group uses the information on their card to write the news story, adding more information if they wish. Remind students to use the passive where they think it would be more appropriate.

5   Groups take it in turns to read out their stories to the class.

6   Give feedback on their use (or not) of the passive and give alternative ways of expressing points if necessary.

Variation

The six stories could be typed up or neatly written out and compiled into a class newspaper.

11A: Happiness

Use: After Lead-in (p. 147) or after Reading Exercise 4 (p. 148)
Aim: To generate interest in the topic of happiness; to practise discussing and trying to reach a consensus
Time: 15–20 minutes
Activity type: Pairwork. Students rank factors that create happiness.
Preparation: Make one copy of the activity (p. 115) per pair of students.

Procedure

1   Ask students if they feel happy today or not. At this stage, try to focus students on superficial things (*it's raining, it's Friday*, etc.). Tell them that in this activity you want them to think about true happiness and contentment.

2   Divide the class into pairs and give each pair a copy of the activity.

3   Check quickly for any unknown vocabulary.

4   Set a time limit of 5–10 minutes. Students work together to decide which points are more or less important and agree on the three which are the most important.

5   Conduct feedback with the class, to compare opinions.

Follow-up

Discuss which of the points in the list are easier or harder to obtain.

11B: Clauses of reason, purpose and contrast

Use: After Language development 1 Exercise 5 (p. 151)
Aim: To practise using discourse markers in clauses of reason, purpose and contrast
Time: 20–25 minutes
Activity type: Groupwork. Students form sentences from prompts to win points.
Preparation: Make one copy of the activity (p. 116) per group of three or four students and cut up into cards.

Procedure

1   Divide the class into groups of three or four and give each group a set of linking word cards (grey) and a set of topic cards (white).

2   Explain that the object of the activity is for students to make sentences using the linking words and the topic words, e.g. *although + music*: *Although I like classical music, I don't often go to concerts.*

3   Students shuffle the linking words (grey) and place in a pile face down, then do the same with the topic cards (white).

4   Students take one card from each pile and use them to make a true sentence about themselves. They can use the word on the topic card or any related to the topic. If students are stuck, they can change one of the two cards by putting it to the bottom of the pile and taking the next one from the top.

5   Other students in the group listen and judge if the sentence is grammatically correct or not, referring any disputes to the teacher. If correct, the student keeps the cards and gains a point. If incorrect, the cards go back to the bottom of the pile. At the end the student with the most cards/points is the winner.

6   Give feedback on students' performance, eliciting more examples of any clause types that are causing problems.

Follow-up

Students choose three linking words from the grey cards and write three sentences about themselves, two of which are true and one false. They then read them out to their group, who guess which one is false.

12A: Connecting ideas

Use: After Language development 1 Exercise 4 (p. 165)
Aim: To practise using discourse markers and participle clauses while telling a story.
Time: 20–25 minutes
Activity type: Groupwork. Students play a game, taking it in turns to tell parts of the same story, but working towards different endings.
Preparation: Make one copy of the activity (p. 117) per group of three or four students and cut up into cards.

Procedure

1   Divide the class into groups of three or four and give each student a card.

2   Explain the object of the game: to finish a joint story with the words on their card. Students tell the same story taking it in turns to tell a part.

3   Select one student to begin the story. Turns then rotate around the group.

4   At each turn, students must follow on logically from what came before but try to turn the story in the direction of their ending by introducing characters, objects or incidents as necessary.

5   Each turn, a student must try to use one of the structures listed on the card which is then ticked off. Each student can use each structure once only.

6   Other students can challenge if they think the link is not logical or the use of the structure is incorrect. If they cannot think of a sentence using one of the target structures, they can make up another sentence, just to continue the story.

7   When someone has ticked off five structures from their card, they can finish the story (with the ending on their card) and win the game.

8   As students are playing, monitor by helping with use of target structures and noting errors to correct at the end of the activity.

12B: Media mistakes

Use: After Use of English 2 Exercise 5 (p. 173) or after
Language development 3 Exercise 3b (p. 174)
Aim: To practise word-building and focus on common
student errors
Time: 20–25 minutes
Activity type: Pairwork and whole class. Students play a
game where they win points by identifying correct and
incorrect sentences (and correcting the incorrect ones).
Preparation: Make one copy of both pages of the activity
(pp. 118–119) per pair of students. Cut up the second page
into cards.

Procedure

1   Divide the class into pairs, give each pair a copy of the
    Common mistakes worksheet and explain the object of the
    game: to win as many points as possible by risking points
    on whether the sentences are correct or incorrect.

2   In their pairs, students first decide if the sentences are
    correct or incorrect and put a tick or a cross in the second
    column of the table. They then decide how many points
    to risk on each sentence, depending on how certain they
    are, and write the number in the third column. They can
    risk 1, 2, 5 or 10 points on each sentence.

3   When they have finished, give each pair a set of game
    cards and ask them to put the *correct* and *incorrect* cards in
    front of them.

4   Read out the first sentence and ask pairs to put one of
    the point cards on either the *correct* or *incorrect* card in
    front of them, to show how many points they have risked
    on the sentence. Select a pair to say why they made their
    choice and to correct the sentence if necessary, then
    confirm the answer.

5   If a pair is wrong, they lose the number of points they
    have put down and put a – sign next to the number they
    have written down. If they are right, they win that number
    and put a + sign next to the number.

6   Repeat the procedure for the rest of the sentences, with
    pairs adding + or – to their score each time.

7   Students add up the total. The pair with the most points
    at the end are the winners.

1 X (**as** a journalist)   2 ✓   3 X (I **used to** work)   4 ✓
5 X (**it** was really boring/I was really **bored**)
6 X (give **each other/one another**)   7 ✓
8 X (anything **illegal**)   9 X (It was **such an** interesting
story/**The story was so** interesting)   10 ✓   11 ✓
12 X (that had **robbed** a bank)   13 X (a bit **depressing**)   14 X
(a **two-year** contract)   15 X (an **inconvenient** time)

Photocopiable activity (Pre-course quiz)

How much do you know about the *Cambridge English: First* exam?

Choose the correct answer (A, B or C).

1 How many papers are there in the exam?

A 4

B 5

C 6

2 What's the pass mark?

A about 60%

B about 65%

C about 70%

3 Do you need to pass all the papers?

A Yes, of course!

B No, passing most of them is enough.

C No, it's the total mark that is important.

4 How many parts are there in Paper 1 (Reading and Use of English)?

A 5

B 6

C 7

5 In Paper 1, Part 1 (Multiple-choice cloze) do you lose marks if the answer is wrong?

A No, so take a chance if you don't know, you might be lucky.

B Yes, so only choose an answer if you are really sure.

C Sometimes – it depends on how the examiner is feeling.

6 In Paper 2 (Writing) do you have to answer all the questions?

A Yes, so write quickly.

B You must answer the question in Part 1 and any one question from Part 2.

C You can answer any two questions.

7 In Paper 3 (Listening) how many times do you hear each part?

A Only once, so listen carefully.

B Twice (or more if you ask the examiner nicely).

C You will hear each part twice before going on to the next part.

8 In Paper 4 (Speaking) do you speak to the interlocutor or your partner?

A You only discuss things with your partner.

B Sometimes to the interlocutor and sometimes to your partner.

C You say everything to the interlocutor.

9 Can you use a highlighter?

A No.

B Yes, but only on the question paper.

C Yes, both on the question paper and on the answer sheet.

10 Which of the following can you take into the exam: a dictionary, a bottle of water, a lucky rabbit's foot?

A all of them

B none of them

C just the water and lucky rabbit's foot

Tick (✓) True or False.

11 All papers are worth the same number of marks.
True ☐   False ☐

12 In Paper 2 (Writing), Part 2, you should write between 120–180 words.
True ☐   False ☐

13 Contractions count as one word.
True ☐   False ☐

14 Spelling must always be correct in Paper 3 (Listening).
True ☐   False ☐

15 You can take Paper 4 (Speaking) on your own if you are shy.
True ☐   False ☐

Photocopiable activity 1A   Lifestyle and families

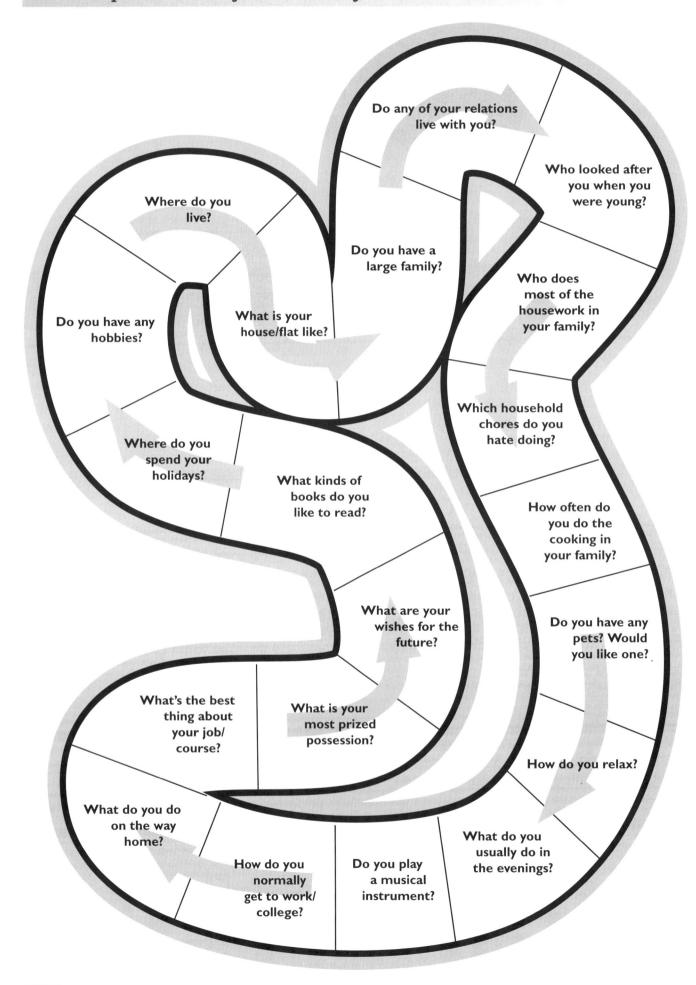

Do any of your relations live with you?

Who looked after you when you were young?

Where do you live?

Do you have a large family?

Who does most of the housework in your family?

Do you have any hobbies?

What is your house/flat like?

Where do you spend your holidays?

Which household chores do you hate doing?

What kinds of books do you like to read?

How often do you do the cooking in your family?

What are your wishes for the future?

Do you have any pets? Would you like one?

What's the best thing about your job/course?

What is your most prized possession?

How do you relax?

What do you do on the way home?

How do you normally get to work/college?

Do you play a musical instrument?

What do you usually do in the evenings?

Photocopiable activity 1B   Adjective + noun collocations

Part 1

unique	final	quick
high	memorable	valuable
strong	natural	domestic
wide	central	exact
hard	guided	slight

opportunity	destination	breakfast
speed	experience	paintings
influence	light	life
gap	heating	date
work	tour	change

Part 2

STREATHAM PALACE

Come for a day out at Streatham Palace. Join our knowledgeable staff on a(n) **(1)** _____ of this magnificent home. There is nothing else like this in London, so this is a(n) **(2)** _____ to learn about **(3)** _____ in the 18th century before the modern era of electricity and **(4)** _____ communication. There has only been a(n) **(5)** _____ to the appearance of the house since it was built sometime between 1760 and 1780 (the **(6)** _____ is not known).

See the **(7)** _____ in lifestyles between the rich house owner and the life of the staff. Staff at the time were used to **(8)** _____ : they worked 12 hours a day, six days a week. Actors in period costume play the parts of the people who lived there, telling you about their lifestyles. After a(n) **(9)** _____ in the kitchen, the staff would start work. One of the first jobs was making up the fires in every room each morning. These were the days before **(10)** _____ !

In the main part of the house, you can see the **(11)** _____ of French design, shown in the choice of furniture and fabrics. Visit the fantastic dining room, where an invitation to dinner would have been a truly **(12)** _____ . In the living room, the large windows fill the room with **(13)** _____ . The house contains many **(14)** _____ by famous British artists of the time. In the main bedroom, see the huge bed that was made in 1825 as a present for an Indian prince but never reached its **(15)** _____ .

The tour continues to the area where the staff lived in the attic and finishes in our tearoom and gift shop.

This is a chance to make history come alive!

Photocopiable activity 2A   Work

1 Which of these jobs do you think is the most stressful?

- firefighter
- prison officer
- football referee
- miner
- actor
- soldier

2 Which of these jobs is the best paid?

- company director
- surgeon
- lawyer
- politician
- accountant
- musician

3 Which of these jobs requires the longest training?

- judge
- dentist
- vet
- ballet dancer
- architect
- chef

4 Which of these jobs would you find the most satisfying?

- pilot
- teacher
- farmer
- midwife
- photographer
- builder

5 Which of these jobs do you think is the easiest to do?

- librarian
- fashion model
- DJ
- traffic warden
- lifeguard

6 Which of these jobs do you think is the most useful for society?

- lorry driver
- dustman
- civil servant
- undertaker
- shop assistant
- TV/radio newsreader

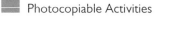

Photocopiable activity 2B   Articles

Story A

The girl and the wolf

One afternoon (1) _____ wolf waited in (2) _____ dark forest for (3) _____ girl to come by. He was very hungry because it had been (4) _____ long time since he had eaten anything. Finally, (5) _____ little girl did come along (6) _____ path and she was carrying (7) _____ basket of food.

(8) _____ girl was happy, (9) _____ weather was good, (10) _____ sun was shining and (11) _____ birds were singing. She loved (12) _____ nature and being with (13) _____ animals. 'What (14) _____ beautiful day!' she thought. She was happy that it was (15) _____ holiday and that she wasn't at (16) _____ school.

(17) _____ wolf asked her if she was going to visit her grandmother and she said that she was. So (18) _____ wolf asked her where her grandmother lived and (19) _____ little girl told him. Then he ran off.

When (20) _____ little girl opened (21) _____ door of (22) _____ Granny's house, she saw that there was somebody in (23) _____ bed listening to (24) _____ radio, wearing (25) _____ nightcap and nightdress. When she was no nearer than ten metres from (26) _____ bed, she saw that it was not her grandmother but (27) _____ wolf – because everybody knows that (28) _____ wolf in (29) _____ nightcap looks nothing like your granny! So she ran out of (30) _____ house and called (31) _____ police, asking them to find her granny!

Moral
It is not so easy to fool (32) _____ little girls nowadays as it used to be!

✂

Answer key

1 a   2 a   3 a   4 a   5 a   6 the   7 a   8 The   9 the   10 the   11 the   12 –   13 –   14 a   15 a   16 –
17 The   18 the   19 the   20 the   21 the   22 –   23 –   24 the   25 a   26 the   27 the   28 a   29 a
30 the   31 the   32 –

Story B

The girl and the shoe

There was once **(1)** _____ poor young girl who was very unhappy. She had to spend all **(2)** _____ day cleaning **(3)** _____ house. She had two big ugly sisters who were unkind to her.

One day, all **(4)** _____ girls were invited to **(5)** _____ party. **(6)** _____ beautiful young girl couldn't go because her big ugly sisters said she had to stay at **(7)** _____ home and do some housework. Anyway, although she loved **(8)** _____ music and **(9)** _____ dancing, she didn't have anything to wear.

Suddenly, **(10)** _____ fairy godmother appeared. 'What **(11)** _____ pity!' said **(12)** _____ fairy godmother. 'Let me help you!' And she gave **(13)** _____ girl everything she needed: **(14)** _____ clothes, **(15)** _____ shoes and **(16)** _____ golden carriage. **(17)** _____ girl went to **(18)** _____ party and had **(19)** _____ great time. She met **(20)** _____ rich young man and danced with him all **(21)** _____ night. At **(22)** _____ midnight she had to leave and was in such **(23)** _____ hurry that she left one of her shoes behind. **(24)** _____ young man kept it and spent **(25)** _____ next few days looking for **(26)** _____ girl who had lost it. Finally, he came to her house and asked her to try it on. **(27)** _____ shoe fitted perfectly! He asked her to marry him. She refused and said that first she wanted to go to **(28)** _____ university and get **(29)** _____ job, then when **(30)** _____ time was right, she would consider getting married.

Moral

These days (31) _____ **marriage is less important than (32)** _____ **career.**

Answer key

I a 2 – 3 the 4 the 5 a 6 The 7 – 8 – 9 – 10 a 11 a 12 the 13 the 14 –
15 – 16 a 17 The 18 the 19 a 20 a 21 – 22 – 23 a 24 The 25 the 26 the 27 The
28 – 29 a 30 the 31 – 32 a

Photocopiable activity 3A   Adjectives and adverbs

Sentence cards

1 I had thought it would be really difficult to find but it was _____ easy.

2 The tour had _____ started when it started to rain.

3 The situation is difficult and the future of the island looks _____ .

4 The town centre is very _____ on a Saturday afternoon when all the cafés and restaurants are busy.

5 The food is good, so it's _____ worth visiting this restaurant.

6 They try really _____ to attract more tourists each year.

7 We received a(n) _____ welcome from the smiling staff when we arrived at the hotel.

8 Plans for the future need to be made now as the population is rising _____ .

9 Unfortunately, it is _____ far from the city centre.

10 The restaurant at the top of the mountain is _____ expensive, so few people can afford it.

11 It is _____ impossible to find a parking space in the town centre but occasionally, you are lucky.

12 We were _____ starving when we got home as we hadn't eaten all day.

13 The castle is worth visiting but the climb up to it is _____ tough.

14 Why don't you come in autumn? The weather is usually _____ good then.

15 Famous residents include Fleming, who is _____ well-known writer.

16 I tried sailing, which was _____ very easy after the first few minutes.

17 The CD was faulty and the case was damaged _____ .

18 If you don't improve safety, someone could be _____ injured.

19 Booking the holiday online was _____ simple and only took a few minutes.

20 The service in the restaurant was _____ slow and when the food did come, it was cold.

Adjective/Adverb cards

surprisingly	pretty
hardly	quite a
bleak	as well
well	seriously
hard	remarkably
friendly	lively
quite	fast
extremely	absolutely
practically	actually
a bit	rather

Photocopiable activity 3B   *-ing* forms and infinitives

Set A

think of	eager	keen on	regret
agree	enjoy	let	remember
apologise for	finish	look forward to	stop
can't help	hard	make	teach
decision	have trouble	opportunity	try
dream of	interested in	refuse	unable

Set B

wear	make	go	learn
watch	build	take	get
play	study	write	buy
feel	work	clean	spend
live	read	tidy up	predict
change	walk	turn down	ignore

Photocopiable activity 4A   Raising money

Your club/society wants to raise money to buy some new equipment. Look at the options below and decide what the best method to raise the money would be. Discuss them and agree on the best way. For each method, think about these questions:

- **How much money would you need to start with?**
- **How long would it take?**
- **How easy would it be for you?**
- **How successful would it be?**

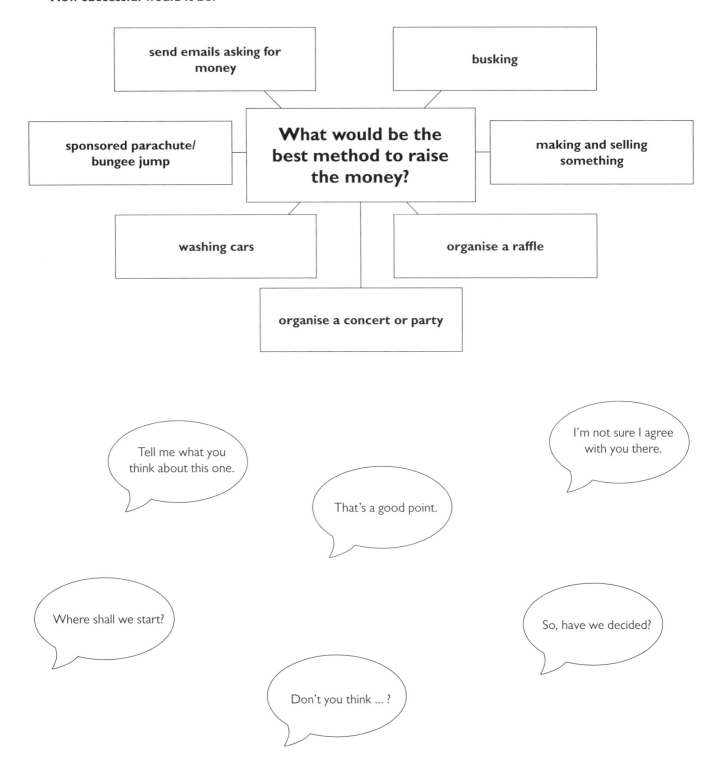

PHOTOCOPIABLE © 2014 Pearson Education Ltd.

Photocopiable activity 4B   Confusing adjectives

Part 1

---

alone: with no one else (physical)

lonely: unhappy; missing friends (a feeling)

---

shy: not confident speaking to unknown people

nervous: worried/frightened about something that may happen

---

imaginative: creative; with a good imagination

imaginary: not real; fictitious

fantastic: very good

---

slim: thin (positive)

skinny: very thin (negative)

---

childish: behaving like a child (negative)

childlike: appearance; quality

---

priceless: worth a lot of money

worthless: worth nothing

invaluable: very useful; essential

---

economic: relating to trade and industry

economical: good value; using money/ time well

---

terrific: very good

terrifying: very frightening

terrible: very bad

---

similar: almost the same (before noun)

alike: the same (not before noun)

familiar: easy to recognise; known

---

convenient: not causing problems

useful: helping you get what you want

---

classic: well-known; typical; influential

classical: traditional

---

high: shows distance from ground

tall: used for people and narrow things

long: horizontal measure

---

foreign: from another country

strange: unusual; different

---

old-fashioned: not modern; not usual any more

out-of-date: no longer useful/correct

---

fun: enjoyable

funny: amusing; making you laugh

---

injured: hurt physically by accident

wounded: hurt with a weapon (e.g. in a fight or war)

Part 2

4 Were you an *imaginative / imaginary* child?

3 What would you say was a *classic / classical* sci-fi movie?

2 Do you prefer watching modern or *classic / classical* dance?

1 Do you prefer working with other students or working *alone / lonely*?

5 Are the times of this class *useful / convenient* for you?

6 Do you think some fashion models are too *slim / skinny*?

7 When you travel, apart from a guidebook, what else is *priceless / worthless / invaluable*?

8 How *high / tall / long* are you?

12 Are you an *economic / economical* person?

11 What would you say are *sensible / sensitive* things to do before an exam?

10 How *alike / familiar* are you and your brother(s)/ sister(s)?

9 Do your friends have *similar / alike / familiar* tastes in music?

13 Are you *sensible / sensitive* to the feelings of your friends?

14 Do you usually feel *shy / nervous* before an exam?

15 What's your idea of a *funny / fun* night out?

16 Can you remember a *terrific / terrifying* meal you have eaten?

20 Have you ever met anyone who was rather *old-fashioned / out-of-date* about something?

19 Have you ever been *injured / wounded* while playing sport?

18 Do you prefer *strange / foreign* films or films from your own country?

17 Have you ever been in a *terrific / terrifying* situation?

Photocopiable activity 5A   The human body quiz

The human body quiz

How much do you know about the human body? Can you answer these questions by choosing A, B or C? If you're not sure, have a guess!

1   At birth, how many bones do you have?
A   68
B   about 150
C   over 300

2   What is the most common blood type?
A   AB+
B   B-
C   O+

3   How heavy is your brain?
A   around 0.6 kg
B   around 1.4 kg
C   around 3.2 kg

4   Your heart is
A   on the left.
B   in the centre.
C   on the right.

5   What is a typical heartbeat for someone resting?
A   40–60 beats per minute
B   60–80 beats per minute
C   80–100 beats per minute

6   The study of how characteristics are passed from one generation to another is called
A   genealogy.
B   jeanetics.
C   genetics.

7   Psychology is the study of
A   mental processes.
B   mental illness.
C   mental intelligence.

8   What percentage of your body is water?
A   less than 50%
B   more than 60%
C   more than 80%

9   Genes are made up of a chemical called
A   ADN.
B   DNA.
C   NAD.

10   The largest organ in your body is
A   the liver.
B   the heart.
C   the skin.

11   How many muscles control your eyeballs?
A   4
B   6
C   7

12   Are there more bones in the hand or the foot?
A   hand
B   foot
C   They have the same.

Photocopiable activity 5B   Forming nouns

ure	excite	ion	encourage
ment	combin(e)	ment	exist
ation	perform	ence	surviv(e)
ance	correspond	al	assist
ence	fail	ance	contribut(e)
ure	hesitat(e)	ion	embarrass
ion	approv(e)	ment	press
al	achieve	ure	organis(e)
ment	appear	ation	protect
ance	clos(e)	ion	attend
ure	refus(e)	ance	propos(e)
al	confirm	al	prefer
ation	depend	ence	imagin(e)
ence	restrict	ation	pleas(e)

Photocopiable activity 6A   Ambition

HOW AMBITIOUS ARE YOU?

1 Do you want to be an important person in your community?
Yes ☐ Maybe ☐ No ☐

2 Do you tend to be lazy?
Yes ☐ Maybe ☐ No ☐

3 Do you compare your ability and performance with that of other people?
Yes ☐ Maybe ☐ No ☐

4 Do you set your targets low in order to avoid disappointments?
Yes ☐ Maybe ☐ No ☐

5 Do you try to do things immediately rather than put them off until later?
Yes ☐ Maybe ☐ No ☐

6 Are you satisfied with your current achievements?
Yes ☐ Maybe ☐ No ☐

7 When you play a game, is it important that you do well?
Yes ☐ Maybe ☐ No ☐

8 Would you prefer to laze on a beach rather than work/study?
Yes ☐ Maybe ☐ No ☐

9 Do you prefer to mix with ambitious and successful people?
Yes ☐ Maybe ☐ No ☐

10 Do you sometimes have days when you haven't done a thing?
Yes ☐ Maybe ☐ No ☐

11 Are you embarrassed if you are caught being lazy?
Yes ☐ Maybe ☐ No ☐

12 On an escalator, do you let it carry you along rather than walking up it yourself?
Yes ☐ Maybe ☐ No ☐

Photocopiable activity 6B   The arts

audience	standing ovation	director
choreographer	curtain	interval
rehearsal	stalls	first night
stage	review	front row
conductor	role	composer
ballet	costume	performance
box office	orchestra	programme
encore	critic	principal dancer
actors	spotlight	backstage
a play	concert	theatregoer

Photocopiable activity 7A   Cultural guide

Cultural dos and don'ts

I In Korea you are *supposed to / not supposed to / not allowed to* write someone's name in *pink / green / red*.

2 In China you *mustn't / aren't allowed to / aren't supposed to* use your *teacher's / partner's / neighbour's* name when talking to him/her.

3 In Japan you *don't need to / are allowed to / must* wash *before / while / after* you have a bath.

4 In Greece you *shouldn't / ought to / are not allowed to* give someone a coin if they give you *perfume / chocolate / a watch* as a gift.

5 In Thailand you *mustn't / ought to / have to* put your foot on a *ball / coin / apple* if you drop it and it is rolling away.

6 In the UK you *don't have to / are supposed to / aren't allowed to* stand *on the left / on the right / at the bottom* on escalators on the Underground.

7 In Japan and Korea you *must / mustn't / shouldn't* use both hands when giving something *valuable / to an older person / edible*.

8 In Spain you *aren't supposed to / ought to / are allowed to* say 'hello' to everyone when you enter a *restaurant / lift / bus*.

9 In Egypt you *must / shouldn't / don't need to* open *gifts / letters / umbrellas* in front of the person who gives them to you.

10 In Germany you *are supposed to / aren't supposed to / oughtn't to* keep your *hands / knife and fork / phone* on or above the table during a meal.

Photocopiable activity 7B   Modals of deduction

1 I've got a great photo of my grandad standing on the ice with lots of penguins. It was taken on a trip to the Arctic.

2 My friend Jorge speaks Spanish as he comes from South America but I can't remember if he's from Brazil or Colombia.

3 My grandfather got his first mobile phone in the 1960s. It was expensive, but very useful.

4 My favourite painting by the artist Edgar Allan Poe is *Girl with a pearl earring*.

5 My cousin recently returned from a holiday in South Africa. He told me all about the strange animals he saw there, such as kangaroos.

6 I think my grandparents got married in 1971 but I'm not sure. I know it was on the same day that people first landed on the moon.

7 My friend had a car accident in Asia. I can't remember if it was Japan or Korea but it was a place where people drive on the left.

8 I remember going to Berlin about ten years ago and seeing the famous wall and wondering how much longer it would last.

9 My brother is working in Italy now. I can't remember where exactly but it is a city with a famous leaning tower.

10 I've been driving for years and have never had an accident. I think I was 15 when I passed my test.

11 The first time I used some euro banknotes in 2000 I thought that they were ugly but now I quite like them.

12 Yesterday I was reading about the type of television programmes people watched in the 1920s – they were very different from now.

13 My friend Lucy is on holiday in Greece. She just emailed me a picture of her in the Louvre.

14 My friend in New Zealand is always having problems. Recently, she was bitten by a snake when she was hill walking.

Photocopiable activity 8A   Reported speech

Student A

Report these last words from famous people to your partner.

> Am I dying or is it my birthday?

Nancy Witcher Astor, British politician (to her family sitting round her bed)

> I am about to – or I am going to – die; either expression is correct.

Dominique Bouhours, French grammarian

> I have had a hell of a lot of fun and enjoyed every minute of it.

Errol Flynn, Australian actor

> I don't have the passion anymore and so remember it is better to burn out than fade away.

Kurt Cobain, American musician

> I have not told half of what I saw.

Marco Polo, Italian explorer

> Tomorrow I shall no longer be here.

Nostradamus, French astrologer (to his assistant)

> I have never felt better.

Douglas Fairbanks, American actor (to his doctor)

> My wallpaper and I are fighting a battle to the death. One or other of us has to go.

Oscar Wilde, Irish author

> I'm going away tonight.

James Brown, American singer

Listen to your partner's quotes. If you don't know, guess! Choose from these answers.

1 Elvis Presley, American singer (at his last press conference)
2 Marie Antoinette, queen of France (to her executioner, as she unintentionally stepped on his foot)
3 Edmund Gwenn, British-American actor (to a friend who asked if dying was tough)
4 Thomas de Mahy, French aristocrat (to a court official, while reading his death sentence)
5 Lou Costello, American actor
6 Louis XIV, king of France
7 Quincy Adams, president of USA
8 H. G. Wells, British author
9 Salvador Dalí, Spanish painter

Student B

Report these last words from famous people to your partner.

I see that you have made three spelling mistakes.

**Thomas de Mahy,
French aristocrat (to a court
official, while reading his death
sentence)**

Where is my clock?

**Salvador Dalí,
Spanish painter**

Go away. I am all right.

**H. G. Wells,
British author**

Pardon me, sir – I did not mean to do it.

**Marie Antoinette, queen of France
(to her executioner,
as she unintentionally stepped on
his foot)**

This is the last of Earth! I am content!

**Quincy Adams,
president of USA**

I hope I haven't bored you.

**Elvis Presley,
American singer
(at his last press conference)**

That was the best ice-cream soda I ever tasted.

**Lou Costello,
American actor**

Yes, but not as tough as doing comedy.

**Edmund Gwenn,
British-American actor (to a friend
who asked if dying was tough)**

Why do you weep? Did you think I was immortal?

**Louis XIV,
king of France**

Listen to your partner's quotes. If you don't know, guess! Choose from these answers.

1 Errol Flynn, Australian actor
2 Oscar Wilde, Irish author
3 Dominique Bouhours, French grammarian
4 Nostradamus, French astrologer (to his assistant)
5 Douglas Fairbanks, American actor (to his doctor)
6 Nancy Witcher Astor, British politician (to her family sitting round her bed)
7 James Brown, American singer
8 Marco Polo, Italian explorer
9 Kurt Cobain, American musician

Photocopiable activity 8B   Leisure activities

You and your friends have decided to spend a weekend together doing something interesting. Look at the activities below and choose the one that would be the most interesting for you as a group.

Photocopiable activity 9A   Conditionals

what / you / do / if / you / go / into the red / next month?	if / you / win / a lot of money / what / you / do / with it?	if / you / start / a business one day / what / it / be?
what / you / say / if I / ask / you / to lend me some money / yesterday?	what / you / do / if you / find / some money in the street?	when / a shop assistant / give / you too much change / what / you / do?
what / you / do / when / this course / finish?	if / you / not do / this course / what / you / do / now?	if / you / not start / this course / what / you / do / now?
what / you / do / if / you / cannot / do / the homework this week?	if / I / have / a party at the weekend / you / come?	if / you / visit / anywhere in the world / where / you / go?
if / you / can change / one law / what / it / be?	if / you / feel / ill tomorrow morning / what / you / do?	if / you / watch / TV tonight / what / you / watch?
when / you / make / your favourite meal / what / you / cook?	if / you / go / to a party / what / you / usually / wear?	when / you / have / a cold / what / you / do?
where / you / go / if / you / have / another holiday last year?	what / you / say / if / I / tell / you / I / want / to change the world?	when / you / get / a headache / what / you / do?

Photocopiable activity 9B   Money vocabulary

Student A

Student B

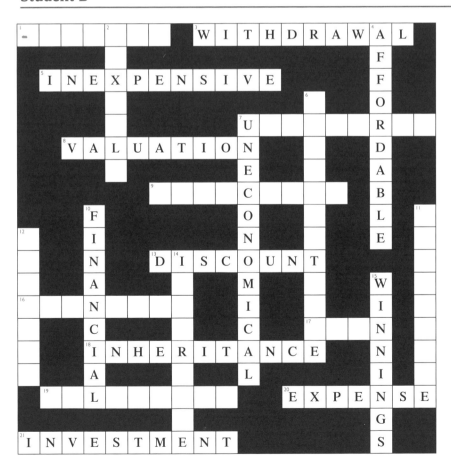

Find the perfect travelling partner!

1 When I'm on holiday, I prefer to
A stay in and relax.
B stay in my country.
C visit a country I know.
D visit a new country.

2 For holiday accommodation, I prefer
A camping.
B youth hostels.
C cheap hotels.
D luxury hotels.

3 I prefer to go on holiday
A on my own.
B with one close friend.
C with a big group of friends.
D with my parents.

4 For the arrangements, I prefer to
A do it all myself in advance.
B let a travel agent do it all.
C make them as I go along.
D just see what happens.

5 My ideal holiday would be
A a safari.
B a tropical beach holiday.
C in an interesting city.
D in the mountains.

6 I like to take
A just a few basics.
B a small backpack.
C a suitcase.
D as much as possible.

7 On holiday, what I like to see most is
A exotic animals.
B famous works of art.
C fantastic sunsets.
D the sights.

8 When I travel, I usually read
A a local phrase book.
B a guidebook.
C a racy novel.
D a magazine.

9 The thing I enjoy most on holiday is
A doing nothing.
B visiting museums.
C physical exercise.
D learning about local customs.

10 I think travel should be about
A history and culture.
B food and drink.
C relaxing.
D looking for adventure.

11 My photos are mainly of
A me.
B historical buildings.
C local people.
D friends.

12 I like to bring back
A lots of photos.
B a few souvenirs.
C traditional local crafts.
D food!

Photocopiable activity 10B   The passive

RECORD CLIMB

Keiko Fujita, a 70-year-old Japanese woman, has climbed Everest by the North Face – the oldest person to do so. A team of local climbers helped her.

Everest facts

- It is the highest mountain in the world.
- The first successful climb to the top was in 1953 by Tenzing and Hillary.
- It is situated on the border of Nepal and Tibet.
- People consider the North Face to be the hardest route to the top.

NEW CAR RENTAL COMPANY

Some people have started a new online car rental company. They call it Simple Cars.

Simple Cars facts

- You must reserve and pay for cars online.
- You can collect a car from 22 airports around Europe.
- They charge customers per hour.
- People say they are the cheapest rental cars in Europe.

RECORD BALLOON FLIGHTS

Diane May has flown a balloon solo non-stop around the world – the first woman to do so.

Flight facts

- A team of experts helped her.
- The wind blew her off course twice.
- A storm almost forced her to crash.
- She equipped her balloon with the latest technology.
- Her friends expect her to try to break another record next year.

NEW HOTEL

A company has announced that they are going to build a new hotel in Cairo, near the pyramids. A famous architect is going to design it and a local company will build it. Tour groups will use it, mainly.

Pyramid facts

- Someone built them 4,500 years ago.
- The government has protected them for many years.
- We think that conservation groups are opposing the plans.

DISCOUNT CARD

Some organisations in London have launched a Tourist Discount Card. They will also give cardholders a chance to book things more easily.

Card facts

- Hotels and train stations sell the card.
- You can use it to get up to 25 percent discount at many places.
- It costs £150.
- Many hotels, travel companies and restaurants in London accept it.
- We think it is the first discount card just for tourists.

HOLIDAY COMPANY IN TROUBLE

Zoom Holidays has announced big discounts on their holidays after losing many customers. They have reduced some prices by 30–40 percent. They will give a free flight to all customers that book this month.

Company facts

- Two men started the company five years ago.
- The company employs 1,700 people.
- Analysts do not expect the company to survive.

Photocopiable activity 11A   Happiness

Here are some things that some people say are 'the secrets of true happiness. Talk to each other about how important each one is and then choose the three that you think are most important.

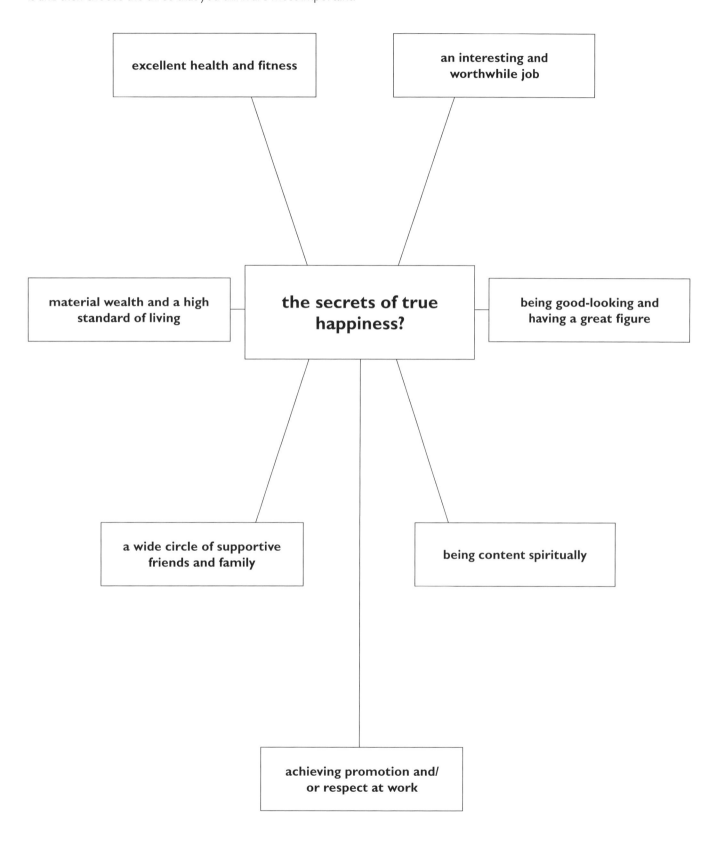

excellent health and fitness

an interesting and worthwhile job

material wealth and a high standard of living

the secrets of true happiness?

being good-looking and having a great figure

a wide circle of supportive friends and family

being content spiritually

achieving promotion and/ or respect at work

Photocopiable activity 11B   Clauses of reason, purpose and contrast

owing to	due to	because of
since	as	so as to
so that	in order to	in spite of
even though	despite	to
whereas	in case	although
money	clothes	friends
happiness	music	parents
work/job	holidays	children
food/drink	lifestyle	school
health	family	weekends

Photocopiable activity 12A Connecting ideas

A

'And that's why he never went to the city again.'

conjunction + clause (e.g. *when, while*) ☐

conjunction + *-ing* (e.g. *before ...-ing*) ☐

modifier (e.g. *so/such a ... that ...*) ☐

clause of purpose (e.g. *to, in order to*) ☐

clause of reason (e.g. *as, since*) ☐

present participle clause (*...ing ... , he/she/ they ...*) ☐

perfect participle clause (*having + past participle ... , he/she/they ...*) ☐

B

'And she never mentioned the incident from that day onwards.'

conjunction + clause (e.g. *when, while*) ☐

conjunction + *-ing* (e.g. *before ...-ing*) ☐

modifier (e.g. *so/such a ... that ...*) ☐

clause of purpose (e.g. *to, in order to*) ☐

clause of reason (e.g. *as, since*) ☐

present participle clause (*...ing ... , he/she/ they ...*) ☐

perfect participle clause (*having + past participle ... , he/she/they ...*) ☐

C

'It was almost midnight by the time they had cleared up all the mess.'

conjunction + clause (e.g. *when, while*) ☐

conjunction + *-ing* (e.g. *before ...-ing*) ☐

modifier (e.g. *so/such a ... that ...*) ☐

clause of purpose (e.g. *to, in order to*) ☐

clause of reason (e.g. *as, since*) ☐

present participle clause (*...ing ... , he/she/ they ...*) ☐

perfect participle clause (*having + past participle ... , he/she/they ...*) ☐

D

'When she got home, she realised it had been in her bag all along.'

conjunction + clause (e.g. *when, while*) ☐

conjunction + *-ing* (e.g. *before ...-ing*) ☐

modifier (e.g. *so/such a ... that ...*) ☐

clause of purpose (e.g. *to, in order to*) ☐

clause of reason (e.g. *as, since*) ☐

present participle clause (*...ing ... , he/she/ they ...*) ☐

perfect participle clause (having + past participle ... , *he/she/they ...*) ☐

Photocopiable activity 12B   Media mistakes

Common mistakes

		✓ / ✗	Points
1	When I left university, I worked like a journalist for a local paper for a few years.		
2	He has hardly worked since becoming a freelance journalist.		
3	I was used to work on radio but now I'm working for a TV company.		
4	There was a very low attendance at yesterday's news conference.		
5	I tried to read the article but I couldn't finish it because I was really boring.		
6	My sisters and I usually give each others books for Christmas.		
7	She's a good journalist because she writes well.		
8	Journalists must be careful that they don't do anything unlegal.		
9	It was a so interesting story that I read it twice.		
10	The problem with some reports is that they are inaccurate.		
11	She had lots of frightening experiences when she was a war correspondent.		
12	The front-page story was about two people that had stolen a bank.		
13	I didn't read the story about the economy – it looked a bit depressed.		
14	They employed the reporter on a two-years contract.		
15	I don't watch the news as it is always on at an unconvenient time.		
		TOTAL	

Game cards

correct

incorrect

1 point

2 points

5 points

10 points

Audioscripts

Module 1

Speaking, page 15, Exercises 6b and 6c

Both of these celebrations are obviously very proud family occasions and they both seem to be for one of the younger people in the family; in this one it's this girl's birthday – perhaps it's a special one – it could be her eighteenth – and this one clearly shows the girl's graduation ceremony.

The main difference between the birthday and the graduation is that this one is very informal – everybody's wearing casual clothes and laughing – whereas the graduation ceremony is a much more formal celebration.

The celebrations are important for different reasons. Although the graduation ceremony is very formal, I think it is an opportunity for the family to share in the girl's success at college. On the other hand, the birthday party is more relaxed and probably more fun than the graduation ceremony – and it's a good excuse for friends to get together.

Listening, page 16, Exercises 2 and 3

I

A: I first came out here to stay with friends for a few months after I left university, and I haven't been back home much! I was astonished to realise that you can eat outdoors for much of the year, which is great and also means you save on heating bills. It's very easy to get to know people as well. The only problem is that it's such a long way away from anywhere and I feel out of touch with what's going on at home. Strangely, the thing I miss most is the seasons – the leaves falling in autumn and the first daffodils in spring.

2

B: I went there to teach English and immediately fell in love with the lifestyle, so ended up staying for several years. Life is very different over there; for example, people regard it as important to take a break at lunchtime and eat homemade food all together with the family, whereas in the USA we just grab something on the move – people are always in a rush. Also, because of the climate, people tend to have a nap or relax in the afternoon and work late. I preferred this. Unfortunately, I ended up spending too much time with other Americans and so I didn't really become as fluent as I would have liked, which is a shame.

3

C: I originally came over here to learn English and then met my husband and got married, so I have been here ever since. Of course I miss my family and the problem is that after all these years here it feels odd to be back in Russia again and yet I don't feel totally British either! The people here are as I'd expected in some ways - they're polite and law-abiding in the way they queue for buses and so on, unlike where I come from. But I'd been told they were unfriendly, which couldn't be further from the truth. They may come across like that at first but once they get to know you, they're really warm and would do anything to help you.

Module 2

Speaking, page 28, Exercise 2b

continuous assessment
curriculum
degree
exams
head teacher
higher education
homework
lecturer
playground
playgroup
strict discipline
tutorial
undergraduate
uniform

Speaking, page 29, Exercise 6a

Now, I'd like you to talk about something together for about two minutes.

I'd like you to imagine that a school is considering making some improvements so that it's a better place for students to study. Here are some ideas they are thinking about and a question for you to discuss. First you have some time to look at the task.

Now, talk to each other about how these changes would benefit the students.

Speaking, page 29, Exercises 6b and 6c

A: OK, shall I start? Well, personally, I think they would benefit a great deal from having more teachers so classes could be smaller.

B: I couldn't agree more. But that means they would need extra classrooms. What about more up-to-date equipment so that students could work on their own more?

A: Yes, I suppose so. Mmm ... actually, I think smaller classes would probably be a bigger benefit.

B: Do you think so? I'm not so sure. Students these days work very well on computers.

A: I know what you mean, but many students are not as fit as they should be and I think extra sports facilities would be even more important.

B: That's true. Many schools have too few.

A: How about more space for play and relaxation?

B: No, I don't think that matters so much. For me, it would be the least important change in a day school. Obviously, it would be important in a residential college.

A: That must be true for food too. Good food would be much more important in a residential college.

B: Yes, I agree up to a point, but even in a day school, you need a good lunch if you are working in the afternoons!

Listening, page 30, Exercise 2

(P = Presenter; L = Leanne)

P: Today we've invited into the studio a university student in her final year, Leanne Wilson, to give tips on surviving those first few weeks. Were you nervous about going off to university, Leanne?

L: In a way. I'd been really looking forward to it but my main worry was that I didn't know anyone.

P: But you made friends fairly quickly?

L: Oh, absolutely. Many of my friends initially were on my course but you've got to be careful you don't stick with just them all the time – you really miss out if you do. And try and be open-minded. Just because people don't speak to you doesn't mean they're unfriendly. They could just be shy. The main thing is to get involved with anything and everything. Even if you can't play tennis to save your life, have a go. Join the Scrabble® club, drama society, whatever – just so you meet a wide variety of people.

P: Which clubs did you join?

L: Well, that's the silly thing. I didn't! And I really wish I'd taken more advantage of the social life in that first week and enjoyed myself more. I think I was a bit scared of getting left behind in my work – when, really, that shouldn't be a priority at first. I didn't have a lot of cash to splash around either. But the thing is, you have to remember that it won't be such a social whirl for the whole term – things do calm down and you won't be spending money like this all the time. The first week you need to get out and enjoy yourself and not worry about it.

P: While we're on the subject of money, how did you manage on your student budget?

L: Well, some people choose to save on food and accommodation by living at home. I live quite near York, so that was an option but I felt it was important to stand on my own two feet, so I was in a hall of residence for my first year. My parents didn't put any pressure on me either way but it was tough at first because our family is quite close. It was the right thing to do for me to leave, though.

P: So did you have to get an evening job in York?

L: The thing is, with my subject, the workload is very high, so a job would mean very little time for a social life. So I just cut costs by sharing books with friends, shopping in charity shops, eating cheaply, that kind of thing. Although I do get a job in the holidays at home, so I can save up.

P: And is going to lectures very different from being at school?

L: It is, really. Where I went wrong at first was trying to write down every word the lecturer was saying and not really listening. In fact, you can normally get the notes online later anyway, so it's really not worth it – unless it helps you concentrate. Some of my friends don't bother going much at all, actually, but personally, I think that – even though you only get a basic overview in an hour – it makes you aware of the main areas that you need to read around.

P: Is it difficult to get used to structuring your day?

L: I found it's very easy to waste time unless you're disciplined. It's not that you aren't interested in the subject but life has a habit of getting in the way and it's tempting to stay in bed late and have a coffee with friends instead of getting stuck into what you have to do.

P: I can imagine! And the worst aspect of university life?

L: Mmm ... I thought it would be the cooking and washing and so on but that's not been too bad – although I do appreciate my mum more in the holidays! Probably, it's getting totally stressed as the work piles up. To be fair, that's only at certain times of year – exam times – but terms are short, so it feels as if it happens more.

P: Well, thanks very much, Leanne, and good luck in your final exams.

Module 3

Speaking, page 43, Exercise 8a

In this part of the test, I'm going to give each of you two photographs. I'd like you to talk about your photographs on your own for about a minute, and also to answer a question about your partner's photographs.

Emil, it's your turn first. Here are your photographs. They show people working with animals. I'd like you to compare the photographs and say why you think the jobs might be difficult.

Speaking, page 43, Exercises 8b, 8c and 8d

(E = Emil; I = Interlocutor)

E: In the photo on the left the man – he's a farmer, probably – is in the country with the sheep, whereas in the other one there's a woman in a white coat – she's a ... a kind of doctor who looks after animals. People bring in ... er ... small animals who live in the home, when they are ill or when they hurt themselves. She has to make them better. Sometimes there are emergencies when animals are injured in car accidents. This must be very ... upset ... it must upset her a lot. Personally, I think both jobs must be very hard work. A doctor for animals has to study for a long time to learn about the different animals and she has a lot of patients in a day. A farmer has to get up very early in the morning and go out in the fields in summer and winter. He has to work a lot – it must be very tiring and not very nice when it's raining hard and very cold and windy.

I: Thank you. Now, Tania, can you imagine doing either of these jobs?

Listening, page 44, Exercise 2b

Thanks, Paul, for the introduction, and hello, everybody.

Well, when I first went out to the Brazilian rainforest, I certainly never intended to stay there for any length of time. It was meant to be a quick visit to research and write a piece about tropical birds for the nature magazine I worked for. While I was there though, I also became fascinated by many of the other inhabitants, such as the huge variety of monkeys and snakes. However, the reason I stayed on was my love affair with the jaguar.

I must admit, at the beginning I found the rainforest environment quite hard to deal with. OK, I knew the forest was going to feel a bit claustrophobic. What I hadn't quite realised was how little daylight actually gets through the trees, which means you spend much of your time in semi-darkness – that took some getting used to. The other challenge was the insects. You get bitten by them all the time! They're massive noisy creatures – a bit like flying motorbikes!

Anyway, the first time I saw a jaguar was very early in the morning, and it was totally unexpected. This awesome animal just emerged from the forest and started walking towards me. It must have been about sixty metres away. Time seemed to stand still and I couldn't breathe. Not because I was terrified but I just felt emotional – she was so beautiful it brought tears to my eyes. She had a drink from a nearby river and disappeared into the forest again, so I didn't get a photograph that time, but I went on to have five more encounters over the next four years.

This may not seem much to you, but remember the jaguar is a threatened species, so it lives mainly in the most remote areas. The Amazon forest extends for thousands of kilometres and the territory of a typical male jaguar is something like 170 kilometres – in exceptional cases as much as 300 or more. It's rare to see one because they are such solitary, shy creatures and move incredibly quietly.

To have a better chance of seeing another jaguar, I went inland into a less populated area, where I met some of the local forest people. By that time, I'd tried all sorts of the local food: monkey's brains, alligators – you name it – but it's the spider I was given as an honoured guest that stands out in my mind on that first visit. It was the size of a small rat, had eight eyes and looked and tasted revolting. But it would have been very rude to refuse to eat what for them is a special food.

The forest people themselves don't see jaguars very often because until recently, the animals have tended to avoid places where humans make their homes. They are rarely a danger to human life and it is interesting that forest people tend to respect rather than fear these powerful animals, regarding them as fellow hunters rather than potential prey.

Unfortunately, in recent years, more and more of the forest has been destroyed, meaning that cattle are being bred in the open spaces which are left behind. This is seen as a source of food for jaguars and as a result, landowners have no hesitation in killing them if they see one near their farms.

Even if they escape being shot, there are many reported cases of jaguars picking up diseases – not so much from sheep or cows but from dogs and other domestic pets. In the interests of survival, therefore, it is much better if jaguars avoid areas of human habitation completely but this is easier said than done these days, if their own habitats are no longer available to them.

Since being back from Brazil, I have replaced journalism with lecture tours as I think they are a more effective way of educating people about the dangers that these magnificent creatures face unless we act now. Jaguars are an endangered species and if we allow the rainforests to disappear completely, we risk losing them altogether.

Module 4

Speaking, page 57, Exercise 4a

Now, I'd like you to talk about something together for about two minutes.

I'd like you to imagine that a college wants to persuade students to take up more sports. Here are some sports they are thinking of encouraging and a question for you to discuss. First you have some time to look at the task.

Now, talk to each other about the advantages of doing these sports.

Speaking, page 57, Exercises 4b and 4c

(C1 = Candidate 1; C2 = Candidate 2; I = Interlocutor)

C1: OK, let's begin with swimming, shall we? I think it's a good sport to do because it exercises the whole body and if the college has an indoor pool, you can swim all year round.

C2: Yes, I agree. I love going swimming but it can be a bit boring just going up and down – although I enjoy swimming in the sea. I think a lot of students would like something a bit more exciting, like judo. It builds up your strength and self-confidence and …

C1: Yes, and as well as that, it is a great discipline. But I don't quite agree with you about swimming. Swimming is good for everyone, male or female, young or old. And it … what do you say … it's very … er, ah, doesn't hurt the body … hurt the muscles so much as some other sports. Like judo, perhaps – I don't know.

C2: Yes, as long as you can swim. So what would you say about horse-riding?

C1: I think it's a bit like judo in some ways. It would appeal to some but not others – probably more to girls, to be honest.

C2: You're probably right but it must be wonderful to learn to look after horses.

C1: I agree to a certain extent but think of the … um … er, ah, it must be very expensive.

C2: It's very good exercise, though. It builds up your muscles and it's a skill you'll have for life.

C1: That's true. All the same, it's really not for everyone. What do you think about basketball? That seems very popular these days and you don't need much equipment – just a net, a board with a ring and a ball, really. You see it played a lot in poor areas, in lots of different countries.

C2: Yes, it's good for making friends. And all that running and jumping is good exercise. It feels like a more relaxed sport than some.

C1: I'm not sure about that. Not if you play to win! But it's certainly more relaxed than running. Don't you agree?

C2: Yes, but you don't have to compete when you run. You can do it on your own, for fun. The great advantage of running is that it's cheap and, of course, brilliant exercise.

C1: You're right! And after a hard day's studying, it gets rid of your stress. Which is just what you need.

I: Thank you.

Speaking, page 57, Exercise 4d

(C1 = Candidate 1; C2 = Candidate 2; I = Interlocutor)

I: Now you have about a minute to decide which sport would be best to encourage.

C1: Well, I think we are agreed that horse-riding and judo are great sports but they wouldn't appeal to everyone.

C2: So does that mean we have to choose the most popular sport, which is probably running – or, at least, jogging?

C1: No, I don't think it has to be jogging. Everyone knows about jogging. It has great health benefits. But it's hard work and a lot of people find it boring.

C2: But it has lots of other advantages. You don't need equipment, you don't need to wait for other people to join you. You can put on your shoes, get into your shorts and just go. I do think people need to be encouraged. Perhaps by having events like fun-runs which include everyone? Don't you agree with that?

C1: I suppose so. And the problem with basketball is you do need other people to make it fun. It's a team game, after all. But we haven't considered swimming. That is a sport for everyone. Well, at least those that can swim, as you said. And those that can't swim should be encouraged to learn. It's a skill for life, like horse-riding.

C2: That's a good point. So, really, what we are saying is that it's between running and swimming. So which one shall we choose? I think I know what your answer will be!

C1: Yes, I think swimming. It's just as good for exercise as running – if not better – because you get fewer injuries and you exercise more muscles.

C2: OK, let's decide on swimming, shall we?

C1: Yes, swimming it is.

Listening, page 58, Exercise 2c

1 My first parachute jump was the scariest thing I'd ever done. Nothing prepares you for falling out of a plane at 180 kilometres an hour. After all, you can't turn back if you change your mind, can you? When it came to actually jumping, I got very nervous. I had no choice but to do it though, because the whole point was to get people to give donations to a medical research organisation. If I hadn't jumped, I wouldn't have got any money for them. Once back on the ground, I realised I'd loved it and that was the beginning of my big hobby, much to the amazement of my friends and family.

2 I grew up surrounded by water – you could see the Atlantic from my bedroom window – and yet I'd never learnt to swim. See, I, I just never fancied it, even though my parents and brother swam like fish. I finally signed up for a five-week beginners' course at the age of thirty-five, I mean, not because I'd changed my mind about wanting to swim but just so that I could see the expressions of amazement on my kids' faces. It was worth suffering those awful lessons just for that! But I must admit that, even now, I'd much rather relax at the poolside and watch them splashing about.

3 I took up skiing while I was living abroad. I absolutely loved it from the word 'go' – the scenery of course, the sense of speed and complete focus on the task. It's fantastic exercise too. I hadn't expected to enjoy it though; in fact, I had to be talked into doing it by my friends. They'd all skied since they were very small and kept on at me until I agreed to give it a go. I'm much older now and, obviously, not as fit as I used to be but if I could find the money, I'd like to take the kids and see if I can still do it.

4 I'm not really into risky sports but I enjoyed snorkelling and quite fancied getting a closer look at exotic fish. My main motive for taking up scuba diving though, to be honest, is because my boyfriend, Tony, said I wouldn't be able to do it. I tend to panic, you see, and in scuba diving you have to remain totally calm or things can get very dangerous. It took me ages to gain the confidence to do it but I was determined to show Tony that he was wrong. So I persevered and I've now passed all my exams and we're off on a diving holiday together soon.

5 I've always been into football – all my friends were, and it was something we could all share. But apart from a few kickabouts in the garden, it tended to be very much a spectator sport. We'd watch *Match of the Day* on the TV, play computer games like *FIFA* and go to Liverpool home matches when we could afford it. Funnily enough, it was only quite recently that I started playing it on a regular basis and that was because I wanted something to help me unwind after a stressful day at work. It's brilliant because it means I have to think about something other than my job.

Module 5

Speaking, page 71, Exercise 4b

(C1 = Candidate 1; I = Interlocutor)

I: Now, I'd like you to talk about something together for about two minutes. I'd like you to imagine that a radio station is planning a programme on useful technology. Here are some ideas they are thinking about and a question for you to discuss. First you have some time to look at the task. Now, talk to each other about what the benefits of these items might be.

C1: So, we have to discuss why each of these items might be useful?

I: That's right.

Speaking, page 71, Exercise 4c

(C1 = Candidate 1; C2 = Candidate 2)

C1: OK, well, straightaway, I'm looking at the portable gaming devices. I think they're fantastic. They're much cheaper than other systems and they take up less space.

C2: I completely agree with you. And, of course, you can take them with you wherever you go. But, really, driverless cars would have a lot more benefits.

C1: I'm not so sure. People say they will cut down on car accidents, yet I wonder if that's true. They depend on satellite technology – and what if that breaks down?

C2: Good point. Still, I wonder, isn't that the case with all technology? That there are dangers? If a driver is tired though, surely, there are more dangers. And you wouldn't be able to go over the speed limit.

C1: I suppose so. And it would be wonderful to be able to do other things like read instead of looking at the boring road.

C2: What about some of the other things like robots?

C1: Robots! I imagine they're fantastic in factories because they don't make mistakes and they can do dangerous jobs.

C2: And they don't need to take breaks or holidays! Still, I'm not sure about in the home. Would you want a robot doing the housework?

C1: Oh, I don't know – it sounds like a good idea.

C2: Yes, but …

C1: No, no, I'm kidding! However, they must be incredibly useful – for example, in car production. They never get tired!

C2: Mmm … Right, let's move on to 3D TV.

C1: OK, what do you think?

C2: Well, the picture is obviously fantastic – it feels like real life. Most people don't like having to wear special glasses though.

C1: But aren't we getting more used to them these days?

C2: A little. Even so, they're still a nuisance.

C1: But if you've ever seen a football match in 3D, you'll never want to go back to an ordinary flat screen TV!

C2: Yes, I can see the advantage for special events but not for all the time.

C1: Of course. And, anyway, you don't have to watch in 3D unless you choose to. So you just use it when you want to.

C2: That's true. Well, lastly, then, ebook readers.

C1: I think they're great for travelling and you can put a whole library on a very small tablet.

C2: Yes, but I think it will take a long time for people to feel comfortable with them. Books are still very attractive.

Speaking, page 71, Exercise 4e

(C1 = Candidate 1; C2 = Candidate 2; I = Interlocutor)

I: Now you have about a minute to decide which item might have the most benefits.

C1: Right, so now we have to make up our minds about which item has the most benefits.

C2: Yes. I think we could find benefits in all of them and, of course, it would depend on the situation. But for general everyday use, I would say that robots have fewer benefits, don't you agree?

C1: Yes, I guess so. And, really, I don't think you are as enthusiastic as I am about the idea of ebook readers.

C2: Yes, you're right. They have advantages but a lot of people still prefer books.

C1: So we won't agree on that one. What about 3D TV?

C2: Yes, possibly. But I think it's more of a luxury item, not really a necessity.

C1: But neither are portable gaming devices. Nice, but not absolutely necessary.

C2: And if you've got a video games console at home and you've got games on your smartphone, they're not necessary at all.

C1: So that leaves the driverless cars.

C2: Yes, you weren't as enthusiastic as me at the beginning but I think you changed your mind.

C1: Yes, I did, when I thought about it. I can see them having a big effect. They would be good for older or disabled people or, really, anyone who doesn't like driving.

C2: And most importantly, they will reduce the number of car accidents dramatically.

C1: OK, so we both think that driverless cars would have the most benefits. Many more than the others.

I: Thank you.

Speaking, page 71, Exercise 4f

(C1 = Candidate 1; C2 = Candidate 2; I = Interlocutor)

C1: OK, well, straightaway, I'm looking at the portable gaming devices. I think they're fantastic. They're much cheaper than other systems and they take up less space.

C2: I completely agree with you. And, of course, you can take them with you wherever you go. But, really, driverless cars would have a lot more benefits.

C1: I'm not so sure. People say they will cut down on car accidents, yet I wonder if that's true. They depend on satellite technology – and what if that breaks down?

C2: Good point. Still, I wonder, isn't that the case with all technology? That there are dangers? If a driver is tired though, surely, there are more dangers. And you wouldn't be able to go over the speed limit.

C1: I suppose so. And it would be wonderful to be able to do other things like read instead of looking at the boring road.

C2: What about some of the other things like robots?

C1: Robots! I imagine they're fantastic in factories because they don't make mistakes and they can do dangerous jobs.

C2: And they don't need to take breaks or holidays! Still, I'm not sure about in the home. Would you want a robot doing the housework?

C1: Oh, I don't know – it sounds like a good idea.

C2: Yes, but …

C1: No, no, I'm kidding! However, they must be incredibly useful – for example, in car production. They never get tired!

C2: Mmm … Right, let's move on to 3D TV.

C1: OK, what do you think?

C2: Well, the picture is obviously fantastic – it feels like real life. Most people don't like having to wear special glasses though.

C1: But aren't we getting more used to them these days?

C2: A little. Even so, they're still a nuisance.

C1: But if you've ever seen a football match in 3D, you'll never want to go back to an ordinary flat screen TV!

C2: Yes, I can see the advantage for special events but not for all the time.

C1: Of course. And, anyway, you don't have to watch in 3D unless you choose to. So you just use it when you want to.

C2: That's true. Well, lastly, then, ebook readers.

C1: I think they're great for travelling and you can put a whole library on a very small tablet.

C2: Yes, but I think it will take a long time for people to feel comfortable with them. Books are still very attractive.

I: Now you have about a minute to decide which item might have the most benefits.

C1: Right, so now we have to make up our minds about which item has the most benefits.

C2: Yes. I think we could find benefits in all of them and, of course, it would depend on the situation. But for general everyday use, I would say that robots have fewer benefits, don't you agree?

C1: Yes, I guess so. And, really, I don't think you are as enthusiastic as I am about the idea of ebook readers.

C2: Yes, you're right. They have advantages but a lot of people still prefer books.

C1: So we won't agree on that one. What about 3D TV?

C2: Yes, possibly. But I think it's more of a luxury item, not really a necessity.

C1: But neither are portable gaming devices. Nice, but not absolutely necessary.

C2: And if you've got a video games console at home and you've got games on your smartphone, they're not necessary at all.

C1: So that leaves the driverless cars.

C2: Yes, you weren't as enthusiastic as me at the beginning but I think you changed your mind.

C1: Yes, I did, when I thought about it. I can see them having a big effect. They would be good for older or disabled people or, really, anyone who doesn't like driving.

C2: And most importantly, they will reduce the number of car accidents dramatically.

C1: OK, so we both think that driverless cars would have the most benefits. Many more than the others.

I: Thank you.

Speaking, page 71, Exercise 5b

(C1 = Candidate 1; C2 = Candidate 2; I = Interlocutor)

I: Can you imagine life without smartphones?

C1: Oh, it would be impossible. We've got so used to them.

C2: I don't know. Not everyone's got a smartphone. Some people just use ordinary mobiles without all those apps.

C1: True. Well, we certainly couldn't do without those.

I: Do you agree, Maria?

C2: Sometimes I think we use those too much too. It's amazing how silly a lot of conversations are. And they're often so public, which is irritating.

C1: But that's always true when people chat to each other.

C2: Yes, but you see people holding onto them all the time as though they're frightened to put them down.

I: Do you think we are too dependent on electronic technology? If so, why?

C1: I get a bit worried about how dependent we are on satellite technology. So many of us now rely on it for finding our way when we drive. It would be a shame if we forgot how to read maps.

C2: Yes, I agree. It would be a pity if we lost the skill to read a map.

C1: And sometimes we lose a satellite connection and find ourselves lost! It's amazing how many things now depend on this technology.

Listening, page 72, Exercise 2

Like all mothers who have full-time jobs, of course I value dishwashers, washing machines and so on but to be honest, people of my generation pretty much take household appliances for granted now, so much so that it's a catastrophe when one of them breaks down. Online shopping is relatively new though and I've really appreciated being able to do my food shopping online above all because that's something I really can't stand doing. Actually, I'm beginning to do more and more shopping online – books, music, household stuff, even clothes, although I still prefer to try stuff on first, particularly shoes – there's no way I'd consider ever buying those online.

I have a laptop and a smartphone, so I can have a quick look at the news headlines whenever I want, rather than wading through the newspaper. To be honest, if it weren't for the crossword, I wouldn't bother buying one at all but I like doing it on the train on my way to work.

I don't use all the facilities on my phone, really, although I do save time by catching up on emails while I'm commuting and it's great for researching and booking holidays. For working people, online banking is also a huge help. I seem to have more money left in my account now I can organise my finances regularly and check that my bills are paid on time.

As for my daughter Lizzie, like all kids, she is never without her mobile phone. She sends text messages to her friends the whole time, even when she's been with them all day. I just don't know what she finds to say to them. I'm totally fascinated by how fast and accurately she texts – the speed is amazing, even when she's doing it under the table at mealtimes! Young people all seem to be able to do this.

And when she's not doing that, she's on Facebook or Twitter or whatever, on her tablet. My son isn't so bothered about the social media but he's permanently plugged into his MP3 player, which means there is loud music belting out the whole time. It's not so much the effect on his hearing – although I do worry about that – it's crossing busy roads that makes me lose sleep because he just doesn't concentrate. Apparently, sixteen to twenty-one-year-olds are the most vulnerable to road accidents because of this.

I enjoy my MP3 player too, mind you; I listen to podcasts when I'm walking the dog and it's great to have all your music in one place instead of on all those CDs we used to have. What I particularly appreciate is being able to pick and choose and download just a few tracks from an album rather than having to buy the whole lot. It has also given me so much more space in the house. All our CDs used to pile up, gathering dust. I'm thrilled to get rid of them!

The kids use the computer at school and to do their homework. Thank goodness for Spellcheck so they can get on with it themselves! I used to spend ages checking their homework when they were younger.

Mind you, there are things I worry about in the computer age: the obvious things, such as safety online, of course, but also, now the school asks them to do more and more research into their subjects, I sometimes wonder whether they just copy down what they read in essays without thinking it through for themselves.

As for my husband, he's probably the one that resists technology the most, perhaps surprisingly. But he's become obsessed with YouTube recently now he's discovered he can watch all the 1980s rock bands that he's so keen on. You'd have thought he'd have lost interest now he's in his fifties, wouldn't you?

In general, I'd say technology is great as long as it doesn't take over your lives, though I do get frustrated with people who can't be parted from their phones or tablets.

Module 6

Speaking, page 85, Exercise 6a

In this part of the test, I'm going to give each of you two photographs. I'd like you to talk about your photographs on your own for about a minute, and also to answer a question about your partner's photographs.

Here are your two photographs. They show different kinds of art. I'd like you to compare the photographs and say why these types of art might be interesting to people.

Speaking, page 85, Exercise 6b

(C1 = Candidate 1; C2 = Candidate 2; I = Interlocutor)

C1: Both pictures show art – they're completely different kinds of art. In one picture we can see classical art, and the other picture is definitely a modern sculpture. In the first one there are not many people but they are all looking at the pictures on the wall, while in the second picture there is just one person, a woman, looking at what appears to be … er … a thing used for rubbish. She seems to be interested but looks a little puzzled. I get the impression that she's not quite sure what it is. Is it art or isn't it?

Why might people be interested? Mmm … well, I think classical art is easier to understand than some modern art. In the first photo, my guess is that the people know what the painters wanted to say but if you want, you can easily learn something about why they were painted. In my opinion, the people who like modern art like it because it's strange or funny. If you look at the second object, what is it? It could be something found in the garden so why is it there? I think a lot of people won't know the answer.

I: Anna, do you think that young people are more interested in classical art or modern art?

C2: Modern art, definitely. Classical art is more interesting for older people, I think. There's no doubt that young people like modern art because the artists are younger and more fashionable. Also, the art galleries for modern art are livelier, whereas the older galleries for classical art feel very old-fashioned.

Speaking, page 85, Exercises 6c and 6d

Both pictures show art – they're completely different kinds of art. In one picture we can see classical art, and the other picture is definitely a modern sculpture. In the first one there are not many people but they are all looking at the pictures on the wall, while in the second picture there is just one person, a woman, looking at what appears to be … er … a thing used for rubbish. She seems to be interested but looks a little puzzled. I get the impression that she's not quite sure what it is. Is it art or isn't it?

Why might people be interested? Mmm … well, I think classical art is easier to understand than some modern art. In the first photo, my guess is that the people know what the painters wanted to say but if you want, you can easily learn something about why they were painted. In my opinion, the people who like modern art like it because it's strange or funny. If you look at the second object, what is it? It could be something found in the garden so why is it there? I think a lot of people won't know the answer.

Speaking, page 85, Exercise 7

(I = Interlocutor; C = Candidate)

I: Anna, do you think that young people are more interested in classical art or modern art?

C: Modern art, definitely. Classical art is more interesting for older people, I think. There's no doubt that young people like modern art because the artists are younger and more fashionable. Also, the art galleries for modern art are livelier, whereas the older galleries for classical art feel very old-fashioned.

Listening, page 86, Exercises 2 and 3

1

Hi, Rachel. Thanks for phoning back. Listen, you're going to see the New York City Ballet, aren't you? … Have you still got the brochure there? … Great. So do they give the exact dates? … Oh, really? I didn't realise it was so soon. Thank goodness I phoned you because I'd hate to miss it. I'd better give them a ring. … You're going next Friday, you say? Shall I see if they've got any for then because that would be nice, wouldn't it?

2

To start with, I must admit that I had my doubts. I didn't think Alex Casey would be able to leave the film-script style behind. But even though the characters are a bit predictable, they are so colourful that you can't help but engage with them. And they're portrayed with a good deal of sensitivity, so you really care what happens to them. Then there's the very unusual plot, which keeps you gripped until the very last page. In fact, it would probably transfer very well to either stage or screen and because it's Casey, you immediately think of that. But actually, it works well enough as it is.

3

A: Can I help?

B: Yes, I'd like to move to the back, so I'm not disturbed so much by the noise of the traffic.

A: Well, it is the holiday period, Madam, so we're fully booked and …

B: I appreciate that. But if I'd known how much noise there'd be, I would've gone elsewhere. I might as well put my bed on the motorway.

A: I'll see what can be done. Would you like to take a seat in the bar over there while I have a word with the manager?

B: I'm just on my way to the dining room, actually.

A: Very well, Madam.

4

A: So what did you think of it?

B: It was all right but, you know, it ... it didn't really live up to the hype, did it?

A: Oh I thought visually it was really good.

B: Well, the special effects were OK, I suppose, but I hadn't really expected all that in this sort of film. If you ask me, though, they'd have done a lot better to stick to the plot of the original a bit more closely. Much as I liked Julia Roberts, it just didn't hold my attention, I'm afraid.

A: Well, I haven't read the book so I don't know but I think she was just brilliant.

5

A: I lent him that CD ages ago. I keep dropping hints whenever I see him in the canteen but either he's forgotten or just doesn't want to give it back to me.

B: Some people are very thoughtless, aren't they?

A: Well, I wouldn't mind, except it was a birthday present and I haven't really listened to it myself yet. My son bought it for me. If I knew him better, I'd ask for it straight out but I don't want to fall out with someone new like that.

B: It's difficult to know what to do, isn't it?

6

Don't get me wrong. It's mostly worthwhile stuff they've got there. It's just the way it's been put together that I don't like. I mean, it would be much better if all the works were grouped in some kind of logical way – you know, according to period, theme or whatever. You can't argue with the amount of background information available, which is very thorough, but if all you want to do is see a particularly brilliant painting or watercolour or whatever, you've got to go past all this other stuff to get to it. Some people will be exhausted by the time they're half way round, if you ask me.

7

A: I was a bit surprised, really. I was expecting something more – I don't know – progressive, I suppose, this time.

B: What, you mean like their last album? That went in a very different direction to the first one.

A: Yes, it was more a mix of genres, wasn't it? It was brilliant and groundbreaking in many ways but this has a completely different feel. The lyrics are really interesting – it has more in common with their original one around ten years ago.

B: That's what I thought – kind of more confident and relaxed. It's no bad thing, though.

A: Absolutely. It could be their best one yet.

8

A: I love going to the cinema but the popular films get booked up so fast – it's totally ridiculous! I mean, if you phone, it's just engaged all the time and by the time you get through, there are no decent seats. You have more chance for afternoon performances and they're cheaper but not everyone can go then, can they?

B: Wouldn't it be quicker to book online?

A: I suppose so but not everyone of our age is that good with computers. And that's if they've got one in the first place.

B: That's true. They should really make sure they have more people manning the phones.

A: Or hold back a certain amount of seats for retired people who can then just turn up on the night.

Module 7

Speaking, page 99, Exercise 7a

(C1 = Candidate 1; C2 = Candidate 2; I = Interlocutor)

I: Here are your photographs. They show people wearing different types of clothes in interview situations. I'd like you to compare the photographs and say why the people are dressed in this way.

C1: I see. You mean you want me to say how the photos are similar and why the people are wearing these kinds of clothes in an interview?

Candidate 1

I: Yes, that's right – but different as well as similar.

C1: Well, in both of these pictures there is someone having an interview. One interview is very formal, even though they are all smiling. The men are both wearing suits and ties, and the woman is wearing a smart white suit with trousers – a trouser suit. One of the men is wearing a light-coloured tie but his suit is very dark. They all look a little stiff and very polite. Er ... in the other picture, the interviewers and the ... er ... person having the interview are more casual but they're not scruffy. None of them is wearing a tie. They have open-neck shirts and quite bright clothes.

Why are they dressed like that? Well, I think in the first picture it is probably a big, traditional company and the person being interviewed wants to make a good impression. It's important when you get a job that you fit in – is that what you say? It would be a disaster if you went for an interview in that company and you turned up in jeans and an open-n ... er ... a shirt without a tie. The other company could be a modern technology company with creative young people – they don't want to appear formal.

I: Thank you. Which kind of clothes do you feel most comfortable wearing ...

Candidate 2

C2: Well, they're both interview situations. This one is kind of funny because it looks very serious. They're all wearing smart clothes. The other one, I like better. It looks like it's a nice place to work. The person having the interview is very relaxed. He's wearing a nice shirt – I've got one a bit like that. I don't know. Let's see ... in the first picture there are three people behind a desk and one person having an interview. Oh, they're all wearing suits, even the woman but hers is white. The men look very conservative. I don't think the woman's wearing jewellery, is she? But she does have some make-up on.

I: Thank you. Which kind of clothes do you feel most comfortable wearing ...

Speaking, page 99, Exercise 7b

(I = Interlocutor; C = Candidate;)

I: Here are your photographs. They show people wearing different types of clothes in interview situations. I'd like you to compare the photographs and say why the people are dressed in this way.

C: I see. You mean you want me to say how the photos are similar and why the people are wearing these kinds of clothes in an interview?

I: Yes, that's right – but different as well as similar.

Listening, page 100, Exercises 2 and 3

1 During the week, when I'm at work, I tend to wear fitted jackets, high heels, straight skirts – you know, quite stylish clothes. The first impression my clients get of me is fairly crucial, so I spend time looking for clothes that are businesslike. I can't afford to spend too much on them, though – I don't buy expensive clothes. It's got to the point where I don't feel right in casual clothes, so even at the weekends I'll still wear the same kind of thing but perhaps swap the jacket and heels for a sweater and flat shoes, um, pumps.

2 I always wear the same things when I'm not at school – tracksuit bottoms, a fleece or a T-shirt and designer trainers. Nearly all my friends do. I've also got three different football kits – Man United, England and Barcelona. In the summer, I sometimes wear shorts instead of tracksuit bottoms but it's always sports stuff. There's no point in dressing up in smart clothes, anyway – they just get dirty. What matters is feeling relaxed and not having to worry about what you look like.

3 Well, I've always had a fairly clear idea of how I want to look. I want to be a designer when I leave school and I'm always flicking through magazines to pick up ideas. At the moment either very short or very long skirts are cool, worn with trainers or wedges – nothing in between. And low-waisted trousers. Strong patterns and crop tops in bright colours – even colours that clash, like lime green and pink – are popular too. I wouldn't dream of wearing anything sort of frumpy or like my mum wears. I even try to adapt my school uniform a bit to personalise it – so I might wear patterned or striped tights with it.

4 I don't think about clothes very much. I suppose I wear what I've always worn – a shirt and tie with trousers and maybe a sweater. I don't spend much money on clothes, so most of them are a few years old. I sometimes go into charity shops and my son gives me things he's fed up with. I'll wear anything as long as it's warm and not too scruffy. I'm certainly not trying to impress anyone!

5 I like clothes but I'm not a fashion victim and I don't dress up. Now I've got kids, my clothes have to be practical, so no high heels and tight skirts these days. Having said that, I don't want to end up living in tracksuits or jeans and baggy jumpers all the time like some mums. I go for casual but well-cut clothes in natural fabrics, like silk or cotton. I do tend to spend quite a lot on my clothes but then I can wear them over and over again and they don't drop to pieces. It's an investment.

Module 8

Speaking, page 113, Exercises 6a and 6b

(C1 = Candidate 1; C2 = Candidate 2; I = Interlocutor)

I: Good morning. My name is Katie and this is my colleague, Mark. And your names are?

C1: I'm Anna.

C2: And I'm Giorgio.

I: And where are you from, Anna?

C1: I'm from Zurich, in Switzerland.

C2: And I'm from Milan, in Italy.

I: First we'd like to know something about you. Anna, how do you like to spend your evenings? What do you do?

C1: Um ... let me think. It depends on the season. In the winter I like to sit in front of a warm fire and read a book. I love thrillers. But in the summer I like to get out in the evenings after a hard day at work and go for a walk in the mountains with my husband. Or sometimes we go round to dinner with a work ... eh ... it's another person who works with me.

I: Giorgio, do you normally celebrate special occasions with friends or family?

C2: Usually with my family because I'm still living at home. You know, in Italy, families are very important, so we always get together for birthdays, but not always at home – there's a lovely fish restaurant by the sea near our house. We go there a lot – we are eh ... how do say ... customers ... mmm ... we go there often and the owner likes to cook us a special dish if we tell him we're coming. Of course, my three brothers can't always get there because they live in different parts of Italy. It's different at Christmas – we celebrate at home and everybody comes.

I: OK, Anna, tell us about a TV programme you've seen recently.

C1: Well, as I said, I like thrillers and I'm fascinated by a French crime series called *Spiral* in English.

I: Why?

C1: Well, you get very involved with the characters. Nobody is completely good, even the police, and there are some very unpleasant people in it. The plots are very complicated but they keep you watching. But I have to admit, it's rather violent.

I: Giorgio, how about you?

C2: Oh, I don't like crime stories very much. I love game shows and reality shows – shows with real people.

I: Thank you.

Listening, page 114, Exercises 1 and 2

(I = Interviewer; S = Simon)

I: Most of us have an interest of one kind or another, whether it's keeping an unusual pet, collecting stamps or gardening. Simon is interested in learning about other people's hobbies – both ordinary people's and those of celebrities. Why is this, Simon?

S: Well, the thing is, if you tell me that the bloke sitting opposite me in the train is a teacher or engineer or whatever, I might be able to guess what sort of things he can do – what he's good at – but really I haven't the faintest idea what he's really like, you know, what makes him tick, whereas if you tell me he's a stamp collector or a leading light of the local drama society, you've pretty much drawn a map of his personality for me.

I: You think people reveal their souls through their hobbies?

S: Absolutely. One of the things you can see straightaway, for example, is whether people are happier in company or whether they prefer solitude. So if they enjoy, let's say, being in a choir, it's often as much the belonging to a group with shared goals as about the singing.

I: And is the same true for people who like curling up with a good book or knitting jumpers? It's not so much the activity itself but the fact they want to get away …

S: Escape from the world for a bit, yes – be on their own, usually in the fresh air, actually. Look at Jarvis Cocker from the band Pulp – he likes nothing more than being out bird-watching. Or Brian May – he used to be with the band Queen but he spends hours looking at the night sky through his telescope, being on his own. Other famous people fly kites or model aeroplanes – I suppose it's a release from the tension of being in the public eye all the time.

I: And what about actors? I suppose they need activities to occupy them while they're filming.

S: There's a lot of hanging around, yes. You get to see some very glamorous film stars doing crosswords or Sudoku, or knitting quietly by themselves to pass the time. What seems to be the most popular at the moment though is to bring along board games and play them together. They all seem to take it very seriously and are all determined to win – maybe it takes their minds off the acting and makes them less nervous.

I: What else do people's hobbies tell you?

S: Well, whether you are intellectual or creative, or practical. For example, the Dalai Lama will spend ages, you know, repairing an old film projector which has no instructions, or with his head under a car bonnet, or taking clocks to bits and putting them back together. He is completely in his element.

I: You wouldn't really expect that of a Nobel peace prize winner, would you?

S: Not really, and rock star Bill Wyman, of the Rolling Stones, is also interesting. He goes around with his metal detector – so far he's found about 300 old coins and even a couple of Roman necklaces. But it's not the actual treasure itself that motivates him – I don't think he even keeps it – he's just fascinated by the process of archaeology. I've heard that a friend is trying to get him to photograph the things he finds so he can publish a book about his findings one day.

I: Let's hope he does!

S: But perhaps the most interesting thing is the hobbies of leaders and presidents and so on. The ex-Japanese prime minister, Koizumi, is fanatical about Elvis Presley. No, really – he has released a CD with his favourite Elvis tunes on and used to sing Elvis songs at karaoke, even when he was on official visits, to the discomfort of his advisers, one imagines. The late North Korean leader Kim Jong-il collected movies and was so mad about them he even kidnapped an actress once so that she would make movies for him! These interests completely take over their lives!

I: What does that tell us about our leaders?

S: Probably that they have very addictive personalities. Still, it's better than doing nothing, I suppose, although we are difficult to live with. I say 'we' because I'm as bad – I follow a rather indifferent football club around the country and it drives my wife mad. The thing is, you'd be surprised how many otherwise normal people have a really weird compulsion – buying rare books, bungee jumping – you name it, somebody will do it!

Module 9

Speaking, page 127, Exercises 6b and 6c

(C1 = Candidate 1; C2 = Candidate 2)

C1: I think some people like to go shopping just for the fun of it. It's very relaxing.

C2: Oh no, I don't think so. It's very stressful. Not only that, I can never find what I'm looking for.

C1: That's probably because you only go shopping when you want to buy something. A lot of people go just to see what there is. They like wandering around and dreaming of what they would buy if they had the money.

C2: That's not for me. Actually, I hate the crowds. I don't understand people who go shopping for fun. I'm sure they buy things they don't need and then get into debt.

C1: Yes, that's true sometimes.

Listening, page 128, Exercise 2

1

How's your general knowledge? Reckon you can outwit the competitors on the TV quiz shows? Well, *Quiztime* gives you the chance to show what you can do. Beat the clock to answer questions on a variety of topics, ranging from football to soap operas, natural history to music, fashion to computers. Throw the dice and race round the board, collecting points as you go. Based on the hit TV programme of the same name, *Quiztime* comes in both adult and junior versions and is guaranteed to keep the whole family entertained for hours.

2

A: All I can do is either give you a jacket in another size or issue a credit note. I can't give you a cash refund unless the product is faulty in some way, I'm afraid, because you paid by credit card.

B: But supposing there isn't a blue one in the longer fitting?

A: Well, I expect there will be if you look – or we can order one in for you. A credit note would be valid for up to six months.

B: But that's no good to me, it's a 100-mile round trip from where I live.

A: I apologise, sir, but those are the rules.

3

The thing is, last month I had a service done and the work alone cost me well over £100. And that's without the parts. What worries me is whether you can trust them or not. I mean, I don't know a thing about what goes on under the bonnet. How do I know they're not just ripping me off and saying they've put new bits in when they haven't? I suppose you'll say I should go to an evening class or something to find out how the engine works but quite honestly, I haven't got either time or interest. I just wondered if you had any ideas on what I could do.

4

A: Right. Here we are ... I'm not so sure that this is a good idea, Miriam. They did say on the phone that there wasn't one. Why don't we go to a shop and buy a map of the area and then get someone to mark the bus routes on it for us?

B: Oh honestly, Tom, why should we spend money needlessly? These places always have maps, it stands to reason. I'm going to go up to that uniformed man over there and ask him to lend me one, then we'll take it next door to the library and photocopy it.

A: OK, but don't say I didn't warn you.

5

Look, I'm sorry. I accept it was a genuine mistake – these things happen but surely, I'm entitled to some kind of compensation. Had I known there was a midday flight, I'd certainly have chosen it. But when I spoke to your employee on the phone, she said there was only one flight a day and, as you know, with these cheap flights, once you've booked, you can't change them. So we ended up having to get up really early in the morning in time to catch the flight she'd booked us on, then had to wait ages at the other end because we were too early – the rooms were still being cleaned.

6

We're on the train and we'll be arriving around six o'clock but what I want to know is whether we've got time for a round of golf before dinner, or whether we're down to eat at a specific time. Yes, I know that you didn't make the booking yourself but I think I read something about the rest of the conference delegates arriving tomorrow morning, so I'm not sure what arrangements have been made for tonight. I seem to have mislaid all the paperwork somewhere, it's probably on my desk somewhere – can you have a look? Or perhaps you could check with the organisers and then get back to me, please? I'm on the mobile number. Thanks.

7

It's the latest idea to hit London. A company called Q4U has launched a new service that takes the tedium out of waiting around – be it for prescriptions at the chemist's, picking up dry cleaning or queuing for theatre tickets. Anything that people waste their time standing in a queue for. Customers pay the company £20 an hour and one of their professional queuers does the boring bit on their behalf. The idea has caught on fastest when there's something to be picked up, especially holiday documents. The company says that, given mobile phone technology, the idea can actually be applied to any time-wasting task. Who knows? Maybe even the dentist's waiting room!

8

For both customers and e-commerce businesses, not to mention the mail-order industry in general, the question of delivery has long been an issue. The problem is simply this: that the people most likely to spend serious money having a purchase delivered are the least likely to be in when it arrives. After all, they are the ones most liable to possess a job and a busy life. It makes you think that if e-commerce had been around first, then the invention of the walk-in shop would have been welcomed as a brilliant new idea. But, fortunately, it looks like a solution is at hand. Tanya Wilde went to investigate ...

Module 10

Module 10B page 142, Listening, Exercise 2

1 About four years ago, during a tube strike, I was in a taxi. I was running late for a meeting because, as usual, at rush hour all the roads were jammed. Suddenly I saw this scooter in the window of a showroom and that's when I had my flash of inspiration. I jumped out of the cab, did all the paperwork in 15 minutes and still got to my meeting on time.

The bike can't go above 50 kilometres an hour but it doesn't seem that slow because you can overtake lines of cars. I must admit it sometimes doesn't start, which is a pain, but when it does go it has shrunk London for me and means I can fit in more business meetings than I used to before.

2 I love my bike – it's quite comfortable, with lots of gears. I bought it second hand from a colleague, so it was quite cheap as well. I started cycling to work around the time of the terrorist attacks on the underground. Like lots of other people I suddenly got very scared and anyway I'd always hated being squashed in with all these other people during the rush hour. It's so much nicer being outside in the fresh air, apart from when it's freezing, of course, and motorists are quite considerate to cyclists these days, although I wear a yellow jacket to be on the safe side. The only problem is all the pollution from the traffic – perhaps I should wear a mask.

3 If I drove a car, people would probably try to contact me on my mobile – riding a bike gives me a breathing space to think about things without being interrupted for once, which is great when you have a demanding job like mine. I find I arrive at places in a much better mood.

I've got a Kawasaki motorbike and I'm a passionate enthusiast. It all began 20 years ago when I was a student and I was looking for something cheaper to run than a car. Now I use it every day, for the same reason. When it's windy or pouring down with rain, it's not very pleasant but I still go out on it, although my family never thought I would stick with it.

4 I'm aware that many colleagues and clients think that lawyers should drive flash cars rather than have a bike. But the great thing about a bike is there's always somewhere to leave it and you don't have to worry about getting a parking ticket. Mind you, I've had a couple of bikes stolen in the last few years, despite having chained them up.

People do often look really astonished when I turn up to important meetings on my scooter, which is great – it's good to challenge people's expectations. Some probably look down on this method of transport but I don't care – the opinions of others don't matter to me in the least.

5 I began cycling again because I wanted to get fit but jogging bores me and I don't like going to the gym. I'm wary of the major roads just from lack of experience – cars seem to go so fast and you feel very vulnerable on a bike – but I think this will pass eventually and I've not had an accident yet, thank goodness.

I'm really glad I took it up again, because it's so convenient – you always know how long the journey's going to take, whereas you can't depend on public transport, and also hopping on a bus or tube is so expensive these days.

Module 11

Listening, page 155, Exercise 6

Thanks for that lovely introduction, Helen. You are doubtless aware that obesity – being grossly overweight – is one of the greatest challenges of the twenty-first century. The instances of this have tripled since the eighties and continue to rise at an alarming rate, affecting around one in four citizens in Europe and the USA. As well as causing physical and psychological problems, excess weight drastically increases a person's chances of developing serious illnesses. Which is why ministers from the European Union convened a meeting this week, specifically to address the issue of healthcare and how long governments will be able to afford to fund this, given the mounting cost of obesity-related diseases.

It's actually not so much overweight adults that's the issue for me; it's the young people who are growing up eating so much junk food. In my view, it's the advertisements for all this stuff that are partly to blame because they target kids. They should be banned!

Obese twelve-year-olds are eighty-two percent more likely to be obese adults. Which is why the quality of school dinners must also be addressed. Most of you will be shocked when I tell you that this government spends four times more per head on prisoners' meals than on those for kids in school – that's how much of a priority they've been! Thank goodness something is finally being done to improve this situation. Although this does involve spending more, it will save us money in the long run.

In order for obesity to be reduced, it is clear that supermarkets also need to take more responsibility for the contents of the products they sell. True, there is much more availability of low-fat food on the shelves these days. Now the World Health Organization has issued new guidelines suggesting that we cut the amount of sugar we consume daily by as much as a half to bring it to a recommended limit of 25 grams per day. Which is less than the amount you will get in just one can of some fizzy drinks or ready-prepared meals.

People often ask me how come the French manage to remain relatively slim despite their love of high-fat cheeses and meat. I'm inclined to think that the key is their approach to food. Because they still tend to have proper sit-down meals, they seem to be less tempted by the high-calorie snacks that are the downfall of many other cultures.

Also, in my view, the fact that lunchtime tends to be the main meal in France, rather than dinner, is also a contributory fact. The earlier in the day calories are consumed, the more opportunity there is to convert them into energy, so we should follow their example and try not to have a heavy meal in the evenings.

Moving on to other parts of the world, why is it that in Japan, for example, life expectancy is much higher than anywhere else in the world? One of the reasons could be that their diet is built around rice and fish and plentiful fruit and vegetables. There is little meat, animal fat or sweets and two thirds of their calorie intake comes from carbohydrates, as opposed to the UK or the USA, where fat accounts for much more than the recommended quarter of our daily calories.

You would think the Inuit in Greenland had very little in common with the Japanese, wouldn't you? And unlike the Japanese, sixty percent of the calories eaten in Greenland do come from fat – even more than we consume – and they eat surprisingly little fruit and vegetables. However, as in Japan, heart disease there is not that common. The difference is that the fat they eat is from oily fish such as salmon and mackerel. This type of unsaturated fat, called omega 3, we already know has huge benefits for the bones. What has only recently been discovered and is therefore less well known is that it is also said to improve mental health.

And for those of us who are worried about forgetting things, scientists are also suggesting that turmeric, a key ingredient of curries, may be a major factor as to why elderly Indian people are less likely to lose their memory than someone in the western world. So perhaps we can learn …

Module 12

Listening, page 170, Exercise 2

(I = Interviewer; M = Mike)

I: My guest today, Mike Morgan, has been a leading journalist on a national newspaper for more than 40 years. Mike, what made you decide to take it up in the first place?

M: I kind of drifted into it. I was always good at English and liked writing stories and so on at school, but I was initially quite keen on a career in business and, in fact, I'd accepted a place to study that at college. It was my father who talked me into doing journalism. He just thought I'd be better at it than I would at going into business.

I: What training did you get?

M: In those days, you were taken on by the newspaper straight from school as a kind of message boy. Rather than doing a diploma in journalism as you would now, you had to pick up the skills you needed actually on the job. You had to follow a senior reporter around and if he went to court, you'd go too and then write up the same story. He would look at it afterwards and give you feedback. It was some time before anything of mine actually appeared in the newspaper.

I: What was your first real reporting job?

M: I was a crime reporter, which meant I had to spend a lot of time with the police. In those days, you just hung around them to find out what was going on. They were terribly suspicious of us at first, I remember, but we were given an enormous expense account to buy them drinks, which helped! And after a bit, they felt sure enough of me to let me go out on jobs with them. Unfortunately, I wasn't always allowed to report the things I heard and saw!

I: Are there rules about what you can and can't report, then?

M: There are legal issues, obviously, with privacy and national security and so on. But there are also unwritten rules. I remember when Prince Charles was at university, he had four bodyguards looking after him but he sometimes used to try and lose them so he could meet a girlfriend. So he might go to the toilet in a pub or restaurant and then get out through the window. We always knew what he was up to, but we never printed it – all the journalists sympathised with his situation and didn't want to spoil things for him. It was an unspoken agreement amongst us.

I: So, what makes a good journalist?

M: Well, obviously you need to be confident and articulate and able to get on with all kinds of people. Being able to write well also helps. However good you are though, this is not as important as having bags of energy and commitment. When a big story breaks, you have to drop everything you're doing and work all hours if need be, often under tremendous pressure.

I: And do you still enjoy it?

M: I do, although I won't be sorry to retire. In my day, it was all going out and meeting people to get stories. Now it's much more office based. We have to be computer literate and we do a lot of stuff that printers used to do. In the satellite age, everything has to be instantaneous. It's still just as exciting, but quite honestly it's not what I set out to do.

I: Would you encourage young people to go in for it?

M: Let's face it. Even working on a best-selling tabloid paper, you're never going to make your fortune but you can earn a decent living. No two days are the same and it's great to be one of the first to know what's going on. In some ways, it's competitive, like all jobs, but actually, that's not such a problem as people might think because there's also a great team spirit when you're working on a story. So, as long as your family commitments aren't going to be a problem, given the long and unpredictable hours – which is something that has to be borne in mind – then, yes, I'd say, go for it!

I: Mike, thanks for joining us today.

M: My pleasure.